JOURNEYS BENEATH THE EARTH

The autobiography of a cave explorer

David William Gill

Copyright © 2020 David William Gill

Revised edition

All rights reserved.

ISBN 979-8-6175497-4-6

Dedication

To all those friends I have had the privilege of venturing underground with, as without them there would be no stories to tell. You will notice that many of the names of cave explorers mentioned in the following chapters are designated as 'the late'. Sadly, they are exploring the great cave in the sky and are no longer with us. It was a great and wonderful privilege to have known them all, including many I have not mentioned, as there are far too many to count.

Also, to all the conservationists I have had the opportunity to work with over many years.

I was lucky enough to have Frank and Ethel as my parents, they were the best. Thank you.

Little Neath River Cave. Photo: Paul Deakin.

Preface

By midnight it was still raining hard, the river was in severe flood, there was no way we could cross back to base camp. The powerful current of the Medalam River was sweeping huge trees downstream, a swirling mass of raging brown water with massive standing waves. We tried a few times to ford a crossing but it was suicide.

Eventually, we gave up trying and trudged on through the dense undergrowth at the side of the riverbank. Park guide Philip led the way slashing at everything in sight with his by now very blunt Parang. We progressed slowly downstream towards base camp, which I judged from a previous trip to be no more than two hours away.

As usual the Gunung Mulu National Park and the Sarawak jungle threw up a few surprises; large poisonous snakes, stinging plants, biting bugs, the usual sort of thing. There seemed to be large numbers of fallen trees that I could not remember being there before. We were tired, wet, cold, hungry and our lights were fading fast. It had been a long but rewarding exploration of a newly found cave discovered by members of the USA Gunung Buda Caves Project. We had set off early with Philip, crossing the river in low flow conditions without any problems. The mapping and photographic trip to this as yet unnamed cave high up on the flanks of the northern side of the Benarat Mountain had been a great success. We had managed to explore over two kilometres of massive cave passage. The cave was huge, 80 metres high in places, with fantastic popcorn calcite formations. We were all running on adrenaline on something of a high which I suppose helped to keep us going. Also the thought of some food, dry cloths, a sleeping mat and the tales we could tell drove us on.

By 3 am we had all had enough. I judged that base camp was still a long way off and we still had to somehow cross the raging river. Thoroughly exhausted, we collapsed beneath a small overhang, which offered a little respite from the rain and the leeches. I tried to sleep but the sand flies were out in force and my feet were a mess. Mulu foot, a dreadful fungal infection that had a nasty habit of creeping up on you, meant that every step was akin to walking on hot needles. Did I really do this for a living? What a strange occupation.

Contents

	Acknowledgements	vii
	Introduction	viii
1	In a Cardboard Box	1
2	Getting Hooked	12
3	1967 Gouffre Berger expedition and a new depth record	22
4	The Caving Scene	32
5	Gouffre de la Pierre-Saint-Martin expedition, 1969	45
6	A Few Cave Rescues	56
7	Gouffre de la Pierre-Saint-Martin, 1971	62
8	The Deepest Hole in the World, 1972	67
9	Gouffre de la Pierre-Saint-Martin, 1973	78
10	Tatra Mountains Expedition, Poland 1974	88
11	Felix Trombe, France, 1975 and 1976	97
12	Sima GESM, Spain, 1981	105
13	Chiapas, Mexico, 1982 to 1983	111
14	V3 Tunnels, Hitler's Terror Weapon, 1983	122
15	The Untamed River Expedition, New Britain, 1984 – 1985	129
16	Tulakan Karst, Java, British Combined Forces Expedition, 1986	167
17	Operation Paddington Bear, Peru Expedition, 1987	173
18	Guangxi Province, The China Caves Project, 1987 – 1988	181
19	Three Counties Expedition to China, 1989	201
20	Gunung Mulu Expedition, 1988	212
21	China Caves Project, Yunnan Province, 1990	230
22	Yunnan, China, 1991	235

23	High Trikora Expedition, Irian Jaya, Indonesia, 1990	240
24	To Russia with Love, 1990	252
25	Gunung Mulu Expedition, 1991	259
26	Bac Son Massif Vietnam, 1992	269
27	Caves of Thunder, Irian Jaya, Indonesia, 1992.	281
28	10 years in the Borneo Rain Forest	286

Acknowledgements

To the photographers, the late Paul Deakin, Robbie Shone, Alan Gamble, Stephen Wood, Rod Leach, Steve Dickinson, Jim Cunningham and Jerry Wooldridge. With many thanks. Also I would like to express my sincere thanks and appreciation to Linda Wilson for proof reading, Alan Jeffreys for kindly providing a second set of eyes and Graham Mullan for typesetting. The cover photo is by Jerry Wooldridge.

The author in Faunarooska Cave, Co. Clare, Ireland. Photo: Paul Deakin.

Introduction

I have attempted to write so the non-caver may gain some inkling into the mindset of the cave explorer, as when asked where I was off to next, the reaction was normally a blank look of disbelief that I was travelling halfway around the world in order to disappear into a hole in the ground.

Back in my local pub on my return from some crazy-sounding expedition or other, when asked how I got on, the looks were again ones of total disbelief and consternation. After little more than a minute or two they would return to their game of pool or darts as the general opinion seemed to be that I was a nutcase and best left alone.

The tales contain in this book are true to the best of my knowledge and belief but are based for the most part on a fading memory and equally fading scribbled notes made in the field at the time. Many of my notebooks are still smeared with dried-out cave mud from years ago. My sincere apologies to the many cave explorers who might remember slightly different versions of the same story.

I have been lucky enough to explore caves over a period of 50 years and in many countries with some of the greatest people on the planet and the best cave explorers in the world. It seems strange that a 25-year-long hobby became an occupation.

Also my continuing work on conservation has brought me into contact with some incredibly dedicated hard-working individuals.

The most difficult thing for a cave explorer to come to terms with in old age is to know what you used to be able to do, in the knowledge that you can't do it anymore.

1

In a Cardboard Box

'The two most important days in your life are the day you are born, and the day you find out why.'

Mark Twain

My first most important day was during the war on the 12th November 1941 at Crossley Salvation Army Maternity Hospital on Pollard Street, Ancoats, Manchester, founded by Francis Crossley of the famous Crossley Motors but sadly demolished in 1985. The baby boom was on and cots were in short supply. As I was so tiny they put me in a cardboard box.

The second most important day is much more difficult to define because the question is "why are we here?" I think the answer is that we are here to find out why we are here. When we do there will be no point being here, so it is not likely to happen.

Thankfully, my birth came after the devastating air raids of August and September of 1940. The worst came on the night of 22nd and 23rd of December when 270 aircraft dropped 272 tons of high explosives and 1,032 incendiary bombs on the centre of Manchester, just down the road from where we lived.

The following night Manchester was again the target when the Luftwaffe, with 171 aircraft, dropped 195 tons of high explosive and 893 incendiary bombs. The centre of Manchester was a mess with 8,000 homes damaged or destroyed, 2,364 people were injured and 684 dead. It did not finish there and Manchester was bombed on a regular basis throughout the war. The main industrial centre at Trafford Park that churned out war machines was the main target; even Old Trafford Football Ground received a direct hit. A V1 flying Buzz bomb was also aimed at Manchester but it missed and tragically killed many people in Oldham.

Beswick and Bradford were dangerous places to live at the time, as they were surrounded by major industrial complexes, all on a war footing and all targets for the German bombers: Bradford Pit, now the site of Manchester

City Football Club; Johnson's Wire Works, now the site of an Asda Store; the Gasometer, amazingly still preserved; Clayton Aniline, a massive chemical factory finally closed in 2007, now a highly polluted building site; English Steel, Openshaw where mother – and later dad – worked, now a housing estate; and the huge coal yards in Ardwick where my father originally worked, again no longer there. There were numerous major engineering works and cotton mills surrounding the area, all long since gone. The industrial heart of Manchester is now little more than a memory. The great Nazi war machine could not destroy it, but successive British Governments succeeded where the greatest military force in history at that time had failed.

Mum and me somewhere in England, 1944. Photographer unknown.

My generation became known as 'The War Babies', the baby boom. We had no toys in those days so we made ones out of pieces of wood. There were no air raid shelters in Bradford so during air raids we slept under the kitchen table. I remember queuing up in a long line with a bucket to get the coal and going to the corner shop to have the lead acid battery for the radio charged. We only had gas lights, no electricity. Of course we listened to the radio and Winston Churchill's speeches. They meant nothing to me and I think my mother despised the man as a war monger. I can't say I blame her, after all as the First Lord of the Admiralty during the First World War; Churchill was directly responsible for the death of her father, as the debacle at Gallipoli was his idea.

The exploration of caves was always regarded as a hobby for strange people but over the years has become far more acceptable as a genuine method of original exploration. I often wonder why I was fascinated with caves. Was it something to do with genetics?

On my paternal side, we managed to trace the Gill family back to the early 1600s originating from St Agnes in Cornwall. Gill seems to be a common name in Cornwall so presumably the family was well established and large. So we are probably Ancient Britons, the original inhabitants of England escaping from the invading Romans. In the 18th and 19th centuries, the main occupation in Cornwall was tin mining but also seems to have been smuggling rum and tobacco and dodging the Excise Men. The numerous sea caves were favourite haunts for storing their ill-gotten gains and they were not averse to luring ships onto the rocks.

So it does seem possible that exploring caves is a genetic thing from my ancestors. How many of the Gill family worked in the tin mines or were captured, shot or executed for smuggling, I would not like to speculate, but by all accounts the Gill families' main occupation in the 18th and 19th centuries was indeed smuggling.

While on holiday exploring the sea caves along the coasts of Devon and Cornwall with father was a great adventure, I always wanted to know what was around the next corner.

My great-grandfather seems to have been an exception. As a teacher, he was offered a job as the headmaster of Waverton School, so that's how we came to be living in the north west of England. While Frank, my grandfather, managed to survive the First World War, few others did around those parts. He lived apart from my grandmother, Gertrude Higginson but just a few doors away. Her brother lived in the same house. The only thing I can remember about my Uncle Alfred was that he was drunk most weekends and would curse "The High Speed Cylinders". I never found out what they were, but I presume he built them.

My father, Frank, named after his dad, married Ethel Harrop, my mum, in 1940 and they went to Llandudno in Wales for their honeymoon. Luckily their hotel was reserved for 'government servants' so they were not thrown out when thousands of tired and bedraggled troops arrived by train having just been evacuated from Dunkirk. Hotel guests were forced to vacate their rooms but still the beaches were full of troops. Residents poured out of their houses offering food, blankets and drink, showing an amazing community spirit, compassion, resilience and bravery.

Are we the men our fathers were? Dad served in the RAF during the last war in the Military Police and also survived. Along with most of the great men of that era, he would not talk much about it. I know that dad was stationed at various airfields and was there during the daring air raid of Operation Jericho, when some very brave men blew the walls down of a prison in Amiens, France so the French Resistance leaders could escape. It was rumoured that most were due to be shot and one of them happened to know the place and date of the D Day landings. Group Captain Percy Charles Pickard (DSO and two bars) was shot down along with his navigator and buried with full military honours by the Germans, Dad said that, uncannily, his dog howled at the same time he was shot down and killed. My father served as a dog handler in England, France, Luxembourg, Belgium and finally Germany, escaping the Battle of the Bulge during his Belgium tour. He was not trained as a dog handler but Bill, his friend in the RAF, finished up with two Alsatians, a bitch called Peggy and another dog called Cheeky, which he gave to my father to handle. Sadly, Peggy did not survive the war as she was badly hurt in a car accident and Bill had to shoot her. Cheeky survived and was demobbed at the same time as my father.

After the war Dad would not go near an aeroplane and flatly refused to fly. He had seen far too many crashed planes and dead air crew. I did not see him until I was about three years old, but was very impressed when this big man with a huge revolver on his belt came home on leave before being posted to France as it was just after D Day.

On my maternal side, the family all seemed to be heroes rather than smugglers. My grandmother, Alice Green, married William Harrop who was in the Territorial Army. He was a musician in the Ardwick Pals, a Battalion of the Manchester Regiment, playing the flute and piccolo in the Battalion's Band. When the First World War broke out he was sent to Egypt and then from Alexandria to the debacle of Gallipoli.

The Dardanelles campaign was a blood bath with the sea running red with the blood of the Lancashire Fusiliers as they stormed W Beach, now known as Lancashire Beach. Out of 1,000 men, they suffered 600 causalities winning six VCs before breakfast. Another six VCs were awarded to the men at V Beach which was attacked by the Royal Munster Fusiliers, Dubliners and Hampshires. This was Winston Churchill's permanent nightmare as it had been his brilliant idea. Grandfather landed on the 6th May 1915 and was killed on the 12th May, only six days later, shot twice by a sniper as he went to fetch water from a well. His surviving mates spotted the sniper and shot him, or so they said. I still have the last letter he sent to my grandmother, Alice. It said: *'You must not worry about me; I shall be alright, and I hope you and the children will be the same.*

He has no known grave as they buried the dead where they fell and just removed the identification tags. I still have his ID tag including the piece of string that hung around his neck.

A few years after the war to end all wars, the War Graves Commission began the gruesome task of trying to identify the dead and remove the bodies they found into mass graves. Grandfather just has a simple epitaph along with 20,000 others, carved in stone on the Helles Memorial, Gallipoli. Harrop W, that's all it says. Mother could not remember him as she was only three years old when he gave his life for his country. I was named after him and am quite proud of the fact. I remember as a little child, the house we lived in was full of women, all either widows or spinsters as my grandmother's sister also lost her husband on the Western Front. There were few men left to marry in those days, most of them were dead. Whole streets in Manchester and many other cities in the north of England were left occupied by widows and orphans. The men volunteered street by street and joined their local Pals Regiments, so died together, side by side. Thankfully although grandfather was killed in his mid-30s and so died young, he lived long enough to pass on his genes to his two daughters, otherwise I would not be here. Many other men during the Great War did not get that chance.

I always wanted to see grandfather's name on the Helles Memorial and the battlefield where he lost his life, but never got the chance when I was young. Then a few years ago I managed to visit Gallipoli with two caving friends, John New and Dave Sims. We located the site of the Ardwick Trench where grandad was probably killed from the old trench maps. The trenches were named after the Battalions; the Wigan trench is just next door. We came across a well not far behind the lines, long ago abandoned, probably where he was heading before he was killed.

Shell casings and human bones can still be found as the local farmers keep digging things up from the once blood-soaked fields. We found two shell casings near a farmer's hut close to the site of the old Ardwick trench. All the area is now a National Monument with the graves kept in beautiful condition by the War Graves Commission and a few trenches are still preserved. The Helles Memorial is an imposing sight that brings a lump to the throat. The Turkish people venerate the place and the Turkish Memorial is spectacular. For many years, Gallipoli has been a major tourist destination for Australians and New Zealanders. Every April the place is inundated with pilgrims arriving to commemorate ANZAC day and quite rightly so. Gallipoli has become not just a National Monument for the Turkish people, but also for the Australians and New Zealanders. The huge sacrifices made forged the identity of their respective countries. I was greatly impressed that Turkish school children are bussed in to see their National Monument, it's a great pity we do not do the same. It really should be a part of the National Curriculum for British school children to pay their respects to the dead of the First and Second World Wars. Without their sacrifice, we would not be here today.

During my visit to Gallipoli I decided to revisit the Helles Memorial one more time while John and Dave were doing their own thing. The buses seemed to have stopped running so I set off walking the 12 miles or so. A Turkish couple in a car stopped and asked if I wanted a lift; they were also visiting the monuments to pay their respects to the Turkish dead. We visited all the Turkish Memorials and I pointed out grandfather's name on the Helles Monument. A young Turkish lad gave me a piece of lead shrapnel, and what moved me most was the famous quote by the first President and father of modern Turkey, carved into the stone. The man who led the Turkish defence of the peninsular, Lieutenant Colonel, Commander of the 19th Division, Mustafa Kemal Bey, better known as Ataturk, ordered his men *'not just to fight but to die,'* in the defence of their homeland and they did, in their thousands. At one point in the conflict, no man's land was littered with bodies, so much so that the stench of rotting corpses and the flies was overpowering. A truce was called to bury the dead, Turkish soldiers and Allies shook hands, dug graves, swapped food water and tobacco, then went back to their respective trenches and carried on killing each other.

Ataturk's famous inscription reads: *'Those heroes that shed their blood and lost their lives... you are now lying in the soil of a friendly country. Therefore rest in peace. There is no difference between the Johnnies and the Mehmets to us where they lie side by side here in this country of ours. You the mothers who sent their sons from far away countries wipe away your tears. Your sons are now lying in our bosom and are in peace. After having lost their lives on this land they have become our sons as well.'*

These are great words, but little comfort for grandmother who struggled on a meagre War Pension to survive and bring up her two daughters with no bread winner. Mother said that visits to the pawn shop to pawn her dead father's gold watch and chain or his best suit were common. I remember as a small child during World War 11 that grandmother always smelt of carbolic; she worked in a soap factory.

My great-grandmother was a very little lady, so she became known to me as Little Gran. Her maiden name was Campbell so I must have six and a quarter percent Scottish genes kicking around somewhere. Her father John Campbell, who was originally a blacksmith, was my great-great-grandfather and by all accounts became a professional soldier. The story goes that he was promoted on the field of battle during the Crimean War and also served in the Boer War in South Africa but I have no details of his life.

Great-Grandmother married a Green, her only son Bill, my grandmother's brother was my favourite uncle, along with his only son, Bill the second. The younger Uncle Bill was called up as a teenager in the last war and served as a Desert Rat in the Eighth Army with General Montgomery. General Field Marshall Erwin Johannes Eugen Rommel, better known as the Desert Fox, gave them their name. After the Middle East, Uncle Bill served in Sicily, then Italy and finally finished up fighting in Greece. None of the family saw him for six years.

They became my favourite uncles as they loved football and took me to Old Trafford to watch Manchester United. Before I was born, Uncle Bill the Younger was made a fuss of in Grandmother's house in Bradford as it was full of females, Bill was the only boy in the family. As a very small child at the end of the war, I can just remember his wedding. He was dressed in his army uniform, dancing with his wife, my Aunty Lilly, to a tune belted out from an old piano. It's strange how certain events remain indelibly ingrained in memory.

I remember visiting my father at an airfield 'somewhere in England' and meeting his huge RAF pals. The war also made itself felt in another way. One day I was with my mother walking through Central Station in Manchester, which had been hit by an incendiary bomb and its soot stained glass roof badly damaged. We were getting a train somewhere, when a load of glass decided to detach itself and missed my head by inches. Mother probably protected me from certain death with her arm, which left her with a nasty cut. I remember the dismay and hurt I felt watching my mother bleeding and having her arm stitched up, even at that very young age it gave me a terrible deep-seated hatred of Hitler and bombs. So, even my dear mother was wounded in the war.

Although the war seemed normal to me as I knew nothing else I was certainly frightened of the terrible sound of the air raid sirens. I refused to go to the outside toilet in the back yard for a pee whenever the sirens went off. Mother assured me I had at least five minutes grace before the bombs dropped. I still dislike the sound of a siren. A young man who lived with his parents next door was in the navy and came home on leave one day with a banana which he gave to me. I had never seen one before but still remember eating it and his kind gesture. I often wonder if he survived the war.

A major event etched forever into my brain is the Victory in Europe Celebrations. VE day was an exciting time as the sun shone on a great line of wooden trestle tables lined up in the middle of the street laden with what little food we had. Everything was of course still rationed. No one had a car then of course so there was no traffic on the streets. It was the flags and bunting which impressed me most and I suppose the relief, joy and happiness expressed by the adults, mostly women.

At last Dad returned in one piece from the war in his demob suit. He had been out of work throughout the terrible years of the depression before the war and had been thankful to get a job as the manager of a coal yard in Ardwick; they gave him his job back. The pay was poor but he was loyal and would not leave, he always said his job was secure and they had given him the job during the depression years when he was desperate. He was made redundant along with a few million others during the Margaret Thatcher years. Our Prime Minister was better known to us as Snatcher Thatcher as she stole the school children's milk allowance.

A year after the war, Dad obtained a mortgage for a 1936 built semi-detached house in Droylsden. It cost the pricey sum of £700 and had a bathroom, electricity and an inside toilet. Great-Grandmother had passed away along with Grandmother's sisters, so Grandmother came to live with us. It was 1946 and I still have the house today. It had a garden, which to a five year old seemed enormous. I had not seen a house with one before as the streets of Bradford were simply row after row of terraced houses with back yards and outside toilets. I was ecstatic and soon made lots of new pals. It made a great change from playing with the rats in the back allies of Bradford.

My father kept in close contact with Bill, his friend from the RAF, after the war and we stayed for a few days in the summer at his beautiful white-washed cottage in Shropshire. He was a professional rabbit catcher and I would join him shooting rabbits. His kitchen had huge hunks of ham hanging from the oak beams, and their water supply was a natural spring in the garden. I loved the outside loo which had two seats, a big one for Mum and a little one next to her for me. When myxomatosis was introduced into the rabbit population it put him out of business and he was forced to leave his beautiful Welsh cottage and live on a housing estate. The butcher's shops with the affordable rabbits hanging outside on hooks were no more.

Grandmother passed away in her 70s, she had had a hard life and suffered from chronic bronchitis from living in the smog of Manchester most of her life.

One of my favourite subjects was geography as I was fascinated by maps and spent hours designing my own fictitious islands and river systems. Even as a young lad it seems I was a little like Slartibartfast who designed worlds in Douglas Adam's wonderful book, The Hitch Hiker's Guide to the Galaxy. Senior school was a nightmare with a deputy head called Heinz. We reckoned he was ex-Gestapo and had worked in a Nazi concentration camp. He took delight in inflicting pain on any kid he happened to see and was never without his short, thick stubby cane. I left school just after my 15th birthday in 1956 after coming top of the class. Looking back, I suppose it did not do me any harm whatsoever as at least I received a good education and with the extreme discipline, I could concentrate on my studies with little disturbance from other boys of an unruly nature. My teenage group of friends had regular fights with hooligans from Clayton, next door to Droylsden.

You might ask what all this has got to do with the exploration of caves, well, there are parallels. The rescue of injured people from caves is carried out by cavers, not by the police or fire brigades as is often depicted in the press. The police, of course, have overall responsibility for life and limb but hand over that responsibility to the voluntary cave rescue teams who are well versed and equipped to carry out a cave rescue of a trapped or injured victim.

The fire service are also on hand if their assistance is asked for.
Members of the cave rescue teams place themselves in a potentially dangerous situation on a cave rescue for an injured victim they do not know and are probably never likely to see again. The members of the rescue teams are all volunteers and do not get paid for their services. This is a classic case of human altruism. Caving expeditions are good examples; a good successful expedition entirely depends on a good team and good team work, not one individual. Of course there will always be the rare egotistical cheater, but they do not normally last long and usually do not get invited again. In other

words, the concept of altruism plays an important role in a cave explorer's life, and it certainly has in mine.

Tolerance and understanding of other people's cultures and religious beliefs must be taken into account when organising an expedition to a foreign country and the team needs to be picked accordingly as team members who act disrespectfully when a guest in another country can spell disaster for the expedition. It's important not to be portrayed as the superior great white colonial master who knows it all, so diplomacy needs to be implemented. If the above is disregarded the chances of receiving a permit to explore caves in a foreign country is greatly jeopardised.

I was not 100% sure what profession to follow at the age of 15 as I had two interests, chemistry and electronics and as I came out of school with a very good report, I could pick and choose. I wanted to be a radio operator in the Merchant Navy, but it was a one year full time course and the officer uniform cost £100, about 20 weeks' salary then. Mother was dead against it, so I looked elsewhere. Not liking the look of the apprentice chemists at the large Clayton Chemical Company, I chose electronics and started work at Fred Dawes in January 1957, just a few days after leaving school as a radio and TV apprentice on a wage of £1.50 per week, or 30 shillings as it was known then.

I gave mother all my wages and then she handed over my spending money. There was not much left. It seemed to me at the time a miracle that sound and pictures could be transmitted through thin air without being seen, so I was curious to understand it all. In the late 1950s and '60s it was easy to get a job and an apprenticeship, today it is damn near impossible. Metro Vickers at Trafford Park employed 1,000 engineering apprentices, probably one of the largest apprentice schools in the world. I went to night school three nights a week but most of the time I found myself falling asleep. It was a long day from 8 am to 10.30 pm before I returned home. I did not last long at Fred Dawes as I was told that I would never make the grade so I moved to Ridings Stores, again as an apprentice Radio and TV engineer. The advantage was that we had a day off every week to attend college. By the time I was 21, I had gained a City and Guilds Full Certificate as a Radio and TV Engineer and was an Associate of the Society of Radio and Electronic Engineers. Colour TV had just been introduced so I studied and received the City and Guilds qualification in Colour TV engineering. I just had to prove the Fred Dawes boss wrong. Eventually Ridings terminated my employment as I was a bit of a rebel but it was so easy to get another job. Just a phone call and the answer was always *'Can you start tomorrow?'*

I started work for Granada TV. It was great that I had a van I could use, wheels at last which made a change from the bicycle. As a young teenager I spent most Saturdays when I was not working with my uncles watching Manchester United playing great football at Old Trafford. The Busby Babes were a delight to watch and the Munich air disaster affected me deeply. I also loved the Speedway at Belle Vue and Stock Car racing. Of course living the life we did in the wilds of Manchester it was inevitable we would get into trouble eventually and we did. I liked playing football but I was useless at it and playing for a pub team against big hairy arsed hard drinkers on gravel pitches resembled a blood bath. I seemed more at home in the countryside.

As an apprentice I made some lifelong friends. Camping in the Peak District every Easter and again at Whit week was a great adventure. While at Ridings, I met my future first wife, Patricia. We went walking in the Peak District every weekend. Getting lost in the snow, wind, rain and often mist on the moors honed my skills in map reading and navigation.

My first trip abroad was with a bunch of friends when we were in our teens. We hired a car and drove to Dover catching the ferry to Calais. We hired a van and drove through France to Spain camping at Tossa de Mar. At the time it was the most exciting thing I had ever attempted. Walking down the street late at night, drunk and singing out loud, we were brutally attacked by a truncheon-bearing Guardia Civil who was hiding behind a wall. This was during the days of the Spanish Dictator, Francisco Franco Bahamonde but still it was a great adventure and served to wet my appetite for future travel to the far corners of the world.

2

Getting Hooked

When asked what surprised him most about humanity he replied,

'Man, because he sacrifices his health in order to make money. Then he sacrifices money to recuperate his health. And then he is so anxious about the future that he does not enjoy the present; the result being that he does not live in the present or the future: he lives as if he is never going to die, then dies having never really lived.'

Dalai Lama

One day in 1965, Patricia and I were waiting for a train at Guide Bridge Station near Ashton under Lyne, near where Pat lived. We were on our way to Castleton in the Peak District intending to hike across Mam Tor and into Edale.

A friend of hers was also at the station along with her boyfriend who was wearing a coal miner's pit helmet.

I asked, 'What the hell you are doing with a helmet on your head in a railway station?'

'I'm a potholer,' he replied.

I had heard about potholers having read the news reports of the tragic death of Neil Moss in Peak Cavern, Castleton Derbyshire in 1959. I also remembered an exciting, fascinating film of cave explorers in France and a Manchester Evening News story of how Peak Cavern had not yet been fully explored. I did not believe that there could be anywhere in Britain that had not been fully explored by man, especially a cave not far from where I lived.

I always thought, I would like to do that, but had no idea how to go about it.

'Why don't you tag along,' the lad said. At last I had met a real potholer who could tell me all about it. We always carried the basic survival gear while fell-walking, map, compass, whistle, waterproofs, food, water and of course a torch. 'You will need a light,' he said.

'No worries I have one,' I replied.

I followed him and his friend down Suicide Cave, Old Tor Mine and a few other caves in Winnats Pass just with my torch and felt a surge of adrenaline. I enjoyed grovelling around in the dark. The following week I joined him again, this time with an old pit helmet and bicycle lamp. Squeezing through a tight crawl in Mam Tor Swallet, I could hear my own heart beating as I was surrounded by rock on all sides. The adrenaline rush was even stronger when I reached the surface. This is for me I thought.

We missed the last train back from Hope Station as the guy I was with kept disappearing into little holes in the ground, so we set off walking. There were no buses and no one wanted to give a couple of very dirty, muddy guys a lift. We decided to take a short cut over Mam Tor, into Edale then across Kinder Scout down into Hayfield. It's not exactly short; it's a hell of a long way but cut out a massive circular route via Chapel-en-le-Frith. I knew the way like the back of my hand which was a good job as it soon went dark. We reached Hayfield about 1am the following day and I immediately found a telephone box and phoned the police to ask if they would let my parents know that I was OK. We did manage to get a lift and I arrived home about 3 am. It became obvious to me that the lad with his pit helmet on his head knew little about caves.

I was enthusiastic and told my good friend Dave Adderly all about my adventures. He wanted a share of the cake so we teamed up and started regular trips to Derbyshire. By this time, I had acquired the work's Granada TV van so getting around become much easier. We read everything we could find on caves and ordered books from Droylsden Library. Norbert Casteret books were avidly read, Ten Years under the Earth and My Caves. Haroun Tazieff on the Pierre-Saint-Martin Expedition in the French Pyrenees, Fernand Petzl's adventures in the classic Pierre Chevalier book Subterranean Climbers, which described the exploration of the Dent de Crolles cave system and best of all, Jean Cadoux's famous book One Thousand Metres Down on the exploration of the Gouffre Berger, the first cave to reach a depth of over one kilometre. The above adventures centred on French cave explorers exploring French caves and made very exciting reading.

For the uninitiated, a few facts need to be explained about caves and areas where caves can be found the general public conception is that caves are very dirty little wet muddy holes in the ground. Some are, but others are far from that belief. Some caves are incredibly beautiful with rivers and streams, adorned with calcite formations, stalactites, stalagmites and columns reaching up to the roof and various other forms of mineral deposits and rock formations. Cave formations are usually referred to as speleothems. Some caves have massive dimensions with extraordinary lengths, some many hundreds of kilometres in length and are labyrinths of passages at various levels. The total length of a cave is all its branch passages measured and added together so as caves are a complex three dimensional maze on multiple levels. A 100 kilometre long cave system can often be found in a block of limestone only a few tens of kilometres square in total area.

In geological terms limestone areas are known as karst, and caves are formed in limestone because of its chemical composition. Some fantastic caves can be found in lava beds from volcanoes, known as lava tubes, but these are rare and cannot be found in the UK. Hawaii is one of the major areas in the world for lava tube development.

Limestone is composed of calcium carbonate that is deposited over many millions of years below the sea by the remains of dead sea creatures; these sedimentary deposits build up to great thicknesses and are compressed into solid rock, later to be thrust up above the surface of the sea by tectonic movements of the earth's crust. Limestone can then be attacked by rain water. This is due to weak carbonic acid in the rain drops, derived from the carbon dioxide found in air, which will slowly dissolve away limestone. Vegetation in surface streams also contributes significantly to carbonic acid content and so carves out caves along weaknesses in the rock. Vertical fractures and horizontal beds are obvious weaknesses where water can flow, enlarging the weaknesses over thousands of years into caves. Rivers and streams flowing into the caves also wear away the limestone into meandering passage shapes.

Where a surface stream or river disappears underground it is known as a sink or swallet. The water normally has to come out somewhere, it does not just disappear and these places where it reaches the open air again are generally referred to as springs, risings or resurgences, and can be many miles away from the source and much lower down in altitude. The majority of rainwater tends to sink underground in limestone areas through joints and fissures. This water is known as percolation water and so limestone areas have no surface streams except in times of heavy rain. The contact between the limestone and other rocks are areas where stream sinks can be found.

If you dig deep enough on any dry land throughout the earth you will hit water. This is known as the water table or aquifer. Wells are an important source of water supplies. Nevada in the USA is built on its aquifer which eventually will run out of water judging by the amount they use. Only rain water sinking in the ground can recharge the aquifer and in limestone areas the same principle applies. The depth of the water table is determined by the geographical terrain. Most mines need water pumps in order to mine deep below the earth, or drainage tunnels known as adits or soughs. In caves when the natural water table is reached, the passages are normally flooded and are known as siphons or sumps. This is where the cave divers come into their own as it is can be possible to dive through with compressed air and emerge on the far side in air filled passages as sometimes these siphons are perched and will rise upwards above the water table. It is sometimes possible just to take a deep breath and free dive through a short and shallow sump, which can be intimidating as the caver has no idea where they are going.

So every cave is very old, different and unique; no two are ever the same. Multiple passages can be developed on different levels depending on their age. The higher levels are the older. Fractures produce vertical drops known as shafts, pots or pits or, in French, puits.

One never can tell where a cave is going or what is around the next bend as unlike a mountain, caves cannot be seen, unless you carry a light and delve into their mysteries. In scientific terms, cave explorers and scientists studying caves are known as speleologists, a name that sounds important and a little more respectable than a potholer or a caver.

The science of speleology is a fascinating and complex subject and in the UK we are lucky enough to have some of the most knowledgeable cave scientists in the world, all passionate about their chosen subject. All are only too willing to present lectures on cave evolution at caving conferences and will spend their precious time talking personally about their latest theories and passing on their knowledge, even to cavers like me with little or no scientific background.

There are a number of major limestone areas in the British Isles containing caves: Derbyshire and Staffordshire, the Yorkshire Dales, North and South Wales, the Mendip Hills of Somerset, the Sutherland region of Scotland, Northern and Southern Ireland. There are a few other isolated areas but these are the major ones.

The books whetted my appetite and I was enthralled by the adventures they contained. I bought David Heap's book on the caves of the Yorkshire Dales, Beneath the Northern Pennines and we searched for caving magazines but never found any. There seemed to be magazines for every subject you could think of, but nothing on caves and caving. It was then that I found by accident Dr Trevor Ford's guide book The Caves of Derbyshire which was the bible of recorded caves in the Peak District.

In later years, attempts were made to produce a cavers' magazine to record the exploits of Britain's cave explorers. The first was The Speleologist, which only ran to a few issues but this was closely followed by Bruce Bedford's magazine, Descent later to be produced and edited by Chris Howes under Wild Places Publishing. This has now become the established cavers' magazine, well produced with colour photographs and is wildly read by all of Briton's cave explorers with a passion for the underground, it also reaches many cavers abroad so has become something of a British cavers' national treasure.

We bought some nylon climbing ropes and stinky Premier carbide lamps. Calcium carbide is a magic material that resembles lumps of coal; when it comes into contact with water, it fizzes and produces acetylene gas. Acetylene gas is highly inflammable and is used along with oxygen for welding. The carbide lamps are made of brass and have a lower chamber filled two-thirds with carbide and a chamber above filled with water. This upper chamber has a tap that allows a controlled water flow onto the calcium carbide in the chamber below. The inflammable gas is then directed via a filter to a tiny jet where it can be lit by a spark like one from a cigarette lighter. The Premier lamp is armed with thin wire prickers so the jet can be cleared of soot. The flame produced can be varied in size; the more water, the bigger the flame. With a polished reflector the light was bright and spare carbide could be carried along with water. If the caver ran out of water, he could always pee into the reservoir; OK for the men but a little difficult for the ladies, although a gentleman can always offer his assistance in this regard. Carbide has a very distinctive smell, hence the nickname of Stinky. The lamps had a hanger so they could be slotted onto a bracket fixed to a miner's caving helmet.

We used this type of lighting and rechargeable lead acid miners' lamps for over 50 years until the recent advent of powerful light emitting diodes, LEDs, which only require small dry cell batteries. Oldham's miners' lamps were commonly used in UK caves but did not stay charged for more than 12 hours or so. Often, after a long trip, the light output reduced to a tiny red glow, it was then that your true caving friends became even closer. Carbide lights tended to be used on expeditions as normally being under canvas at the top of some mountain or other, facilities for recharging lead acids is not usually available. On the other hand, carbide can be obtained in most countries of the world and water is freely available, unless you live in Britain where it rains a lot and they charge us for it.

As the two of us were novices, we had no ladders for climbs within the caves so used our ropes, climbing hand over hand. An epic trip down Perryfoot Cave when our lights went out brought home the dangers involved in caving when we knew damn all about it. We groped back to daylight in total blackness feeling our way by touch alone. It needs to be pointed out that there is zero light within a cave, leaving behind absolute blackness. The only creatures that can navigate through caves without any form of lighting are bats and cave swiftlets with their echo sounding capabilities, and unfortunately humans do not have this amazing ability. These little creatures have a brain the size of a pea where we need rather large machines. Troglobitic insects can do the same using chemicals and receptors to find food and a mate. What this means for a cave explorer is, no light, no life. We reached the surface and lit a cigarette relaxing in the beautiful sunlight and from then on always carried spare carbide or a candle.

Thumbing through the Derbyshire guidebook, it became apparent that if we wanted to take our chosen sport one step further, we needed to join a caving club, but the question was which one, as at the time there were many.

The club that seemed to have the majority of references quoted in the guide book was the Eldon Pothole Club based in Buxton. And as Buxton was the closest place to Manchester with a caving club, I wrote to the late Dr Hugh Kidd, the secretary and he invited us down.

John Needham taught us to climb electron wire ladders and to safely lifeline each other at a quarry in Buxton. The way of negotiating vertical drops in caves was to hang a wire ladder down, attached to a solid protruding rock; such ladders have aluminium rungs and sway around as they are flexible, so take practice to climb without using too much effort. A rope lifeline is attached to the climber and held by the man at the top, so if the caver falls, his friend can hold him on the line preventing his death or serious injury.

The big attraction of joining the club was the Eldon Hostel at the back of a pub on Hardwick Street, Buxton. The hostel, with a row of rickety bunk beds, was a den of iniquity occupied by a bunch of eccentric caving characters the likes of which I had never met before. On the wall was a map of the Gouffre Berger. The late Dave Allsop, one of the founders of the Eldon Pothole Club, had led a successful expedition there and reached the bottom of what then was the deepest cave in the world. Even the great legend of cave exploration, Norbert Casteret was an honorary member. It looked like I had joined the right club.

We were voted in at the next general meeting and from that day forward I was hooked, both line and sinker. My fate was now well and truly sealed.

I caved in woollies and cotton oversuits but froze to death most of the time. The temperature in caves is determined by the average temperature in the specific area wherever they happen to be, so the cold conditions in the Peak District caves necessitated warm clothing. Passing the bailed-out water-filled sump passage in Giants Hole was a pain but you soon became warm racing down Crab Walk. A concrete dam had been built some way inside the cave at a flooded section of tunnel. This had been constructed by the original explorers of Giants Hole, so the sump could be back-bailed with buckets to give a small air space above the solid rock roof. It was then a case of wallowing through very cold water with your nose pressed against the roof so you could breathe in some air. After about three hours, the sump filled up again with water, so speed was essential.

Some had Goon suits, ex RAF survival suits designed for pilots ditching in the sea. Ex-Army and Navy Stores were our main shopping centres. The Goon suits were bulky and usually leaked like a sieve so I invested in some neoprene rubber and glued a wetsuit together of the type normally used by scuba divers. Life underground became much more pleasurable, although the wetsuit did have a habit of falling apart. But the beauty was that you could just patch it up again by gluing it together. Although you still became wet in a wetsuit as the name implies, the water held in the pores becomes warm due to body heat, so it insulates you from the cold, providing of course you keep on the move. Inactivity for a long spell and the water held in the pores soon cools down then shivering commences.

Only a few months after I joined the Eldon, the big split occurred. The hierarchy, the older members whom had formed the club in the 1950s also ran it. The caving for the most part was carried out by the younger guys, most of them eccentric lunatics, heavy drinkers, party goers, hell raisers, but good, tough competent cavers. A general meeting was called and a proposal to terminate the membership of certain hell raisers was defeated. The committee, comprising the original founding members, stood up, resigned and walked out. I found myself as the treasurer and not much later took over the job of secretary as well. After just a few months of membership, I was running the club. The next meeting divided the club assets and the founders of the Eldon formed the Buxton Speleological Group.

I could not cave every weekend as I was on a roster system at Granada but managed most Sundays. Patricia came to Derbyshire with me most of the time and sat patiently in the van waiting for my return or came underground with me. I caved mainly with the late Gordon Parkin and my first major caving trip that earned the name hard was down Nettle Pot to the bottom of Elizabeth Shaft on ladders with Dave Adderly and Bob Dearman. The shafts are deep and tiring to climb back out on thin wire electron ladders. We returned very tired late at night so I slept most of the next day in the hostel and found I had missed going to work, something I had never done before. I could see that caving was going to interfere with earning a living and I was proved correct many times in the years to come.

The Eldon Stomps must be mentioned as they became famous, with a very loud rock band, heavy drinking and the inevitable stomp when everyone joined forces and arms in a great swaying circle. I lost count of how many glasses we broke and how many pubs we were banned from. The favourite was the White Lion just off Hardwick Street in Buxton. If the windows were open, clouds of steam from lots of very sweaty drunken and half naked cavers poured out into the frosty night air. Down below the plaster fell off the ceiling with the heavy stomping and the local drinkers covered their beer with beer mats. The beer was cheap then and tended to be thrown over anyone and everyone. Some cavers not knowing the consequences of Eldon Stomps arrived in suits and went home in rags.

The Easter trip to Ogof Agen Allwedd, a long and complex cave in South Wales was not to be missed. The SAS training ground was close by and collections were made of blank and live ammunition. Rockets, flares and stun grenades were the favourite collector's pieces, spectacular when thrown on the bonfire. The caving was good too and in later years I became a leader for Dan yr Ogof, partly a show cave open to the public but with huge passages going on for miles, reserved only for the cave explorers.

We had a nice armour piercing shell in the Eldon Hostel as a trophy for many years, thinking it was a dummy. We were surprised when a marine visited us and pronounced it live. I am not sure what we did with it, it probably got dumped on a policeman's doorstep.

The late Dr Ken Pearce of Gouffre Berger fame, who led expeditions to the deepest cave in the world, liked digging Biza Passage in Ogof Agen Allwedd at the end of the notorious Southern Stream Passage. The aim was to bypass the upstream choke of fallen boulders, a huge pile of rocks blocking the obvious way on. Southern Stream passage was over a mile of arduous low crawling that seemed to go on and on forever. Ken was a big man and would tear off at great pace then slow down at the tight sections of cave, then once through he would shoot off at speed. Those following him had to keep up and it seemed to be a deliberate ploy to tire them out.

Alan Gamble one of my great caving partners needed to prick the jet of his carbide lamp.

'Give it to me,' said Ken and snatched it out of his hand. He pushed it into the mud and ran off leaving Alan in the dark with no light and no chance of lighting it.

When the team arrived back on the surface they asked where Alan was. Ken said, 'Still in the cave.'

By midnight, he had still not turned up so a few of his friends started looking for him. They found a very angry Alan near the First Boulder Choke which consisted of many tight squeezes through boulders, impossible to negotiate in absolute blackness.

Ken was known as Black Pearce. A powerful imposing figure, a giant but a caver of exceptional ability but he loved to write off fellow cavers, more in fun than anything else. Of course, Alan was never in any danger as it was Ken's way of teaching initiative. It worked for many, but failed for many more.

On the Whit Week holidays we always travelled to the Mendip caving region in Somerset and enjoyed trips down many of the area's finest caves, the caving songs in the Hunters' Lodge being one of the high spots of the occasion.

One day, we had a mass trip into Oxlow Caverns in Derbyshire and I took Patricia with me. Pat was a good caver and came with me on many underground trips. After the trip we all retired to the pub and then went on our separate ways. Gordon Parkin was with us in the cave and I remember he went to fill his carbide lamp with water but he was not travelling at the time with me, someone else had given him a lift to Oxlow. Usually after the pub Gordon began his long arduous hitch hiking to get back to London where he lived and worked, arriving dirty and tired just in time to clock on at work so no one missed him thinking he had set off early. On Monday night, his mother became worried when he did not return home from work.

She gave his caving friends a ring in Buxton. 'Have you seen our Gordon?' But no one had seen him since the Oxlow trip.

One of the lads went back to Oxlow and found his clothes in a plastic bag behind the farm wall. Gordon's carbide lamp had gone out and he had been unable to light it as one of his friends was carrying the spare calcium carbide. Left in the pitch dark in Oxlow Caverns, on his own for 36 hours or so, he passed the time singing songs to himself knowing that eventually someone would miss him. We got some stick for that episode but he did forgive us.

Regular trips were made to the finest caving region in England, the Yorkshire Dales. My first trip was Simpson Pot with two members of the Eldon, both tragically killed years later, one in the mountains and one driving to get to them.

A trip into Lancaster Hole, in the Yorkshire Dales, turned into an epic when we decided to swim the final 30 metres into the main underground river draining into the downstream sump. A sump is where the river becomes completely flooded and the passage is filled to the roof with water. Only cave divers with compressed air can penetrate beyond, a very dangerous pastime with no room for mistakes.

The current was strong and the late George Cooper and I found ourselves being swept into the sump and a watery grave. I am a strong swimmer, or was in those days, and just made it back to the shingle bank. George finished up clinging to a tiny ledge with his fingertips. There was no way I could swim back with him against the current. I floundered exhausted on the bank and shouted for a rope but no one had one. The guys did not seem to know what to do so I sent someone back to the main chamber to bring a rope. Speed was essential as George would not be able to cling on for long as he was being hit by a strong current of water. The guy I sent floundered and moved very slowly so I set off at a cracking pace leaping over boulders. I reached the chamber, grabbed a rope and raced back. I expected not to see George again but he was still there clinging on in desperation.

I threw the rope at the nearest man and shouted for him to tie on and swim to the rescue.

The reply was, 'I can't swim.'

No one seemed to want to jump in and grab George. By this time I had expended a great deal of calories but it was a case of shit or bust. I tied the rope around my waist, handed it to the group on the bank and jumped in. Within seconds I had been washed downstream and reached George, By this time his knuckles were white. Tying a loop while treading fast-moving water was not easy, but I managed it and placed the loop over his shoulders and shouted the boys to pull. They all pulled but far too fast, so 20 metres or so we spent under water. George sang hymns all the way out.

I started diving with the British Sub Aqua Club and enjoyed the open water but decided cave diving was akin to committing suicide, so I dropped the idea.

Patricia and I liked to travel, and I could not resist visiting the Caves of Drach in Majorca and the Postonja Cave system in President Tito's Yugoslavia, now an independent Slovenia. Travelling is a bug I have never been able to throw off. I was to do an awful lot of it in the years to come.

One day, Paul Deakin happened to mention that Ken Pearce was organising another expedition to the Gouffre Berger, and did I fancy it? There was no need for an answer so we went to see Big Black Pearce. So began another chapter of my life that continues to this day.

As I said previously, I was never very good at sport as a schoolboy, but had finally found something I was reasonably good at. I had at last discovered my true vocation in life.

Speedwell Cavern, Derbyshire. Photo: Paul Deakin.

3

1967 Gouffre Berger Expedition and a new depth record

'It is only in adventure that some people succeed in knowing themselves and finding themselves.

Andre Gidé

The book One Thousand Metres Down by Jean Cadoux describing the exploration of the Gouffre Berger was enough to inspire any young caver, and it certainly inspired me. I still consider this as one of the best caving books ever written but it seemed at that time that the Berger was well beyond my reach. Surly this cave was the reserve of only the very top internationally well-known cave explorers. The entrance to the cave was originally discovered by Joseph Berger on the 24th May 1953 and subsequently explored over a period of a few years by some of France's top speleologists.

It came as something of a surprise on joining the Eldon Pothole Club to discover that Dave Allsop, Ken Pearce and other leading lights of the Derbyshire caving scene had actually led expeditions to this mighty 1,122 metre deep cave, the deepest in the world, the Everest of the underworld. It appeared that I had unwittingly joined the right club.

Within a year of joining the Eldon, Paul Deakin suggested I might be interested in Ken Pearce's next expedition to the Berger. With no hesitation, we both knocked on Ken's door. The sight of Big Black Pearce, as he was affectionately known, was enough to strike terror into the heart of any budding caver. He was a huge, powerfully built man with an equally powerful personality, not a man to be trifled with. Within a couple of weeks, we found ourselves along with John Sinclair, Henry Mares, and Alastair Watt plus Big Ken on a windswept moor in the Dales armed with a mountain of electron ladders and ropes. I remember little except for a dirty great big dark wet 67 metre pitch.

Pearce lifelined us to the bottom. John went up the electron ladder first but for some unknown reason started to climb back down again. Curious, I thought. He then proceeded to climb back up again. Even more curious. It was my turn next. Usually on a deep pitch the man at the top will give a good pull on the lifeline rope in order to help the man climbing up on the ladder. All the way up, I appeared to have a large loop of lifeline hanging by my side. At last I reached the top with arms like lead weights but Ken growled at me not to get off the ladder and to climb back down until I say stop. I proceeded like a fool to make a painful way back down. About three metres from the bottom of the pitch, the shout came for me to climb back up, there was no chance of getting off the ladder for a rest. On reaching the top, he graciously granted me permission to get off the ladder and stand on solid ground. Paul underwent the same exercise without hesitation. Alastair complained bitterly but succumbed to Ken's growls and did it as well. Henry, on the other hand, told him where to go.

On reaching the surface, Ken pronounced that Sinclair, Deakin and Gill were OK for the assault team. Nodding in the general direction of Alastair, he pronounced that he was suitable for the support party. He gave Henry a black look, meaning you can't come.

On our return to Derbyshire, the horror stories about Dr Ken Pearce's previous expeditions to the Berger started to be aimed in our direction. We were considered to be stark raving mad as his dictatorial style of leadership was too much for most. The tales of cavers dousing their carbide lights and hiding behind boulders as Ken Pearce passed by, pretending to refill their carbide or pricking the jet just to gain some respite from the rigours of caving with Big Black Pearce. Blistered feet and Berger hands as it became known, hands that went soft and rotten after being constantly wet for weeks, living underground for three weeks without seeing the light of day and subsisting on tinned carrots. Cavers returning to the surface and burning their gear, vowing never to go caving again. For many the Berger was their very last caving trip.

A great tale was when Ken asked Bob Toogood to return to the surface for more fuel for the stoves as Bob was about the only one that could be trusted to return. His famous quote to Bob was that when he got to the top of Aldo's Pitch he was to pull the ladders up so no one could escape. The best one of all just has to be one of Ken's quotations.

The caver, lying on the surface exhausted with bleeding hands and blistered feet, was told, 'OK you, back down the cave with those 30 bags.'

The reply was that the caver had not slept for three days.

'If you're not hard, sonny, you shouldn't have come,' said Ken.

I suppose this summed up the man. He never asked you to do something he could not do himself so therefore commanded complete respect. Strangely, the stories did not put us off and the next few training meets were just as much fun as the first. The saving grace was that we were caving with the new breed of hard Yorkshire Dales cavers, the Happy Wanderers.

It was then that tragedy struck, when some of the team members were swept to their deaths in Mossdale Caverns, in the Yorkshire Dales. This cave is many miles long and arduous with low flood prone tunnels. The weather forecast did not anticipate a heavy thunderstorm but the weather broke and the stream flowing into the cave became a torrent. The cave flooded to the roof and all of the men exploring the cave lost their lives.

The effect on the rest of the Berger expedition team was devastating. We were all cut to the core. I normally caved in the Dales every couple of weeks with the Eldon Pothole Club and the Happy Wanderers Caving Club and for some unknown reason decided not to go on that particular weekend. I never did fathom out why, maybe fate had something else in store. As soon as I could arrange my off day at work by swapping with my friend, I raced up to Mossdale. There was nothing anyone could do except keep an eye on the water level. A dam had been built and some of the rescue team very bravely went down Mossdale Caverns in an attempt to find our friends but they were all dead. It was decided on safety grounds to leave our friends where they lay; retrieving their bodies would put all the underground rescue teams in great danger from further floods. Some years later their remains were buried in one of Mossdale's chambers by their friends.

The aftermath of this tragedy lasted for many years and was particularly felt on this 1967 Berger Expedition. Many deserted the field unable to come to terms with what had happened to their pals.

The expedition objective this time around was to get five divers plus diving compressed air tanks to the normal end of the cave, which was a sump at 1,122 metres below the entrance; this was where the underground river became flooded to the roof. In 1963, Ken had passed this Sump 1 to dry passage but hit another sump at a depth from the surface of 1,135 metres, a new depth record. He returned with a strong team in 1964 but was beaten back by flood water. The intention this time around was to dive through both sumps and hopefully reach dry cave passage on the other side and break the world depth record.

We were to set up two underground camps where we would sleep and eat, Camp 1, near the Hall of the Thirteen and Camp 2 situated just above the Grand Canyon. Ken having dived through the sump on his last expedition, considered that with more tanks of compressed air and a team of experienced cave divers, the second sump could be passed to dry cave beyond. He considered the Gouffre Berger as the greatest challenge facing cave exploration at that time.

I spent many weekends at Ken's cottage near Chapel en le Frith in Derbyshire working on the expedition equipment. At the time, I worked at Granada TV as did one of the cave diving team members and asked for my two weeks annual holiday entitlement plus one extra week without pay. The boss declined and said I could not be off work at the same time as the diver. I had no alternative but to resign, there was no way I was going to miss this trip.

After the traumas of the preceding months, no one quite knew what to expect. Over 30 team members had assembled on the plateau close to the Berger entrance. This time we had permission. It appeared that Ken Pearce's last expedition never received the required permit from the local mayor and Ken and his team just disappeared down the cave to reappear three weeks later much to the dismay of the French. After all, it was their cave.

Ken hired a bus and we piled it high with equipment and food, all packed in ex-army stuff bags and bright yellow fibre glass boxes with slots where a carry frame could be attached. These were packed with our food supplies to prevent them from getting wet. The compressed air bottles were packed in similar yellow fibre glass, as a tube with a ring attached where a rope could be fixed to facilitate lowering down the shafts. We drove through the night on the way to the French Vercors and tried to sleep curled up on top of the bags. The Vercors scenery is spectacular with numerous gorges, canyons and twisting mountain roads. From the road head it was then a pleasant walk across the plateau, through the limestone pavements and fir trees to our intended base camp situated not far from the entrance of the Gouffre Berger. Carrying all the equipment to base camp was a pain, and blisters became a common complaint as the loads were heavy and numerous.

Much media hype accompanied the run up to the expedition and the expedition itself. The newspapers were well represented on the plateau at base camp. Ken had been described in the press as 'The Iron Man of British Caving.' 'He gets his men up at 6 am and forces them to carry a heavy load from the road head to base camp before breakfast,' was the report in the British press. At least that much was true.

On the plus side, there were two British teams working in the cave at the same time. Besides Ken Pearce's team, there was a large strong contingent from the Nottingham based Pegasus Caving Club. They had agreed to rig the cave and lay a telephone line as far as the underground Camp 2, situated above the Grand Canyon, a huge tunnel full of boulders that had fallen from the roof. Dr Harold Lord was in charge of communications and had developed the first transmitter-receiver molephone, using long radio waves via a large loop of copper wire; messages could be transmitted through solid rock and received underground. This ingenious system was successfully tried and tested in the Berger.

The first trip down the many vertical drops of the entrance series of passages lasted an exhausting 36 hours, with all the equipment and food supplies being piled high at the bottom of Aldo's Shaft. Everything appeared to be going well. One of the normal thunder storms occurred while we were underground and as the limestone acts like a sponge, a short flood pulse livened things up and the team waited it out while the flood water receded before climbing back up the shafts. Trying to climb up a shaft on wire ladders under a powerful waterfall usually results in drowning or severe hypothermia and has resulted in fatalities on a number of occasions.

The second trip was going to last for over a week. Twenty-five men descended on their way to Camp 1 that day where they intended to sleep. As there is no night and day in a cave, it did not matter when one slept or worked, it's always dark so 36 hour continuous work was not uncommon.

The problems started almost immediately as many felt totally uneasy in the cave. Everyone knew it was prone to extreme flooding at the onset of rain but with the phone line manned over a 24 hour period sufficient notice could be given of an impending thunder storm before a push to the bottom where it was very likely you could become trapped by flood water or caught out while climbing a ladder. There are many places where it is possible to get out of the underground river and sit it out until the flood receded. I have done this on a few occasions in various caves in different parts of the world; long, often hungry, cold and boring waits, watching the river either rising, which is worrying, or receding, which is a relief. Many years later a number of cavers lost their lives exploring the Berger when a flood pulse hit and they were unable to make it to dry land in time.

The Gouffre Berger has claimed the lives of six cavers over the years. On one occasion a young man from the Derbyshire area called Alex Pitcher lost his life. Becoming bored while waiting for his friends, he wandered off climbing into the roof of a passage near the entrance. Finding a small ongoing passage, it appears he fell down a vertical drop along with some falling boulders and was killed. The French rescue teams searched for many days before he was found.

The aftermath of the Mossdale tragedy was felt by all and began to take effect. The late Pete Livesey went missing in the Meanders, a narrow twisting passage where one needs to traverse hundreds of feet above the floor. A slip could be fatal as it's too narrow at the bottom of the trench to make progress. Someone was sent to search for him, but Pete was found safe and back on the surface. Those sent to search for him did not return, nor did Pete.

Four of us, including Paul Deakin and my diving friend from Granada TV, were assigned to work all night while the rest of the team, about 20 men, retired to their sleeping bags at Camp 1. Ken only had 20 sleeping bags so we were classified as the night shift. Our job was to ferry the equipment along the Petzl Gallery from Aldo's Shaft where we had previously left all the equipment at the Great Rubble Heap and from there, if we were still standing, to Camp 1. The Great Rubble Heap was, as the name suggests, a vast chamber full of house-sized boulders that had fallen from the roof, something of a tall order for just four of us to move the mountain of equipment. I suppose it was something of an honour, as Ken must have trusted us to do the job without skiving off. We worked throughout the night, backwards and forwards. Pick up a bag or an enormous great big heavy yellow fibre glass box, carry it down, dump it in a safe place where it would not get washed away, return and pick up another one.

And so the night wore on. Before long my friend, the diver from Granada TV who was one of the four, caught the jitters and asked Paul to lifeline him up Aldo's Shaft. He had had enough and wanted out. Paul obliged, so then there were three.

I was the first to reach Camp 1 with the first load. One of the team crawled out of his sleeping bag and asked where the rest were. I explained the situation. He seemed to understand and said he was off out to persuade the diver to return, yet another said the same. As I ferried equipment down the Great Rubble Heap, people kept passing me on the way out. Panic had set in big time. Before Ken emerged from his sleeping bag his team of 20 had reduced down to about ten. At this point, I felt that after carrying the third load down that I had to wake him up and explain the desertions. I was worried he would bite my head off but Ken was quite calm about it as I am sure he understood the general feelings of disquiet. He called a meeting saying that as we were not strong enough to get him to the bottom with the diving gear, the expedition is abandoned. Most of the divers had deserted and there was no arguing with Ken, his decision was final.

We began the long trek out carrying the gear back to Aldo's, all that hard work had amounted to nothing. We stashed the gear at the base of Aldo's Shaft and retired to the surface. The three of us had been on our feet with little sleep for almost three days.

Back on the surface, Ken Pearce approached Peter Watkinson, the Pegasus Caving Club leader, and asked could he join them, plus his diving gear. They respectfully declined but agreed to rig the cave with ladders and ropes to the bottom.

A small group of us had a meeting. I had resigned my job to come on the expedition as Granada TV had refused to give me three weeks off and all the work and effort seemed to have been for nothing. The remaining stalwarts still interested in getting to the bottom of the Berger approached Ken with a scenario. A group of nine, mainly from the Wanderers, which included Stewart Whitmey who was to lead the trip, and Jim Cunningham, would descend and carry Ken's diving bottles to Camp 2. If successful in establishing Camp 2 we would use the telephone line and call Ken to join us for the trip to the bottom. With little choice, he agreed. The trip to Camp 1 and 2 was uneventful and enjoyable compared to the previous week's work, a group of friends working together for a common aim with no dictator. There was no need for a leader as everyone knew what to do. Two days later, I phoned Ken from Camp 2, asking him to join us the following day as the day after we were off to the bottom with his diving bottles. The following day, Ken Pearce arrived with Dave Taylor. Pearce seemed amazingly docile.

A call to the surface brought the news that the weather forecast was good. The trip was on. The way to the bottom was cold and wet, descending pitch after pitch, most with waterfalls pouring down alongside. It was impossible to keep out of the spray. Swimming through a long canal leading to the sump trying to keep the water out of our flimsy dry suits proved difficult, if not impossible. The suits had been designed with a drain hole near the feet, just in case they filled with water, which they did from around the neck seal. As the suit filled with water, our legs filled up like balloons with the icy cold water weighing us down. By removing the plug, the water could be drained, otherwise your legs weighed a ton and it was impossible to walk. The temperature within the cave is little more than one degree above freezing so it is essential to keep warm otherwise exposure can set in with dire consequences.

We arrived at the sump, the lowest point in the cave normal cavers can go, 1,122 metres below the surface. Ken Pearce had already kitted up with his diving equipment and disappeared into the flooded tunnel.

Cave divers usually use twin side-mounted tanks and work on the rule of thirds, one third of air to go forward, one third for retreating. The remaining third is held in reserve for emergency use. After one third of the total air supply is used, the diver turns around and comes out. A diving line is laid through a sump as often the visibility is so bad the diver cannot see his hand in front of his face. To lose the line can be fatal as the diver can become disorientated in the pitch blackness and can stir up sediment in the flooded passage, so often his dive light does not penetrate far ahead. If he loses the line he has little idea which way is up, down, out, or in.

We waited shivering in our wet clothes for Pearce to return from the sump after we'd stopped paying out the thin line attached to him. He eventually emerged after a long dive smiling.

'Well, Ken what happened?'

No answer, was the firm reply.

All the way back to Camp 2, he refused to say, he merely rocked backwards and forwards to keep warm, and grinned.

The trip out was good. For a change, Ken told no one what to do; we just got on with it. There was some banter between this team and our now docile leader.

Ken's normal behaviour was to lie in his pit at the underground camp and growl out his orders, 'Cunningham, stove; Gill, water; Deakin, pots.'

Now it was our turn. 'Pearce, breakfast,' we cried as we had a lie in.

Even more fun was had when Ken contacted his wife on the surface by the telephone link and spoke in code, 'The Mayor of Sassenage is having dinner tonight.' This was his secret message that he had been successful and wanted to dive in the Cuves de Sassenage, the resurgence for the Berger where the underground river emerged into daylight. Of course permission was refused point blank as it's the water supply for the town. Harold Lord had great fun pretending to be working with the French Resistance as messages went backwards and forwards. 'The biscuit is broken in three pieces,' and 'My wife is wearing her blue panties.' The banter was endless.

Our small party that reached the bottom of the Berger consisted of Julian Coward, Frank Barnes, John Huntington, Jim Cunningham, Dave Fisher, John Rushton, Stuart Whitmey, the deputy leader, Dave Taylor, John Shepherd, Ken Pearce and yours truly.

The successful bottom party. (Back Row L to R) J Coward, F Barnes, K Pearce, JS Huntingdon, DW Gill, J Cunningham. (Front Row L to R) D Fisher, J Rushton, SME Whitmey, DJ Taylor, J Shepherd. Photographer unknown.

Back on the surface after a trip lasting about a week, Ken tried to sell the story to the newspapers, as far as I know without success. After a few days he eventually told us that he had passed through the two sumps with steeply dipping open river passage beyond and arrived at a pitch, a vertical drop he could not descend without a ladder, thus breaking the world depth record, or so he thought at the time. He reached a depth of 1,135 metres below the surface but of course this was only an estimate as an accurate measurement required a cave survey map with length, bearing and slope angle. It transpired later that French cave explorers had reached a depth of 1,171 metres in the Pierre-Saint-Martin cave system in the French Pyrenees in 1966.

The official history published in both hard copy and digital format on the internet suggests that Ken Pearce descended and broke the world depth record with the Pegasus expedition under the leadership of Peter Watkinson. This is not the case. He descended with his own team as described above. This does not detract from the commendable work and efforts of the Pegasus team as they were responsible for rigging the cave with ladders and ropes to the bottom and were an important part of the overall effort. In fact, a great deal of the rigging of the cave was undertaken by 'Wingnut' Huntington, a member of my club, the Eldon Pothole Club, who had joined the Pegasus expedition team.

This was to be Ken Pearce's last expedition as his dictatorial style of leadership had been destroyed. Democracy or anarchy now ruled. Alan Gamble, one of my caving partners always said, 'There is only one rule, there are no rules.' I did not agree as some rules are required for a successful expedition, but democracy needs to be implemented, as the consideration and aspirations of the team are important factors for success. This expedition taught me a lot, what to do and what not to do and before long I was leading my first expedition, and the first British expedition, to the, Pierre-Saint-Martin in the French Pyrenees, which had regained the world depth record.

The greatest lesson I gained from Ken Pearce, without doubt, was to know myself. It was a good trip and an important learning curve.

Ken sadly died some years ago. He was a sick man with a bad back, a heart condition and I believe, diabetes. He went diving in Tenerife and decided to go deep. We do not think it was an accident; he probably wanted to go out doing something he loved. The late Ken Kelly spread his ashes over Kinder Scout from a helicopter and placed some in the Giants Hole streamway so Ken could do the through trip to Russet Well in Castleton where the cave stream emerged into daylight.

I have not thought it necessary to give a blow by blow description of the Gouffre Berger as many books and reports cover the same subject, but it should be pointed out that the Gouffre Berger has become one of the great classic caves of the world. It has everything to challenge the cave explorer: long and short dry pitches and impressive waterfalls with some very wet pitches, meanders, traverses, canals to swim through, beautiful calcite formations and even a lake in times of wet weather. The history of the cave is also a major attraction. The present depth of the cave has been accurately measured at 1,323 metres below the entrance.

It was considered to be the Everest of the underground but has since been overtaken by many other caves and is no longer the deepest cave in the world but every cave explorer worth his salt has an ambition to descend to the bottom. It ranks without doubt in the top five classic caves of the world and quite rightly so.

It was a privilege to be a part of the history of exploration of this wonder of the underground, the Gouffre Berger.

Lake Cadoux, Gouffre Berger, France. Photo: Robbie Shone..

4

The Caving Scene

'Only those who will risk going too far can possibly find out how far one can go.

T. S. Eliot

It was four weeks before I returned from the Gouffre Berger. As I had no job to go to, three of us decided to travel around Europe in a Land Rover. Patricia was not pleased that I had deserted her for a month.

I soon picked up an old clapped out MGA sports car, which I loved, and also a new job at Bolton Technical College as a Senior Technician in the Electronics Department. The wages were rubbish and on £11 per week it was impossible to pay a mortgage on a house. After courting Pat for six years we decided to get engaged and I had managed to save enough cash for a deposit for a house in the Derbyshire I loved. Doing some night school teaching helped but not enough.

A good friend suggested working at the factory where he worked, Hawker Siddeley Airfield in Woodford. I obtained an interview as an electronic technician and had a glimpse of one of the first electronic computers, a massive machine running on punched paper strips. The money was poor so I turned it down. On the shop floor in the giant hangers they were building the Nimrod. The money there was good but it was piece work. A time was given by a parasitic rate fixer, but do the job in half the time and you earned a good bonus. I started working on Nimrod aircraft as an aircraft electrician, first on armaments, which I did not like as they killed people, then on the main circuit board distribution panel on the starboard side, near the cockpit. I had over 1,100 wires to connect to the right place and unlike me, the other electrical technicians did not seem able to handle the complexity of the job. The Nimrod was Britain's Submarine Hunter, a cut down version of the famous Comet Jet Airliner and it was packed with sophisticated electronic hardware that no one seemed to understand. We always reckoned that all the highly classified technical drawings had first been passed by the Kremlin before being issued to the workers.

The rate fixer offered me 300 hours to complete the job but I argued the toss for a week basing my assessment on the time given for the port panel, which was half the size. They did not even know how many wires were involved and refused to give me a time trial as they knew they would lose. It was so easy for friends to stop you working as I blocked the entrance to the cockpit. I could have dragged it out for 600 hours or so. I managed to sign the job for 500 hours and became one of the top earners in the hanger earning £20 per week, completing the job in about 240 hours.

Patricia and I were married in 1969 and moved into a stone built detached cottage in Chinley, Derbyshire which was a dream come true. It cost me £2,980 and broke the bank as the deposit was £420. It had taken me ten years of working to save up for my own house. One attraction was the Chinley Conservative Club, right opposite my front door. We could fall out of the pub and fall into the house. Although I was never a Conservative, the annual subscription was cheap, the beer cheap and good along with the clientele.

We had little but managed all right as Pat obtained a job close by as a secretary. The winters were the worst as we could not afford to switch on the gas central heating for long. We collected wood for the fire and when I could afford it, a bag of coal. We grew quite a few of our own vegetables as we had a big garden and I enjoyed pottering about.

The trouble with working at Hawker Siddeley were the constant strikes as the workers were rather militant, there were more strikes in the summer when the sun shone. Of course, you had to be in the Trade Union but they reminded me of sheep, no one dared to go against a strike. Money was of course lost, and we often wondered if the management engineered the strike action to obtain more time to complete the contract, which was for 39 aircraft.

I hated the job, clocking on at 7 am, clocking off at 4.30 pm, clocking on and off jobs, trying to beat the rate fixer's time. In the winter, going to work at 6.30 am in the dark along the A6, freezing cold, coming back in the dark and never seeing the light of day for five days during the week.

The other trouble with working in the cockpit was that all the guys managed to get their respective wives pregnant; the cockpit was the place to work if you wanted to produce. Soon Pat was expecting her first child. It was a very difficult birth and the boy refused to enter the world, maybe he did not like the looks of it. Mark Stephen finally was forced to give up the struggle and was born via a caesarean. Life became even more difficult as Patricia was now a full-time mum.

We got a puppy dog which I wanted to call Split as she was a bitch. Pat didn't like it so we called her Pip. She was a long-haired cross between a sheep dog and something else and proved to be good at sniffing out caves. Pip's Cave in Blackwell Dale, Derbyshire was one of her discoveries and she became a part of the family and later my best friend.

Our Prime Minister, the infamous Snatcher Thatcher decided to cancel further contracts. By the time I started aircraft number 30, redundancies began. The Shop Steward gave me the bad news a few months later, 'Your time is up, leave on Friday.' The following day the boss came into the cockpit and asked me to make a start on aircraft number 36. When I said no, he became rather agitated. I told him the news and he went storming off, saying, 'We will see about that.'

A few hours later the Shop Steward popped his head into the aircraft, 'You're not leaving Friday, it's been rescinded, who the hell have you been talking to?'

When I had finished aircraft number 38 my time was truly up. There were two of us left to go. The Shop Steward put the case. 'We are going on strike to keep the last two,' he said.

'No one is going on strike on my behalf,' I replied. 'I will leave providing my other colleague is not made redundant.' The management agreed and I was hailed as a martyr, but after two years working there, I could not wait to escape. I thought I was on my feet and by now, with luck, could manage.

I received two weeks redundancy pay, one week for each year of service and I signed on the dole. It proved impossible on the meagre dole money to pay the bills and the crippling mortgage as the building society kept increasing the interest rates, so I started doing odd jobs to make ends meet, repairing radios, TVs and the odd electrical wiring job. As I was honest and mentioned it at the employment office, they threatened to stop my dole money so I became self-employed. For the first time in my life I was my own boss. No one to tell me what to do or how to do it, I felt a freedom I had not experienced in 13 years of working. Trying to make a living was near impossible just repairing TVs and radios so I concentrated on the electrical engineering side and found I could make ends meet. I remained in the business for 27 years. This gave me the freedom in later life to lead many expeditions to remote and exotic parts of this wonderful world.

Living close to the caves I loved, I soon became involved in caving politics as the Conservation and Access Officer for the Derbyshire Caving

Association, attending the inaugural meeting of the National Caving Association, the forerunner to today's national body for all caving matters in the UK. Later I worked as the newsletter editor, probably for around 16 years or so. I also became much more involved with the Derbyshire Cave Rescue Organisation as a controller, a post I held for over 20 years.

Just weeks after my return from the Berger, myself and John Randles agreed to take groups of scouts on a few caving trips. I took my group down P8 without any trouble but John's group, down Oxlow Caverns, had a problem. One of the boys tripped over his shoelace and cut his head. The cave rescue was called out in order to help him to the surface. The following day I thought I would take a very small group to a cave where an accident could not happen, so we went down Axe Edge Cave on Stanley Moor near Buxton. An easy grovel around and they enjoyed it, trouble was one of them was a little on the large side and got completely trapped in the upwards squeeze near the entrance. All attempts at pushing and pulling him with the occasional kick, failed to move him an inch in the right direction. The poor boy began to panic. We needed some assistance probably with a cow harness, some strong lads and a rope. I sent my assistant out to call the cave rescue. We managed to extricate the boy, but did I get some stick!

After that episode, I always took extreme caution when taking novices underground. Over the years I probably took hundreds and thankfully never had any further problems. I considered it good experience for youngsters, a good adventure for city kids who would not normally get the chance, I only wish I'd had that opportunity as a young boy, an adventure I craved. So I fully supported the introduction of a professional qualification for cave instructors. Many years later it came back to bite me when I became involved in helping handicapped children. 'Sorry you can't help with taking them caving, you are not qualified.' I think a kind friend sent me a Local Cave Leader's Certificate just to shut me up.

The Eldon were of course involved in digging various caves in Derbyshire. Digging in caves is for most people hard to understand. Long gone are the days when you could explore a previously unexplored open cave entrance or cave passage within a cave in the UK. There were plenty of caves and passages within known caves, where the obvious way forward was blocked with sediment or fallen rocks. By digging it is possible to enter previously unexplored caves and passages. Whenever a breakthrough occurred, the excitement of a new discovery was extreme.

The Peak District is riddled with old abandoned lead mine shafts, many now in a dangerous state of collapse and many of them intersect natural cavities. 'T'owd Man' as he is affectionately known seemed to get everywhere in his search for lead ore known as galena. Caves have been found by searching the old miners' records as they recorded their mining activities. The crown owned the mineral rights, but the Barmote Court based in Wirksworth controlled the industry that gave the local community free range to search for lead anywhere within the Peak District, except for orchards, maybe the king liked his apples? The court is still in existence to this day and it is still possible for a person to 'nick' a mine which has been abandoned by presenting the court with a 29 kilogram dish of ore from the said mine workings. The mine is then registered in their name and they have free rght of access even across private farmland. Lead mining became something of a cottage industry for many hundreds of years. Cave explorers often descend mine shafts in their search for natural cave passages as many of the Peak District's important caves have been entered via old mine workings.

The Peak District Mines Historical Society concentrate their efforts on research, preservation of old mining artefacts and digging into long abandoned lead mines, producing some excellent periodical papers on the subject. They even have their own mine open to the public and a museum at Matlock.

One such investigation was instigated by my namesake, David Icarus Gill. Ribden Mine is an abandoned 55 metre deep lead mineshaft situated in the Hamps Manifold catchment area of the Peak District. Some research done in 1965 indicated that the mine intersected a natural stream sink, a swallet situated close by. The Eldon Pothole Club decided to investigate this around 1965 and Dave Icarus Gill (no relation) was allotted the pleasure of the first descent.

Two hundred feet of electron ladder was attached at the surface and threaded down the shaft. Dave, on a sturdy lifeline, descended. Within 10 minutes shouts came from way down below asking for 'Hughy.' As the Eldon had no members with that name confusion reigned. After a great deal of shouting down the shaft, the answer came back which appeared that Dave was asking for 'Bill.' Bill was not present at the time, which caused even further confusion. The surface team eventually deciphered a shout from below, 'Up, up,' and we began to haul on the lifeline. After about 100 foot of rope was pulled in the rope seemed to be covered in a green very smelly slime. Dave continued to ask for Bill and Hughy for most of the way up. He emerged looking very pale, covered in slime and stinking like a very dead rat. 'Hueeee, Biiiill' went Dave and vomited all over the grass and the lifeliners.

In the gloom at the bottom of the shaft, Dave had stepped off the ladder and sank up to his waist in lots of dead smelly things. At first, he thought they were dead babies but soon discovered they were hundreds of dead turkeys. He found the natural stream inlet but due to the unhealthy nature of the place and the state of his constitution, he beat a hasty retreat. Washing Dave, the rope and 200 feet of electron ladder was not a pleasant experience.

Somehow the Eldon lost interest in Ribden Swallet but six years later when the turkeys had reduced to bones and been washed away, the Peak District Mines Historical Society continued with the work.

The climb up into the mostly six-inch-high flat-out bedding plane called Jim's Crawl in Oxlow Caverns was heading straight for Nettle Pot so a connection between the two caves was on the cards. The problem was the passage is hundreds of feet wide with nothing supporting the roof. How it stays up without collapsing is a mystery. Many weekends were spent blowing pieces out of the floor to make it just high enough to crawl through, but we never made it through to Nettle Pot. This bedding plane, as they are known in caving terms, seemed to go on forever with no end in sight.

The explorer of a newly discovered cave or passage within a cave is under an obligation to map it, not just to prove its existence but also to find out which way it is heading. This is known as cave surveying. Later the map, along with a description, is normally published in expedition reports, caving club journals or in caving magazines.

To map the cave, measurements are taken with a tape measure of a length from one station to the next, also recording passage width and height. The direction is measured with a compass and the slope, the angle of the passage leg going either up or down, with a clinometer. All this information is recorded in a notepad and sketches made of the passage shape, streams, boulders, cave formations and any other relevant information the surveyor sees fit to include. We first started cave surveying using prismatic compasses and Abney levels to measure the slope angle but later Suunto in Finland brought out the excellent range of compasses and clinometers which are still widely used today. These are encased in aluminium, are waterproof, shock proof and could be sighted by looking through a small glass aperture and reading off the bearings.

In the early days of cave exploration the co-ordinates or position from the entrance for each leg of the survey had to be calculated with trigonometry log tables or a slide rule, a very long winded business, but when calculators came on the market things became much easier as tangents, sines and cosines could be calculated, we could then throw our log tables in the bin. Once the explorer had all the co-ordinate data of how far the passage progressed to the north, east, south or west and the vertical distance from the entrance, they could plot a line drawn on graph paper then fill in the details. It is a lengthy process but enjoyable when you view your finished map.

Programmable calculators in later years could churn out east, north co-ordinates and depths just by entering the length, bearing and angle. With the advent of desktop and laptop computers, some very clever cavers produced cave survey programmes enabling co-ordinates to be printed out and with plotting programmes that can draw the line drawing on the screen. Some programmes can draw in the walls and three-dimensional effects can be produced on the screen in colour.

The tape measure is now considered Stone Age technology as waterproof laser measuring devices are predominantly used. Life is now much more fun for the cave surveyor. The latest technology being developed is the use of three-dimensional laser beam scanners. As caves are three dimensional mazes it is always difficult to portray a cave in a two dimensional form drawn on a piece of paper. Normally a cave map will consist of a plan and an elevation, which is how the cave looks as viewed from the side, the map becomes difficult to draw and understand in a very complex and long cave system so the concept of three dimensional interpretation is a step forward but at the end of the day, we still have to produce the map on a flat piece of paper. Cave surveying has come a long way since our first efforts.

The mapping and re-survey of Giants Hole, one of Derbyshire great caves was commenced under the leadership one of the most competent cavers in the Eldon Pothole Club, the late Paul Deakin. Paul worked for the Coal Board as a Mine Surveyor. I tried to model my style of caving on Paul's, fast, light and safe, and have lost count of the number of caving trips we did together, mostly photographic trips, as Paul was a brilliant cave photographer. The late George Cooper, Paul and I camped overnight in Giants Hole and spent many happy hours surveying half metre lengths in Crab Walk, a long, narrow and twisting passage, little more than a foot wide in most places with a pleasant tumbling stream. The only way to make progress is crab-like, hence the name. It was good practice for what was to come.

We realised from the survey mapping data and the maps that Paul had calculated and drawn, that a long low crawl passage in the upper passages of Giants Hole was heading directly for Oxlow Caverns. It terminated in a section which was too small even for me to get through. In Oxlow Caverns, we had noticed a corresponding crawl which seemed to be heading in the correct direction. The flat-out crawl in Giants Hole was not easy to traverse as it had a number of water-filled sections where the passage was completely flooded, known as ducks. These ducks can be free dived without diving bottles as they are only a few metres in length but once in the water there is no room to manoeuvre. It's just a matter of taking a deep breath, filling your lungs, holding your breath, saying a prayer and diving under the water to get through, hopefully popping up the other side in air filled passage. The possibility of a connection looked good which would elevate the system to the deepest cave in Britain.

We started a dig in Oxlow, low wet and pretty horrible. I chiselled away at the calcite and gravel floor for many hours and managed just get my head into the Giants Hole section but did not fancy pushing through as there was no room to turn around. Reversing the squeeze would be impossible. The following week the late Henry Mares enlarged the squeeze and the connection was made. The Oxlow-Giants cave system became the deepest cave in the British Isles. Paul had a lot more surveying to do as the cave system now became as one. I did one of the first through trips with Clive Westlake from Oxlow to Giants Hole; it was not easy as the ducks are low, tight, intimidating and muddy.

We had some success down a number of Derbyshire caves, Dr Jackson's Pot and Waterfall Swallet, finding a few new sections of cave passage not previously explored and I also started work with the late John Beck and Paul Deakin surveying the new finds around Stoney Middleton. John kept digging and finding new caves and extensions that kept us busy for a while. The connection from Merlin's Mine to Carlswark Caverns and the relevant extensions were all surveyed along with Yoga Hole, Streaks Pot, Layby Pot and Sarah's Cave to name a few.

We spent considerable time and effort in Lathkill Dale, with passage extensions in Lathkill Head Cave and Lower Cales Dale Cave. These caves could only be explored during the dry summer months, as in normal weather they were flooded to the roof. I had great fun with Noel Christopher enlarging Dawke's Crawl in Lathkill Head Cave which was heading towards Cales Dale Cave. Using explosives, we only had a short wire so lay flat out with our mouths open so we did not burst our eardrums, then we beat a hasty retreat to avoid the poisonous fumes. Critchlow Cave was another long flat out crawl where we dug and blasted rocks out at the furthest point with Peter Mellors.

Along with Clive Westlake and other members of the Eldon, we forced the connection between Knotlow Caverns and Hillocks Mine. We explored downstream in Knotlow, which proved desperate on the return journey as the water backed up in front of your face. The passage was very low and almost full to the roof with fast running water so as you moved forward it created a wave which came over your head. The only way to progress without drowning was to stop moving to allow the water to flow past your body thus creating an air space, take a deep breath of air, then move forward under water until the air in your lungs gave out, then repeat the process. Sadly, this cave claimed the life of a young man who drowned trying to do the same thing. Clive and I also did a great deal of surveying in the Derbyshire's Caves, P8 cave and Blue John Mines to name a few with Clive drawing all the maps.

The dye tracing with Jenny Potts of the Hamps and Manifold rivers with Seven Trent Water Board proved interesting. We placed a non-toxic dye, fluorescein, into the sinks where the rivers went underground and tried to detect where the dye came out by placing activated charcoal detectors in the likely risings. The detectors can then be tested for traces of the dye as fluorescein glows green under ultraviolet light. We were successful in tracing the Manifold River to a large rising called Ilam and the Hamps to a nearby rising. We also finally found the missing rising for Waterways Swallet where the underground stream sinking in the cave returned to daylight.

Caving and digging with the late Keith Bentham, who later became the Secretary of the Eldon Pothole Club was always an experience except he hated me whistling down a cave. It was unlucky, he said. Keith had many successful digs in Derbyshire, and I was one of the first to explore Winnats Head Cave with him when he broke through a choke of boulders to discover a large chamber. We explored and mapped around 300 metres of fine cave passage. Keith did not bother going to work; he spent all his time digging Derbyshire's caves, a true fanatic. He tragically died from lung cancer but never smoked in his life.

Caves in the Derbyshire region and elsewhere in the world can have a build up of radon gas, which is radioactive, and many of our caves in Derbyshire have high concentrations. Too much exposure can result in permanent damage and was the probable cause of Keith's untimely death. Dave Edwards, a caving instructor at Whitehall Outdoor Pursuits Centre in Derbyshire suffered the same tragic fate, again he never smoked. Dr John Gunn's investigations into radon produced safety guidelines for the number of hours in a specified period that instructors or cave guides should spend underground. Ventilation systems were also installed in some of the British show caves open to the public, so those who like to have tourist trips into caves need not panic, their exposure will be so small as to be undetectable.

The midweek evening digging trips were something we all looked forward to down Snelslow Swallet in Derbyshire. Snelslow is a completely blocked cave with a small stream flowing into the entrance, situated near Giants Hole. We hoped it would lead us into a large cave system heading for the risings where the water emerged into daylight at Castleton, many miles away.

As I worked at the dig one night, I turned and said, 'Chuck us a bucket, Dave.' I was pelted with five buckets are there were six Dave's on the digging team. We dug it for many years, but it did not enter the hoped-for passages of our search but we enjoyed it all the same. It was here that I honed my skills with explosives, thanks to the late Mike Jeanmaire. Blowing things up became a passion and 'bang' as we all called it was easy to obtain as this was well before the Irish Troubles began with the bombs going off in unexpected places. Now of course it is very strictly controlled. After every digging trip we finished up in the pub, arriving just before closing time. The headaches from the bang fumes were just a part of the enjoyment.

A cave was dug into just at the back of a row of terraced cottages in Dove Holes by the Disley Underground Group which we investigated in an attempt to explore beyond the end point. For the most part, this was a flat-out awkward crawl along a small stream way and terminated in a concrete plug. The cave passed beneath the road where you could hear the cars rumbling overhead. We found out that the concrete plug was directly beneath the cellars of the public house on the other side of the road. Attempts to gain entry into the cellars and free beer failed as when a hole had appeared in the cellar floor, it had been filled in with a few tons of concrete. On the way out it was noticed that the small stream entering the cave from a crack in the roof was soapy; when the lady of the cottage above had a bath, the bath water drained into the cave. We emerged smelling of roses.

The Dove Holes railway tunnel was reported to have streams issuing in from the brick lined roof, the water probably originating from the stream sinks at Dove Holes. Dodging the trains, we investigated and found that the tunnel had intersected the natural underground drainage routes which would normally drain towards Ashwood Dale near Buxton. A culvert had been constructed draining the water to the end of the tunnel into the river which drained to the west. This had in effect changed the position of the natural catchment from the River Trent to the River Mersey, from the east coast of

England to the west coast. Unfortunately, only small impenetrable caves were found.

Our regular winter trips every two weeks with Garry Kitchen to Peak Cavern added more cave passage to this impressive system and the system was eventually connected to the nearby Speedwell Caverns. Over the past 20 years, this system has grown with determined diggers constantly finding new unexplored sections.

Elsewhere, one of our regular trips to Ogof Agen Allwedd in South Wales forged the Grand Circle connection. With Clive Westlake and Paul Deakin some digging began in the choke heading towards Biza Passage, Ken Pearce's old dig, mentioned in an earlier chapter. The three of us spent many hours making loud noises accompanied by lots of smoke. After every explosive charge, we gingerly removed the debris and placed another charge. After many hours progressing slowly upwards, we could see a dodgy-looking route through into a black space. With extreme care not to dislodge any loose boulders we popped out in Biza Passage. We had made the connection. After shaking hands, we headed off at great speed downstream in the magnificent river passage section to the start of the long, low, strength-sapping Southern Stream Passage. It was late at night and we were hungry and tired having been underground for a very long time, when I discovered a mouldy Mars bar on a ledge. It seemed like a gift from heaven, a true miracle as we devoured it between us in seconds. The first round trip had been completed.

I became something of an expert on the caves of Derbyshire and assisted the late Dr Trevor Ford with revisions of two editions to his guide book. It did not seem long ago I had found a copy and marvelled at the descriptions of the caves and now here I was writing it.

I wanted to do a grid reference index for the Caves of Derbyshire which was an impossible task using conventional means. I had a friend who worked with one of the first commercial computers. These were large machines fed by a ticker tape paper input which would then sort through a million numbers. In the end, I finished up with a role of thin punched paper a thousand yards long, but it worked and the Derbyshire Caving Association published the first ever grid reference index.

When Trevor gave it up, the late John Beck and I did a complete re write with area maps and called it the Caves of the Peak District as the cave areas extended into Staffordshire. The guides were always published on behalf of the Derbyshire Caving Association, which helped with funding for conservation and access projects.

The late Paul Deakin and myself decided to write a book called British

Caves and Potholes, illustrated with black and white photographs of British caves. Bradford Barton Ltd based in Truro, Cornwall produced a series of books of black and white photographs on various subjects and agreed to publish. Colour printing was far too expensive then. We spent many happy months photographing some of Briton's classic caves in the different caving regions and it was finally published in 1975. It is only by photography that a true perspective of a cave can be seen, as then our caving lights were feeble but lit by multiple flash guns the true size and beauty becomes apparent. Now with high powered LED caving lights we can see ten times more than we could years ago.

Streaking was in vogue at the time with naked men and women racing across cricket and football fields, much to the amusement of the crowd and the commentators. On one of our trips to the Mendip caving region of England we decided to do the same in a cave. One of our team who shall remain nameless but came from Luton was persuaded to take his clothes off for the camera. The sight of a large naked caver wearing just his helmet and lamp battery strapped around his waist and a large pair of boots was simply too much. How Paul managed to take the photographs with tears of laughter running down his face, I will never know. We had a very nice young lady with us at the time who we had not met previously as she had asked if she could join us to assist. She was persuaded to do the same and she did, much to the consternation of the leader of the trip from a Mendip caving club who sat on a rock with bulging eyes wondering what the hell was going on with these weird Derbyshire cavers and a beautiful naked lady. The photographs were considered mildly pornographic in 1974, so out of respect were not published. Of course, they did not go in the book as I doubt Bradford Barton Ltd would have appreciated the cavers' sense of humour. Paul later did produce some tasteful glamour photographs published in the caver's magazine, Descent.

Paul used a Rolex and later invested in a Hasselblad camera and did his best to teach me the rudimentary techniques of cave photography without much success. Of course, with caves having no light whatsoever, flash guns are used positioned in various places to give the best effect. An artistic flare is required in order to compose a good shot underground. This was before the advent of digital cameras so the results could be hit or miss, finding out the success or failure only when the film was processed. Without doubt, caves are the worst places in the world to take a camera as caves are often muddy, wet and with high humidity. Cameras are delicate items of equipment and liable to damage.

When Paul sprained his ankle in a South Wales cave, I did my best to get a few reasonable shots in Dan yr Ogof cave with my wife Patricia as the subject. The photographic trip to County Clare in Southern Ireland was memorable for the hot toddies in the morning before we set off underground in O'Connor's Bar in Doolin, probably one of the best bars in the world.

We received the princely sum of £75 each for the book. It did not cover the costs but we had much fun doing it.

The above selected stories are by no means all and they are in no particular chronological order, being spread over a period of 20 years or so. During the times mentioned above I led several expeditions and took part in many more. Our annual holiday tended to be centred on some caving expedition or other. How my wife Patricia put up with it all, I have no idea but she did for many years.

After several traumatic miscarriages, Patricia gave me another son, Leigh Simon. I took the boys caving of course when they were old enough but thankfully they did not follow in their father's footsteps and by my standards became quite normal.

Yes, it seemed true, the newspaper article I read all those years ago did not tell a lie. Caves could still be found in Derbyshire awaiting exploration, but they were hard to find and required many years of digging effort, but that was a major part of the attraction and fun with a bunch of like-minded enthusiasts. The achievement and thrill of just a few metres of hard won previously unexplored passage was beyond description. It really was like the first footprints, walking on the moon. Where else in Britain could you be an original explorer, the first light to shine in the everlasting darkness, the first map to be produced, the first photograph ever to be taken? Only in caves is this possible and after all, we are just ordinary people.

5

Gouffre de la Pierre-Saint-Martin expedition, 1969

'Do not go where the path may lead, go instead where there is no path and leave a trail.

Ralph Waldo Emerson

The books by Haroun Tazieff and Norbert Casteret about the explorations in the Pierre-Saint-Martin cave system in the Pyrenees, France had fired my imagination when I first started caving. The finding of the entrance shaft when the French cave explorer Lépineux noticed two crows flying out of what looked like a small hole had become something of a legend. Of course, crows nest over a long drop, the drop in this case proved to be over 1,000 feet and ultimately led into the cave system that had been postulated for many years beneath the mountain. An underground river and huge tunnels interspersed with massive chambers followed but tragedy was not far behind. In 1952, the French cave explorer Marcel Loubens fell to his death while being winched up the Lépineux shaft on a wire rope. His body was retrieved a year later and was brought to the surface, the story being well documented in the books.

I received a report that a higher entrance had been found leading into the Pierre Saint-Martin, called the Tête Sauvage, entering the system up stream of the Lépineux Shaft. The cave was now the deepest in the world beating the Gouffre Berger by a few hundred metres at over 1,171 metres in depth. For the uninitiated, cave depths are measured from the highest point to the lowest, so if a higher entrance is found the total depth increases.

The idea of descending and exploring into the unknown in the deepest cave in the world was to me like red rag to a bull. I had just got married to Patricia, so I thought it would be a nice place to spend our honeymoon, although I am not too sure Patricia did. I was still working at Hawker Siddeley and although money was tight, could just afford the budget I had worked out. The great beauty of caving expeditions is that they are cheap, far cheaper and a lot more fun than a boring package holiday to Benidorm. The

British had never been to the Pierre Saint-Martin, so it was about time an expedition was mounted to this mighty cave. It became generally known over the years as the PSM, the French name being rather too long winded.

I set about organising my very first expedition; it was not to be my last. How to organise an expedition to a place you had never been to before seemed to me to be simple logic.

First, decide on a place and objectives, then do the research, work out a budget, pick a team, arrange the dates, transport, equipment and food. I have always used the same system and it seems to work. The hardest part is usually the research and the budgets as allowance needs to be made for the unforeseeable, a contingency sum. The same goes for the plan and the objectives as the best laid plans of mice and men is a quote to be seriously considered, so the plan needs to be flexible and achievable.

The place was already decided, next came the research. We had no emails, internet or even fax machines in the 1960s and '70s so it was all down to writing letters and waiting for the snail mail to arrive. Organising an expedition could take years. Today with our modern communication systems and internet access organising an expedition is a much simpler matter.

I wrote to the great cave explorer Norbert Casteret, having had my letter translated into French; after all he was an honorary member of my club, the Eldon. I received a reply and he was very helpful with much information. He put me in touch with the late Professor Max Cosyns another famous cave explorer and the leader of the original expeditions. Max was the founder and President of the International Speleological Research Association of the Pierre-Saint-Martin, ARSIP for short.

Max wrote back to me in English and invited us to explore and map upstream in the cave. We now had an objective. Two major inlets had been found, the major one – containing the majority of the underground river – terminated at a waterfall that needed climbing. The passage could be seen continuing beyond. The second became small with much breakdown and loose boulders. Again, there was a stream way. He asked if we could map any new cave found. I, of course, agreed but wanted to visit the end of the cave.

The original cave exploration had terminated in the largest cave chamber so far discovered on the planet, the Salle Verna. The river disappeared sinking in boulders and emerged into daylight at a large resurgence far below. The river at this point was large and the Electricity Authority of France, the EDF, had drilled a one kilometre long tunnel from the mountain into the Verna intending to build a hydro electric plant by diverting the river through the tunnel and running it into a turbine many hundreds of metres below in the valley, at a small world's end village called Sainte-Engrâce. The project had been abandoned for technical reasons; the tunnel had been drilled in the wrong place, too far above the river but in 2008 the project was revised to produce four megawatts of electricity.

It was therefore possible for a good strong team to do a through trip. Descend the Tête Sauvage, camp underground at the Salle Susse for a few days; complete the exploration and survey, then to exit the cave via the EDF tunnel. Max agreed and the expedition was on.

It proved easy to get a team providing the budget was small; no one had much money in those days. Some of my Berger friends from the Happy Wanderers in the Dales were keen to join, along with members of the Eldon Pothole Club and we organised a few training meets to get to know each other better. For fun, I tried the Ken Pearce method asking them to climb the wire ladders twice, they all did it with a smile. I was introduced to the late Jim Eyre, a famous Dales cave explorer in a pub and when introduced he looked horrified as he expected a giant of a man like my predecessor Black Pearce, instead he met a little guy he needed to bend down to talk to.

On one of my regular trips to the Yorkshire Dales, I was driving my beloved MGA sports car with its twin carburettors. Patricia was huddled up in the front seat wearing her new coat as it was in the dead of night and mid-winter. I hit a patch of black ice near the river bridge in Settle and the car started to spin like a merry go round, completely uncontrollable. A mini-van following close behind did the same. He was heading straight for me unable to control the erratic movement of his van. I have no idea how it happened, but I shot backwards through an open gate at the side of the road, missing the stone wall and went careering backwards down the slope towards the river.

I remember Patricia's words at the time. Not as I expected, I'm going to die but: 'Oh, I'm going to get blood all over my new coat.' Strange how some women think more about their clothes than their life. I stopped short of the river and the driver of the van came running down the hill expecting to see two seriously injured people.

We emerged unscathed and the driver said, 'Wow, what a fantastic piece of driving, how the hell did you manage to steer backwards through an open gate, if you had not made it, I would be mangled up in my van as there was no way I could have missed you.'

'Oh it was nothing,' I replied.

We managed to get a tow up the hill and travelled on to Ingleton very slowly.

Our main problem was transport, getting all the ladders, rope and food to the French Pyrenees. The Tête Sauvage was a series of deep shafts dropping down to the underground river, over 360 metres below the surface. Some fixed aluminium poles with bits of steel sticking out either side had been fixed in the entrance pitches but we still needed a great deal of ladders and ropes for the lower sections of the .Tête Sauvage We scrounged these from our own caving club stores of tackle. Food supplies we just purchased in bulk from wholesalers.

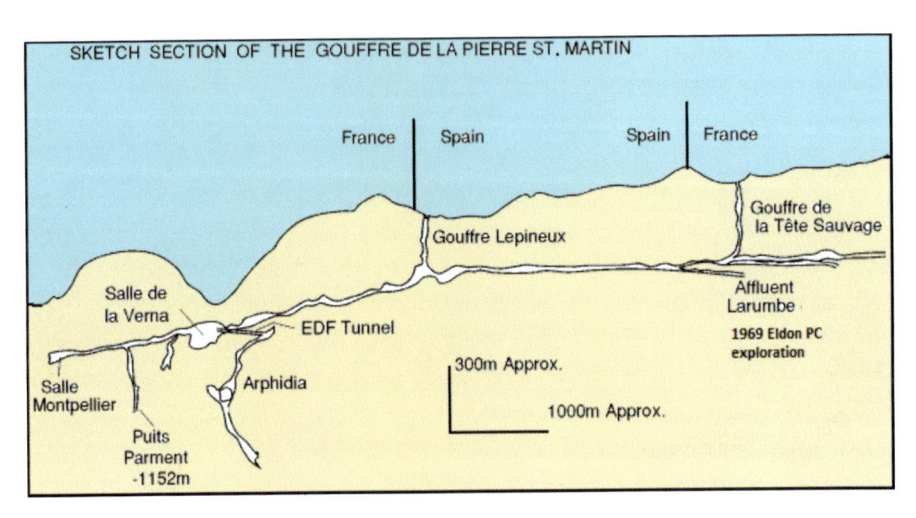

Cross section of the Gouffre de la Pierre St. Martin.

The team comprised, from the Happy Wanderers: Jim Cunningham, our photographer, Dave Fish, John Southworth and his girlfriend Jane Howarth. From the Eldon: Paul Deakin, our cave surveyor and his girlfriend Eileen Hartle who, being a domestic science teacher, agreed to organise the food, the late Ian Gasson, Anthony Cornish our climber and his girlfriend, Carol Thomas, Bob Dearman, another climber of exceptional ability, the late Henry Mares with his internal plastic pipes, Paul Hitchings and myself along with my newlywed wife, Patricia. This was going to be our honeymoon.

John agreed to drive his campervan loaded to the gunnels with equipment. Pat and I along with John and Jane piled in for the long drive down to the Pyrenees. The team were to camp on the plateau near the Tete Sauvage entrance, a tin hut had been built where equipment and food could be stored. A small spring of water about half a mile away could be used for our water supplies.

We set off on Friday 25th July 1969 for the 930 mile journey arriving on Monday 28th July. The other team members made their own way there in private cars. Max had a jeep that we borrowed to ferry some of the equipment up the steep mountain road to the Arête, the furthest point up the mountain that can be reached by road. From there, it was pleasant walking over the mountains with help from a donkey. It took us two days to ferry all the equipment to Base Camp and at last exploration could begin.

Surface karst landscape near the PSM. Photo David Gill.

The pure white limestone mountains of the Pyrenees are a spectacular and beautiful landscape. The area is covered in fractures, deep clefts and shafts and dissolved rock formations known as clints. Most shafts reduce to small impenetrable cracks as the carbonic acid in the aggressive rainwater becomes less aggressive as it progressively dissolves away the limestone, thus losing its carbonic acid content. The Tête Sauvage was an exception in that the rainwater continued to dissolve the limestone down to the base level intersecting the underground river. Some very narrow sections had been enlarged with dynamite.

Before the start of the underground exploration we sat around Base Camp listening enthralled to Max Cosyns' stories.

Cosyns was born in 1906 and died in 1998. He was a Belgian physicist, inventor and explorer, the assistant of Auguste Piccard at the Université Libre de Bruxelles. On the 18th August 1932, he participated in the record-breaking ascent into the stratosphere to 16,200 metres, which was launched from Dübendorf, Switzerland. For this he was awarded the Cross of the Knights of the Order of Leopold by the Belgian king in 1932.

On the 18th of August 1934 Cosyns, together with his student Nérée van der Elst, piloted a balloon to an altitude of 52,952 feet. Following a take-off from Hour-Havenne in Belgium, they flew over Germany and Austria before landing near the village of Žloat, now in Slovenia. They were unsuccessful in maintaining satisfactory radio communication with ground, but were able to make observations of the currents in the stratosphere as well as investigate the nature of cosmic rays. They failed to beat the height record but stated on landing that they were fully satisfied with their discoveries. A large bronze monument in the shape of a balloon was erected in 1997 on the spot of their landing in Ženavlje to commemorate the event.

In the Second World War Cosyns joined the resistance and was captured and imprisoned in Dachau concentration camp. After the war, he was co-director of the 1948 FNRS-2 bathyscaphe expedition in Dakar. In 1952, Max was in charge of the speleological expedition to the Gouffre de la Pierre Saint-Martin when French speleologist Marcel Loubens lost his life in the accident with the winch, which Max had designed. Many people blamed Max for the accident, but his story of the true events shed a completely different light on the subject.

The stories centred on his war time experiences. Max was a communist and as a member of the resistance did the normal saboteur tricks of putting sawdust in the fuel tanks of the German army transports but one of his most remarkable stories concerned the orders to destroy an electrical plant that was feeding the German war machine factories. They discovered that 90% of the power was directed into the German grid and only 10% into the Belgium grid. A dial indicated the amount of power flowing into the two grids. Max switched the dials so it appeared that someone had changed the amounts of power flowing into Germany. The operator switched them back so for the rest of the war, 90 percent went to Belgium and 10 percent to Germany.

When he was captured, he was due to be shot along with ten others. The Germans had ten firing posts so shot ten and forgot about him. He finished up in Dachau concentration camp where the life expectancy was no more than a month or two. He survived for years by growing bacterial moulds on what little food he had.

His wife was fond of the British as the RAF bombed the area where he was due for execution just at the time he was walking towards his death.

One of his most remarkable tales took place near the end of the war when Max and many inmates were forced to dig a large pit, they were all dosed in petrol and as the guard drew the match they pleaded with him not to light the fire. They said they would speak up for him in his defence when the Allies arrived. He did not light the match and Max survived the war.

After giving evidence at the War Trials Commission in Munich, Max was a marked man and could never show his face in Germany. He swore that the winch cable attachment point that had come apart when Loubens was killed had been tampered with deliberately. It was his turn to descend on the winch cable and this was an assassination attempt. He never divulged the name of the suspected assassin but I always suspected it might have been the German ex-commando and war hero, Otto Skorzeny or a member of his post war organisation, as they were up to much mischief around this time and Otto was in exile in Spain.

One funny story concerned Max and his friends exploring a cave in the Pyrenees along a stream passage. They came to a shaft going upwards to daylight and proceeded to climb it, but it was rather smelly. They emerged in a nuns' toilet in a very old nunnery where no man had ever been before.

Max was a brilliant rubber technologist and had several patents to his name. There was a rumour that he became involved in the manufacture of sex toys, but I have no idea if this was true. After the expedition, we made Max an honorary member of the Eldon Pothole Club, we just had to have a man like that in our club.

Bob Dearman and Ian Gasson had arrived a few days before the main expedition party and had been busy in the Kakouette Gorge. Here a large river poured out of the side of the cliff from a cave entrance. Max and his team had succeeded in entering the cave many years previously by flying around in an old bi-plane; trying to spot a likely place they could mount a winch from the top of the cliff as they were unable to climb the cliff to gain the entrance. They found a place just above the resurgence and one of the team descended on the end of the winch cable. Unfortunately, the cliff overhung the entrance and he was a good few metres away from gaining access to the cave. He then proceeded to swing in mid air towards the entrance managing to push in a steel peg used as protection for climbers into a crack. With every swing he hit it with a hammer, finally making it secure enough to hang a rope ladder from. They could then climb the ladder from the bottom of the cliff face into the cave. Unfortunately, the passage was completely flooded after a short distance. Bob and Ian re-climbed it from the base of the gorge and left a fixed rope hanging down so divers could gain access to dive the sump.

On Wednesday 30th July, Etienne Lemaire and his friend arrived from Belgium to join in the fun and games and along with Henry they laddered the pitches below the fixed ladders to the top of the big 100 metre pitch which led to the river. The rest of the team began carrying bags down the entrance shafts and finished the job following day. Meanwhile Etienne completed the job of rigging the rest of the ladders to the river at 380 metres below the entrance.

A good-looking shaft nearby designated E6 was investigated and an offending boulder blocking the way on was demolished using explosives supplied by Max Cosyns. This was descended for 50 metres but the way on was unfortunately blocked by boulders.

On Friday 1st August, the team of nine men descended with camping equipment and food supplies packed in a further seven bags, picking up the rest of the bags on the way, 18 kit bags in all. Bob, who did not fancy camping underground, decided to stay on the surface and join us later with Ruben Gomez, one of the leading lights in ARSIP.

I was ferrying the bags at the bottom of the 100 metre pitch along a traverse at a depth of 370 metres below the entrance when there was an enormous bang and a flash of bright light travelled from my gloved hand to the wall. The shock knocked me off my small perch and I landed on a sandy floor without injury. I raced back to the bottom of the pitch to find some very disturbed cavers wondering what the hell had happened thinking that there had been an explosion of some kind. One was descending on the electron ladder at the time when the shock wave hit him but luckily was held from falling by his rope lifeline. We realised after much discussion that a lightning strike had probably hit the cave entrance travelling down the fixed iron ladders and our electron steel wire ladders on its way to the underground river. Ionised and humid air found in caves can offer a path of least resistance and wet walls will probably contribute, but little research seems to have been undertaken on this subject. It was pretty frightening at the time.

By 1.30 am the following day, we had established an underground camp close to the river at the Salle Susse a dry chamber, not quite as windy as the main river passage; from here we could begin our explorations in the river inlets.

By 1.15 pm Bob, Ruben, Jean and Etienne arrived at the camp and confirmed the lightning strike hitting the cave entrance. A telephone cable leading from the entrance to base camp had disintegrated in a puff of smoke. Jim Cunningham began taking the expedition photographs and by 3.30 pm, John, Henry, Paul Deakin, Paul Hitchings and myself headed off to Salle Cosyns, a chamber at the start of the furthest upstream inlet.

We explored for approximately 900 metres to a cairn, which was the furthest point reached by the French cave explorers. The passage continued until the steam divided into two inlets, the first terminated at a large aven, a shaft going upwards probably to another possible entrance. The second stream was followed for approximately 500 metres in an area of shattered rock reducing in size and terminating in an upper level and a descending pitch of about 10 metres. As we had no spare ladders, we retreated back to camp, leaving a note on a rock, terminus 1969. In later years, another entrance to the PSM was discovered named SC3 which intersected this passage and increased the depth of the system as it was at a higher altitude to the Tête Sauvage entrance.

The second group progressed downstream from the camp and entered the main river inlet. After a couple of hours, they reached the cascade, the furthest point reached by the French. The waterfall cascaded down from an obvious passage 10 metres above and the climb up accomplished in two sections proved easy. A nice stream passage was followed to a junction, right terminated at a large aven after a total of 518 metres, which could not be climbed without placing numerous bolts in the rock wall. The shaft had a strong draught which indicated without doubt that it led to another entrance many hundreds of metres above. Left contained the main stream but was not followed to a conclusion as it was very immature and narrow. A few years later, armed with our survey data, the French found a surface shaft they named M31 that connected into this high aven and again the depth record was increased to 1,332 metres. The two teams returned and settled down at camp by 2 am the following day. Etienne, Jean and Ruben returned to the surface to a comfortable bed.

The following day, the team spent their time taking photographs and repairing torn skin and wet suits. On Monday 4th August, Paul, Henry and Ian began mapping the main inlet above the cascade. When Ian had finished, he joined Bob and I to explore the narrow twisting inlet river. We passed two small chambers to a further 8 metre waterfall after a distance of about 300 metres. This was climbed by Ian, but the passage became too narrow to progress beyond.

On Tuesday 5th August, we packed up the camp and moved all the equipment back to the base of the 100 metre pitch and when Etienne and Ruben arrived set off at 1 pm for the through trip to the EDF tunnel and daylight. The downstream passage, normally a series of deep water canals a couple of kilometres in length was a delight with little water. We had with us rubber dinghies as the water levels were normally much higher and the water is just above freezing so swimming for long distances is not recommended. A low gloomy section followed and the dreaded Tunnel de Vent. The Tunnel of the Winds consists of a number of freezing cold deep lakes in low passages where in flood the water reaches the roof; this is where the dinghies came into their own. The main problem was the howling gale that blows through these low sections causing waves, and as you paddle forward a few metres, the wind blows you back an equal distance. Ropes attached to the dinghies pulled by anyone lucky enough to reach the far bank helped to get all the team across. The base of the Lépineux Shaft where Loubens met his death was at last entered. A small inscription and cross marks the spot.

The rest of the huge passages and chambers through massive boulder piles passed quickly proving hard to appreciate with our small stinky carbide lights and masses of steam from wet bodies. The Salle Verna did not seem real as you can see nothing but blackness, rather like a mountain in the dead of night. We all exited the EDF tunnel by 9.30 pm, an eight hour journey from our underground camp. The French were surprised as the last through trip had taken 24 hours to complete. We reached the hut at Sainte-Engrâce one hour later but had some trouble transporting all the team to the village of Licq Atherey where our ladies were camped. Etienne had left his car at Sainte-Engrâce and, after repairing a puncture, took John and Paul to Licq in order to pick up the rest of our transport. It was 3.30 am the next day before we crashed out in our sleeping bags.

All the bags of equipment were retrieved from the base of the 100 metre pitch on Thursday 7th August and carried across the plateau back to the road head the following day.

On the way back home, John's campervan - being overloaded - kept complaining, with John doing an amazing job to keep it going.

It had been a very successful expedition and everyone enjoyed the experience. It was not to be my last involvement of the exploration of the Gouffre de la Pierre-Saint-Martin as I was under pressure to organise and lead more.

A very sad episode did occur sometime later when my great friend and caving partner Ian Gasson lost his life. Ian was a member of one of Britain's most respected caving clubs, the University of Leeds Speleological Association (ULSA), and also a valued member of the Eldon. We did many caving trips together and he was highly competent at everything he did. On an ULSA caving trip to County Clare in Southern Ireland, some of the group went swimming off Doolin Beach. Here the sea has a very strong current and Ian was swept away unable to reach the shore. His body was never found.

6

A Few Cave Rescues

'There comes a point where we need to stop just pulling people out of the river. We need to go upstream and find out why they're falling in.'

Desmond Tutu

Cave rescues in Derbyshire had always been dominated by Team A, which was led by the late Dave Allsop with a team mostly composed of Buxton cavers who were now members of the breakaway Buxton Speleological Group. The Eldon Pothole Club very rarely became involved, although we volunteered many times.

A few cave rescues are memorable. One of the first I was involved in happened to involve a young man who became stuck fast in the Iron Maiden squeeze in Perryfoot Cave; it was impossible for him to move either forwards or backwards. It was named for obvious reasons and threatened to become his permanent grave as no one could get near him to help. The late Dr Harold Lord of the British Speleological Association had reached a small chamber just before the squeeze with a jack hammer. The trouble was that he could not get through into the next tiny chamber where it may have been possible to use the jack hammer to crack the rock and free the victim. Bob Toogood, one of the most experienced cavers in Britain, was a small but powerful wiry man, and still is. He offered his services but was told they were not required so he went back home to Sheffield.

I arrived at the scene on my way home, late at night after the pubs had closed and was told the same thing. 'You are not needed as you are not a team member'. I was just about to leave when the late John Smith, better known to us as Shag, who was one of the cave rescue personnel, appeared out of the entrance and grabbed me.

'Just the man we need', he said. 'Get down that hole and help Harold.'

The controller relented and I soon joined Harold, who explained the situation. I squeezed through into the very small space where, doubled up into a tiny ball, I could just manoeuvre the jack hammer. The victim held the jack bit inches from his face to stop me drilling through his brain while I gave the rock some stick cracking it on my first attempt. The problem was the split rock would still not budge, being trapped between his body and the rest of the rock that entombed him. He was cool and did not panic as I hammered the rock with a lump hammer, chisel and electric jack hammer but after three hours the victim was still stuck fast even though I had removed a lot of rock.

I needed another double jointed Tich who could manage to move an arm and a leg in this egg box. I was knackered and needed a break but there was no one else who could squeeze into the tiny space.

'Where the hell is Bob Toogood,' I asked.

'Oh, they sent him home.'

'Well get the police to get him back now,' I replied.

When Bob turned up at last from Sheffield, where the police had managed to wake him up, disturbing his night's sleep, he took over and succeeded in removing the offending rock I had managed to spit. After many hours, the young man was at last freed from his rock tomb.

The journalists were out in force and our now rescued victim did not want a fuss, so as he could still walk, we made him carry a load of equipment. When he reached the surface he calmly walked past the journalists pretending to be one of the rescue team and jumped in the ambulance. The journalists went bananas as they had been waiting all through a very cold night for a photograph and interview.

There was a valid reason we did not like the journalists at the scene of a cave rescue, they always gave cavers a bad press. 'Police and Fire Brigade have rescued cavers, at great expense and danger.' Cavers rescue cavers on an unpaid voluntary basis, sometimes missing work, losing wages and often at great risk to themselves. Some of the various Cave Rescue Organisations' personnel, who shall remain nameless, did have a problem with their ego and liked to see their picture in the papers but that was rare.

The breakthrough that joined Oxlow Caverns to Giants Hole made by the Eldon Pothole Club members produced the deepest cave in the UK as recounted earlier. Many trips were attempted by cavers who were not capable of passing the intimidating 'ducks' found in the connecting passage and became either stranded or trapped. One such event happened while I was caving in Oxlow. The caver was completely trapped in the squeeze and the stream was backing up in front of his face. He was unable to move either forwards or backwards. In danger of drowning, all I could do was bail water from around his head while someone went back to the surface to call out the cave rescue to return with digging tools.

It was many hours before one of the rescue team in the form of the late Peter B Smith turned up with the desired tools. PB as he was known was one of the great characters of the Derbyshire caving scene for probably more than 30 years but tragically lost his life when he fell just a few feet off a scaffold on a building site. When I left the victim, he was still alive and eventually PB and other Derbyshire Cave Rescue personnel did retrieve him from a certain watery grave.

One of the worst rescues I was involved with was in Maskill Mine which connects to Oxlow Caverns, Derbyshire. We were attempting the through trip, Maskill Mine into Oxlow Caverns and then to Giants Hole, the deepest through trip in the UK. No one had done this long arduous trip before. We had a very strong team from the Eldon Pothole Club and the Happy Wanderers Caving Club, a well-established caving club based in the Yorkshire Dales. Whenever we were caving in the Dales, like them, we stayed at the hut at Braida Garth, so we knew them all well.

We reached the lead miners' old stone walling near the final pitch. This consisted of stone blocks stacked on top of each other and such things are often unstable as they have been there for hundreds of years, stacked by the lead miners. The late Henry Mares looked over the edge and the whole lot collapsed. Henry hurtled down with tons of boulders following him. I heard the terrible sound of the rumble near the entrance to the mine. By the time I got to Henry, the guys had dug him out but he was in a bad way, semi-conscious.

The cave rescue was called out and we managed to get the stretcher down to Henry without dislodging more rocks. The late Dr Hugh Kidd pronounced him still alive but only just, with internal bleeding. We had to get Henry out and fast. The decision was made to lower the stretcher with Henry strapped inside down the final pitch of Maskill Mine and from there up into Oxlow Caverns and back to day light. This decision was made due to the unstable nature of Maskill Mine, it was considered too dangerous to extricate Henry that way. We began lowering the stretcher but every few feet it became snagged on protruding rocks. The danger was another rock fall with sure fatal consequences for Henry. There was only one alternative, someone had to descend on an electron wire ladder and guide the stretcher around the protruding rocks while hanging on the ladder at the same time.

I volunteered for this potentially hazardous operation. Henry fought me all the way as he managed to get one very bloody hand free and was delirious. Every few feet required a stop and manoeuvre. Held on by a tight lifeline I could use both hands to pull the stretcher away from protruding rocks providing those on top could hold my weight which was no problem as I am very light. About two thirds of the way down I received a shout, they had reached the end of my lifeline rope and I was still hanging a long way from the bottom. By this time my arms felt like lead so the chances of climbing back out was going to be slow and painful. Also, Henry was still a long way from the cavers waiting at the base of the shaft for the stretcher to arrive. Carrying on down without a lifeline was out of the question so I managed to swing the ladder and reach a tiny ledge where I perched in order to get the circulation back in my arms. From there I could direct the lowering of Henry to the bottom. It worked and I climbed the rest of the way down without a line. I was reasonably strong in those days as we had competitions on who could climb furthest up and down an electron ladder with just our arms, not using our legs. Paul Deakin and the late George Cooper were champions, but I was close behind.

Henry survived, although full of plastic pipes. 'Don't get too near the fire Henry, you will melt,' was the favourite line. He survived long enough to bottom the Gouffre Berger not long after his accident. Henry sadly died for the second time in a far-off land. He lived life to the full and had no intention of becoming an invalid, packing more life in a few years than most men achieved in a lifetime.

One life threatening rescue occurred in Giants Hole during a flood pulse. The Crab Walk has a very tight section about a mile into the cave, two thirds of the way along. The passage narrows to such an extent that large cavers have trouble squeezing through. On his return out of the cave, a young man became trapped in the squeeze known as The Vice. The flood water hit and being trapped, he was in danger of drowning as the water was backing up in front of him. The rescue team were called out and managed to get him out of The Vice and onto a small ledge before he drowned. By this time, he was suffering from exposure as the force of the water had ripped his caving clothes to pieces. The small team that reached him had little chance of getting him to the surface with the raging stream becoming fiercer all the time. They retreated to the surface leaving him shivering on the ledge. Tony Jarratt emerged with little of his wet suit in one piece, the bottom half being completely torn to shreds by the force of the water.

I was in charge as the controller on the surface and went underground to access the situation. Team A had stationed themselves at the head of a short vertical drop called Garlands Pot, not far inside but no one wanted to descend as Garlands Pot was like a toilet being flushed. Normally a small stream, this was now a raging river. The few team members who had reached the victim returned with their wet suits in tatters, torn to bits by the force of the flood, no way were they going back down the cave in those conditions. It was vital that someone reached the victim with an exposure bag as soon as possible, exposure is lethal as the internal body temperature decreases, the heart stops. The exposure bag is a type of rubber sleeping bag which, when zipped up with a hood to cover the head, can save a life. The victim's own body heat cannot escape so the temperature inside the bag increases.

George Cooper, Paul Deakin and Roger Martin arrived, all good cavers. I explained the situation and they volunteered to try to reach the victim before he died.

'Hand over control on the surface, Dave, we need you to come with us,' said George.

I handed over and asked the controller to call out the Fire Brigade as they could supply heavy duty water pumps; we could pump the flood water down the valley, bypassing the cave entrance.

The four of us with the exposure bag descended, fighting the river all the way. We were lifelined down Garlands Pot and by holding our breath, we reached the bottom, but trying to make progress along the narrow Crab Walk was impossible as the water was three feet deep and moving very fast. As we tried to move downstream the water was coming over our shoulders and threatening to wash us away. We managed to get over this problem by traversing above the river for all of its length, jamming our bodies against both rock walls until at last we reached the by now delirious victim who was suffering from extreme exposure. We managed to get him inside the exposure bag and sat on him to increase his dangerously low body temperature. After about four hours we were suffering from exposure and he was stewing. The water level began to recede but we had no communication with the surface so had no idea what was going on until some of our friends arrived from the Sheffield based team with a caving suit for the victim to wear on his way out. The Fire Brigade succeeded in drastically reducing the amount of water flowing into the cave. The lad lived to tell the tale.

There were some strange rescues over the years. One young man we rescued about three times always with the same problem, a dislocated shoulder. Dr Hugh Kidd used to say to him, 'Now this is going to hurt' and put it back in place for him. We convinced him in the end that caving for not for him and definitely not a good idea.

One accident down Rowter Mine, a deep mine shaft, involved an injured caver groaning in pain at the base of the shaft. Alan Gamble arrived and started to examine him for broken bones.

'Are you a doctor?' he groaned.

'No, I'm a bloody brick layer but it's the best you're going to get, son.'

Alan always had a great sense of humour even in extreme circumstances.

Probably the saddest rescue was retrieving the body of our friend John Smith who died while diving a sump in Merlin's Mine. All the rescue personnel knew him well, having caved with him for many years. These are the most difficult rescues of all and unfortunately happened more than once.

A very strange and sad episode occurred when the secretary of the Pegasus Caving Club fell to his death down Eldon Hole. He climbed down to the ledge, slipped and fell. He was well known and well liked. He claimed he came from Finland and spoke with a pleasant Finnish accent and was a competent caver, always good company in the pub. It was not until the funeral that we discovered the truth when many people attended, all from different backgrounds. It appears his real name was Paul and he was well known to various groups under various names. He had done 'time' for some misdemeanour or other and did not think the caving community would accept an ex con as a member. I corresponded with him many times and for years he never allowed his Finnish accent to slip.

One of the funniest of the reoccurring cave rescues involved Mike and Liz Jeanmaire's dog. This little dog loved to escape the house and go chasing rabbits. Derbyshire rabbits are smart and would deliberately run towards an open abandoned lead mine shaft. Of course, they would jump over and the dog would fall in. Amazingly the dog survived and a search and rescue operation would find a whimpering dog at the bottom of some mine shaft or other.

The above cave rescues are in no particular chronological order as they took place over a period of 20 years or so and there were of course many more not recorded here. I served as a controller for The Derbyshire Cave Rescue Organisation for over 20 years up to the age of 50 but had to resign when I started work as a full-time speleologist at the Gunung Mulu National Park, Sarawak.

7

Gouffre de la Pierre-Saint-Martin, 1971

'Behold the turtle. He makes progress only when he sticks his neck out.'

James Conant

Some of my caving friends in the Derbyshire Caving Club based in Stockport proved very persuasive and I fancied another short expedition to this splendid cave system.

The Derbyshire Caving Club had a hard core of highly competent cavers who would remain friends for many years to come. The secretary at that time was Stan Gee, well known in Derbyshire caving circles as a joker. He built his toilet with a window facing Kinder Scout so he could look over the mountains he loved while doing his duty. One day he became fed up with the church bells on a Sunday morning, they did not actually have bell ringers but a record with a powerful amplifier. Stan sneaked in the church one day and changed the record to the Beatles, She loves me yeah yeah yeah.

One of his best jokes was the hole in the road near his house; where he built a cardboard bomb and buried it in the hole. The whole street was evacuated until the bomb squad arrived. Stan died as he lived on the dance hall floor and when he left us we buried his ashes on Kinder Scout and built a huge cairn over the spot but a Park Ranger made us knock it all down; it was probably another one of Stan's jokes.

Being broke, along with most cavers, we could only manage one week at the Pierre-Saint-Martin. A long way to go just for seven days. In that time I knew we could achieve little. Many expedition cavers wanted to visit this world class cave with its fascinating history as most cavers had read the books. The story of the Gouffre de la Pierre-Saint-Martin it is a part of caving legend.

I contacted Ruben Gomez and Max Cosyns and they suggested a trip to the bottom of the Arphidia Cave which had been intersected by the EDF tunnel. The furthest point reached by the French had only been visited once, so it was hoped the original explorers had missed something. There were several areas which had not been fully investigated and upstream had a good chance of connecting to the main system which would increase the total depth if a natural connection was found. The cave consisted of a series of deep shafts extending to a considerable depth. This plan also gave the team a chance to see the massive main cave passages as they would be entering through the EDF tunnel.

I hired a van and a very strong team of highly experienced cavers set off from Stockport on Saturday 18th September 1971. The long drive to the Pyrenees was uneventful and the team arrived at Licq the following day. The team amounted to nine men: Alan Gamble, Phil Burke, Dave Sinclair, Rod Mumford and Jasper from the Derbyshire Caving Club and Jim Dale, Ken Lloyd and me from the Eldon. The odd one out was one of Britain's most experienced and famous cave divers, the late Mike Wooding. Mike was one of the pioneers of cave diving exploration using compressed air. He had been on our team to the Gouffre Berger as one of the diving team with Ken Pearce but had decided quite sensibly not to dive with Pearce.

On arriving on Sunday 19th September at 4.30 pm, Ruben asked if we could assist in a cave rescue at a nearby cave called Gouffre Berret. A caver was injured a few pitches down the cave and was a stretcher case. The cave was only about 120 metres deep but the injured man was at the bottom of a 72 metre pitch. We, of course, agreed. 9 pm saw us down the cave helping to rescue the injured man, it was 3.30 am the following day when we emerged from the cave and 4.30 am before we crawled into our sleeping bags in the wooden hut near the little hamlet of Sainte-Engrâce, feeling somewhat tired after our long drive from Northern France. The expedition had not started well, a foreboding of what was to come.

On Monday 20th September, after a late start, we sorted out the keys for the EDF tunnel as ARSIP had decided to lock it to prevent unauthorised access The mountains of ladders and ropes were packed into kit bags, all we would need in order to descend the Arphidia.

The following day we carried all the bags up to the EDF tunnel and began the descent around 4 pm After the fourth pitch, a twisting awkward vertical descent followed at around 200 metres below the level of the entrance. Enthusiasm waned as the team wanted out, so the descent was abandoned as the chances of reaching the bottom became nil as time wore on. It became apparent that the team's real interest was to explore along the major tunnels of the Pierre-Saint-Martin, rather than spending all the remaining few days descending the Arphidia with probably little result. It was 6 am the following day before we all exited the cave.

On Thursday 23rd September, Rod, Dave, Alan, Phil and Jasper had a trip as far as the Lépineux shaft taking a few photographs on the way. Ken, Jim and I spent the day grovelling upstream in the Arphidia searching for a route through to the main passages of the Pierre-Saint-Martin. The area was a complex of passages but no draught could be detected. If the system connected to the main passages, there would certainly be a very strong wind.

A steel door is fitted on the EDF tunnel to keep the airflow at the normal level. If the door is open for more than a few minutes, it takes two people to close it, as the wind increases in intensity to gale force. If a draught is detected in a cave entrance, cave passage, dig or choke of boulders it indicates that there is a way on. If two passages are found, follow the one with the draught and the passage will most likely continue for a considerable distance. Caves do have air circulation especially if there is more than one entrance as there will be a difference of barometric pressure between the two entrances. The lower you are the higher the air pressure; it's the same way a chimney works. A cave with a high entrance and a low altitude exit will have a howling wind, certainly enough to blow out the flame of a carbide lamp in a narrow space. Sometimes if we are trying to connect two caves together, we conduct a smoke test. With a team at each end of the presumed connecting passages, the team with the inward draught lights some damp paper to see if the other team can detect it. This has worked on several occasions. On the way out, Mike Wooding and I crossed the massive Salle Verna chamber, at that time the largest natural chamber in the world.

When the EDF tunnel was completed, this gave access for the French speleologists to easily enter the lowest section of the cave, the Salle Verna. They had noticed a passage high above on the far wall and had climbed into a large tunnel they named Aranzadi. A small stream entered not far inside and flowed into a series of short pitches then down a massive 70 metre deep pitch. They used a winch to lower someone to the bottom, but he returned pronouncing the shaft choked with boulders. He named it the Maria Dolores after his wife. Beyond the Maria Dolores lay a long series of meanders, named the Meander Martine. This consisted of a few kilometres of strength-sapping traversing on small ledges above drops where it was too narrow to progress, arriving at the Montpellier Chamber. A further series of very wet pitches named the Puits Parment descended to the lowest point in the system of the deepest cave in the world. The report indicated that the ongoing passage was too narrow to progress further. Beyond the Montpellier the passage continued for a considerable distance to terminate at choked chamber called Ballandraux. Mike and I made what was an easy climb up into the roof of the Verna and did a reconnaissance of the way on. The stream came from an inlet which needed climbing at the start of the Aranzadi. We retreated and carried a few bags of tackle back to camp.

On Friday, we completed ferrying the tackle bags back down the mountain then set off back to the UK. Although the expedition achieved nothing, it did serve a useful purpose as we were able to familiarise ourselves with the route to the lowest sections of the system. Little could be done in just five days.

Ian Gasson had expounded the virtues of the Pierre-Saint-Martin to his caving friends from ULSA before he was tragically killed and they were keen to explore in the deepest cave in the world. Also, the only caving filmmaker in the UK, Sid Perou, contacted me to see if permission could be granted from ARSIP to make a film of an expedition. We had a discussion on the possibilities and went caving together down Pippikin Pot. I was keen to see Sid make a film on this fantastic cave as he had made a few caving films for British television. This good publicity was gradually changing the face of British cave explorers from the idiots that got stuck underground to serious minded individuals in the pursuit of new discoveries. A good image could only be to the advantage of British cavers.

I contacted ARSIP and permission was granted, the aims and objectives were the descent of the Puits Parment, the wet series of shafts leading to the lowest point in the cave. The reports suggested that the end was too narrow to progress deeper; to ULSA that was a challenge in itself.

ULSA had a very strong team of cavers involved in the new golden age of discovery in the Yorkshire Dales. They explored many new caves, most of them of a very serious nature, being difficult, wet, tight and mostly for the hard men.

I could not obtain much enthusiasm from the Eldon as it seemed I was obtaining something of a reputation. I managed to recruit one Eldon member in the form of Richard Townsend and also had Mike Wooding who was keen to continue with the work after seeing the meanders. In a pub in Buxton I was introduced to the late Mike Boon by Bob Toogood. I had met Mike before many years previously in the Yorkshire Dales and knew something of his idiosyncratic ways. He was an exceptional cave explorer with many credits to his name. His lone exploration of Castleguard Cave in the Canadian Rockies was legendary. He had hiked through the mountains on his own and explored this icy cave for miles before the main team could get there, much to their annoyance. Boon was heavily criticised for his daring.

The year before, a new cave in Iran had been explored by a British team, the cave was named Ghar Parau, but they ran out of ladders at 740 metres below the entrance. This year, 1972 another expedition to Ghar Parau was planned as there was a good possibility that it could become the deepest cave in the world. Much publicity surrounded the expedition and the team had signed the book rights. Mike Boon asked to join the team and was told NO in capital letters. Considering our expedition also had a chance of breaking the cave world depth record, ours was the next best thing. I of course said yes as I love strange eccentric characters.

While Mike stayed with me at my house in Chinley, I received a phone call. The ULSA members had not returned from a major new passage discovery in Langcliffe Cave, situated in the Yorkshire Dales. The cave was a serious proposition being a long, wet crawl in a stream way that went on for miles through the Yordale limestone series. Clive Westlake, I and quite a few other members of the Eldon had attempted trips down this cave on several occasions after Ian Gasson expounded its delights. We seemed to make a habit of descending any cave that was considered ridiculously hard. Each time we had been beaten back by bad weather or some other life-threatening considerations and had never reached the boulder choke leading to larger passages. I phoned the cave rescue and they asked that considering we knew something of the system and no one else did, could we attend. Considering that the majority of the forthcoming PSM expedition team members were in serious trouble, I had little choice but to say yes. I recruited Peter Lord from Sheffield and the three of us drove through the night to the scene.

We were dispatched with ex-army ammunition boxes full of hot tomato soup and grovelled weighed down for a few hours until someone ahead turned up. They were all safe. The boulder choke had collapsed trapping them beyond and they had finally managed to squeeze through by tying the offending boulder up with a shoe lace.

For the next expedition there was to be no leader as such, which seemed strange for many to understand, but there was no need for one as all the team were completely motivated to a common aim and not the types to act egotistically. I hired a small van from Manchester and the four of us set off on Saturday 29th July 1972.

8

The Deepest Hole in the World, 1972

'Strength does not come from physical capacity. It comes from an indomitable will'.

Mahatma Gandhi

We arrived in the town of Tarbes on Sunday 30th July and met up with Max Cosyns, then set up our base camp at Sainte-Engrâce. The ULSA team were already there and had started the work of rigging the pitches in the Puits Parment.

The following day we set off walking up the mountain track to the EDF tunnel carrying our personal equipment and a few ladders. It was about 5.30 pm before we got underground with about five electron ladders in 25 feet lengths, approximately 38 metres. This was before the introduction of the metric system so all caves, ropes and ladders were measured in feet, a much nicer measurement for the mapping of caves rather than the metre.

The four of us, comprising my small team entered the Salle Verna and climbed the steep slope up to the Aranzadi Passage. A further eight ladders, 60 metres in total, were picked up on the way in, weighing us down somewhat as the Meander Martine traverse is awkward. Two hands are needed in order to negotiate this winding cleft so the ladders are hung around the shoulders on a sling. ULSA had fixed three ladders on short pitches along the Meander Martine and on the third pitch we found yet another three ladders so carried them along with the pile we already had. Dave Cobley, Steve Crabtree, Andy Eavis, Tony White and John Donovan arrived on their way out. They had placed a ladder on an eight metre pitch into the Montpellier Chamber and had started rigging in the Puits Aziz down to about 60 metres, a couple of pitches and a few cascades in total before they ran out of ladders and retreated. Ropes had been left on all the pitches in order to lifeline the climber.

We continued where they left off, but Mike Wooding had a sudden desire to get to the bottom before anyone else, so took 120 metres of rope, intending to abseil down to the lowest point but ran out of rope. Abseiling was not normally done in those days as the ropes were not designed for such use as they were twisted rather than plaited, so they tended to twist into a massive knot on the way down. We had just started to experiment with what in later years became known as single rope techniques, or SRT for short, where we could put our electron ladders in the museum and just use ropes alone.

The next few pitches were rigged and a few cascades freeclimbed and we soon met up with Mike waiting at the bottom of one of the pitches for us to rig with ladders, so he could climb out.

We now calculated we had enough ropes and ladders to reach the bottom but as we had been underground for about 12 hours, hunger had set in. We usually carried peanuts, chocolate and other light rations underground just to keep the sugar levels high, but we had scoffed the lot. We all retreated back along the endless meanders, arriving back on the surface at 9 am the following morning and back at camp by 12 noon. We had been on the go non-stop for 28 hours.

On Tuesday 1st August, Alan and Dave Brook with a further three continued rigging but found themselves just 5 metres short of reaching the bottom of the Puits Parment.

On Wednesday 2nd August, they finally reached the end point but the ongoing rift passage was far too narrow even for Dave Brook. Only the use of explosives would engineer a way through for person to pass but Dave did have the honour of having the deepest Wellington boot in the world.

We still had plenty of time left and I had no intention of giving up the search for a possible way on, so decided to take a look at the Maria Dolores, reported as being 110 metres deep to a boulder blockage. On Thursday, Richard Townsend and I returned to the Aranzadi Passage. We first needed to help Sid Perou as he could not get his little vehicle, a Mini Moke, up the track with some ladders and ropes which I needed to make a start. We walked back down the track and retrieved 40 metres of ladder and a couple of ropes.

It was 6 pm before we got going and on entering the Aranzadi we had a good look at the main stream inlet for the Maria Dolores series of shafts. A passage could be seen continuing above the cascade. Richard is a tall guy so by standing and balancing on Richard's shoulders I managed to grab a good hold with one outstretched arm and haul myself up, reaching the overhanging passage about five metres above with the small stream tumbling down. I then rigged a ladder from a good belay point for Richard to follow. Another cascade followed immediately about seven metres high and succumbed to the same ridiculous method. After only 30 metres of nice stream passage another much larger cascade presented itself, about 13 metres high. I gave it another try but could only free climb halfway without some rope protection. I had noticed a steel scaffolding pole in the Aranzadi, probably used during the descent of the Maria Dolores, so went back to pick it up meeting Mike Wooding on the way.

The three of us carried the pole to the third cascade and, placing it against the rock, I climbed the pole monkey-style and reached the top, rigging a ladder so my two companions could follow.

Yet another small three metre cascade could easily be freeclimbed followed by a short traverse above the stream. A side passage entered on the left which was later explored by Mike to a large chamber he called the Salle June. Another short side passage on the right led to yet another nice chamber which I named the Salle Gasson after my good friend Ian Gasson who lost his life in Ireland. An oxbow in the passage followed and our discovery terminated in another large chamber with two small inlets entering at the base, both far too immature for a normal sized person to progress further. The chambers are what we call avens, high chambers with probable ways on at the top, often with small streams flowing down the walls.

We had explored some 370 metres of very nice stream passage, a good start as at least the expedition had discovered some previously unexplored cave. Dave Brook later mapped this extension and it was named the Reseau Anglais. We were all back at camp by 8 am the following morning.

On Saturday 5th August, Richard and I began working in the Maria Dolores while Dave Brook's team of five men started the mapping of the Puits Parment and attempted unsuccessfully to force a way through the narrow passage at the end. Another team were to set off later to join Dave and help de-rig this section of cave, bringing the ladders and ropes back to the surface.

I picked up a 12 metre ladder from the small wooded hut situated just outside the EDF tunnel. Sid used this hut to store his filming equipment and, when returning from the cave exhausted, team members could get their head down for a while before trekking back to camp. We descended at about 4 p.m. and managed to scrounge another few ladders and a couple of ropes. The entrance to this Maria Dolores series involved a few free climbs down cascades, arriving at an eight metre drop on which I placed a ladder. A few other cascades followed, all free-climbable to the head of the big pitch where the French had used the winch. This was approximately 50 metres below the start of the Maria Dolores.

We had no idea of the depth but suspected it to be around 60 metres. The shaft was large in dimensions and certainly it appeared to be deep. It could be laddered in the dry avoiding a drenching from the stream which cascaded down the giant shaft. The take-off was a slope, not vertical but at an angle, this meant that the ladder lay against the rock and did not hang free.

The problem with this kind of take-off is that you cannot get your fingers and feet in the rungs of the ladder unless you pull the ladder towards your body using your knees as levers. This is a difficult manoeuvre when hanging in the dark, 60 metres above an unseen floor. Attaching 35 metres of ladder to a sound rock belay, I descended life-lined by Richard, but on reaching the end of the ladders I was still a long way from the bottom although I could just make it out with my feeble carbide lamp through the spray.

The following day, on Sunday 6th August, accompanied by Richard and a French caver called Bert, I scrounged another 30 metres of ladders and attached them to the end of the 35 metres already rigged down the pitch. I descended but still found myself five metres off reaching the bottom. A small ledge allowed me to free-climb the last few metres and I arrived at the bottom of this splendid pitch amongst a fine spray from the stream cascading from way above down the 70 metre shaft.

The old winch was rusting away at the bottom; the French explorers must have thrown it down in disgust. Behind the winch was an obvious way on through boulders, well, obvious to me anyway, but it appears it was not as obvious to the original French explorers. I free-climbed down through the boulders and entered a passage with solid walls. A narrow rift type passage intersected the small passage I found myself in, but I continued forward and to my surprise discovered a further vertical drop which the French had completely missed. I estimated it to be no more than ten metres in depth and there was a good draught, which indicated interesting possibilities of further extensive passages. Communication from the base of the big shaft to Richard and Bert at the top was good, so I attached myself onto the life-line and free-climbed the five metres up to the end of my ladders.

On the way out we met Mike who had climbed a high aven at the end of the Aranzadi Passage that contained a small inlet stream flowing down into the meanders. He reached a height of about 26 metres but the way on was too narrow for further progress although there was a strong draught.

The following day, Mike Boon helped Sid with his filming and brought out some of the equipment while Andy Eavis investigated the end of the meanders in the final chamber called Salle Ballandraux but only two small inlets were found, not large enough for a person but again with a draught.

There was much interest now in my discovery, so on Tuesday 8th August my team had swelled to include the late Dave Yeandle, Paul Everett, Steve Holcroft and, of course, Richard.

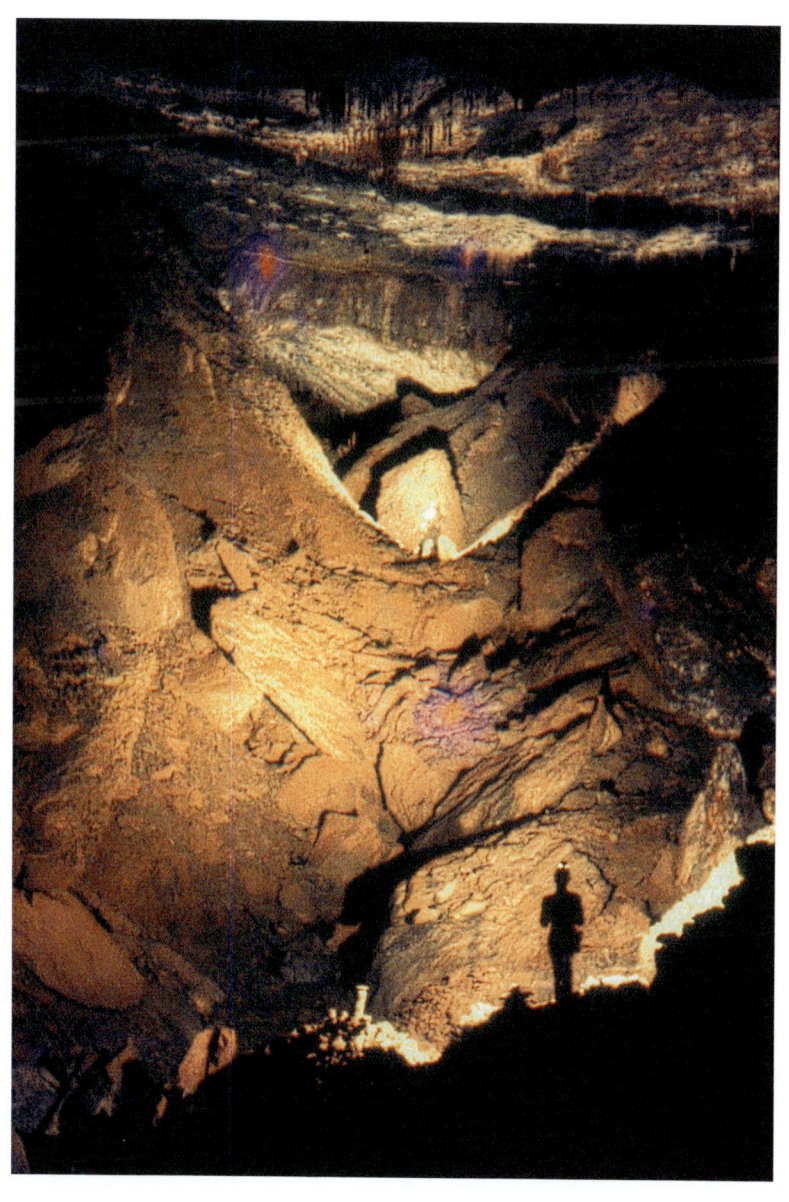

Larumbe inlet, Gouffre de la Pierre Saint Martin. Photo: J Cunningham

We were underground by 3 pm after collecting seven ladders and 36 metres of rope and proceeded to descend the big pitch. I was engrossed reading Tolkien's book, The Lord of the Rings at the time so christened this wonderful shaft Puit Galadriel. Richard and Steve elected to remain at the top of the shaft in order to life-line us back up the pitch as it was impossible to rig a double life line through a pulley at the top, thus enabling all the team to descend. It would be a long and cold wait for them. A great deal of trouble was experienced trying to lower the ladders, ropes and survey equipment down the shaft, as the equipment kept getting snagged on protruding rocks, but we managed it after considerable difficulties.

I descended the 12 metre pitch I had discovered on the Sunday and descended a few free climbable drops at the end of the ladder under a small waterfall. The shaft was a narrow rift but the way on was too tiny to follow further. Dave had a look but could not make further progress. While waiting for me grovelling around in the pitch, Dave had followed the intersecting rift passage and discovered a further vertical drop of about 12 metres. This was laddered and led to a tight rift passage which was followed to a further drop estimated at 25 metres with a very narrow take off at the top. Water could be heard falling beyond. Halfway down the 12 metre pitch, later christened Puit Pooh, there appeared to be another two possibilities both with a draught of air, both led to further vertical drops. By this time, we had run out of ladders and rope so we returned to the surface leaving the tackle in situ. Steve and Richard had been waiting for us for six hours at the top of Puit Galadriel.

Before Richard and myself exited the cave, I took Richard for a trip into the main passages as far as the Metro Tunnel, we were due to go home in a couple of days and this would be Richard's last chance to see something of this world class cave system. Richard had diligently been working with me for the whole time and had not yet had the chance of a tourist trip. We exited the cave at about 2 am Wednesday 9th August.

On Thursday 10th August, the team had swelled once again as excitement was now prevalent to explore new ground. Sid of course wanted to film this discovery as his contract from the BBC appeared to be in jeopardy. The expectation was that this very strong team of some of the most experienced cave explorers in the UK would break the world depth record, but so far we had failed. The discovery of the new passages in the Maria Dolores offered a chance of success.

After some organisation on the surface it was 6 pm before we set off underground. Sid had been filming all the previous day and throughout the night in the meanders and the Puits Parment an incredibly difficult task.

Helped by Dick Ellis, Steve Calvert and John Donovan, Sid filmed Dave Yeandle and I on the climbs from the Salle Verna chamber up to the Aranzadi and the entrance passages of the Maria Dolores.

The team consisted of Andy Eavis, Paul Everett, Richard Townsend and Mike Boon with a support team of Alf Latham, Steve Holcroft, carrying more ladders and ropes. Dave, John and I caught them up around 9.30 pm after four hours of filming. Again, there was great difficulty in lowering the equipment down the big shaft, the Puit Galadriel.

Andy, Paul, Richard, Mike, Dave and I arrived at the bottom of the shaft in one piece with a mountain of ladders and ropes hoping to break the world depth record, excitement was intense.

The first objective was a good looking 37 metre pitch situated half way down Puit Pooh, I descended followed by Andy but it was far too narrow at the base to follow, the stream flowing down the Puit Galadriel reappeared in this shaft. The next one was the 25 metre drop with the tight take-off where a stream could be heard rumbling away enticingly. Paul descended the ladder but again although he could hear the stream it could not be reached as, once more, the bottom petered out in a small rift. These pitches all seemed immature with sharp, corroded limestone.

Dave had better luck and found the other pitch leading off from Puit Pooh. This looked much more promising being in solid-looking black limestone. Followed by Mike, Dave rigged three nice pitches with ladders, a ten metre, a 12 metre followed by a 22 pitch. These led to a large passage terminating in a huge sloping pitch which seemed to be following the steeply dipping beds of this black limestone area. Andy, Paul, Richard and I followed with the ladders and ropes needed in order to descend this shaft which we all hoped would pass the present deepest point in the Pierre Saint-Martin.

Again after The Lord of the Rings we called it Puit Sauron. Mike descended this 61 metre deep pit, followed by myself. We were disappointed to see the bottom, just a large high aven with a small stream coming from way above in the roof. Another small stream entered at the base from a tiny crack and disappeared down a four inch slot. Climbing back up the pitch, I noticed a continuation of the large passage but at the other side of Puit Sauron, and it would have been a major climbing project to reach it. We were not very far short of breaking the world depth record. It was 12.30 pm the following day before we all reached the surface.

I will not go into the detail of Sid Perou's epics filming this expedition as it is well documented in his book, Thirty Years as an Adventure

Cameraman, Book 1, Light into Darkness, but the story does not end there. Along with Ruben Gomez the ARSIP coordinator, all the team congregated at a nice restaurant for the last supper in the village of Licq. Too much was had to eat and far too much to drink and on the way back late at night, the most sober of the four, Richard, was delegated the job of driving us back to Sainte-Engrâce. He took a bend far too fast and hit the steel barrier of a bridge. Luckily the bridge barrier held and we did not plunge into the river gorge far below but the front of the vehicle was in a mess with a heavily damaged radiator. We patched it up and limped back to Sainte-Engrâce and from there the following day drove slowly to Calais.

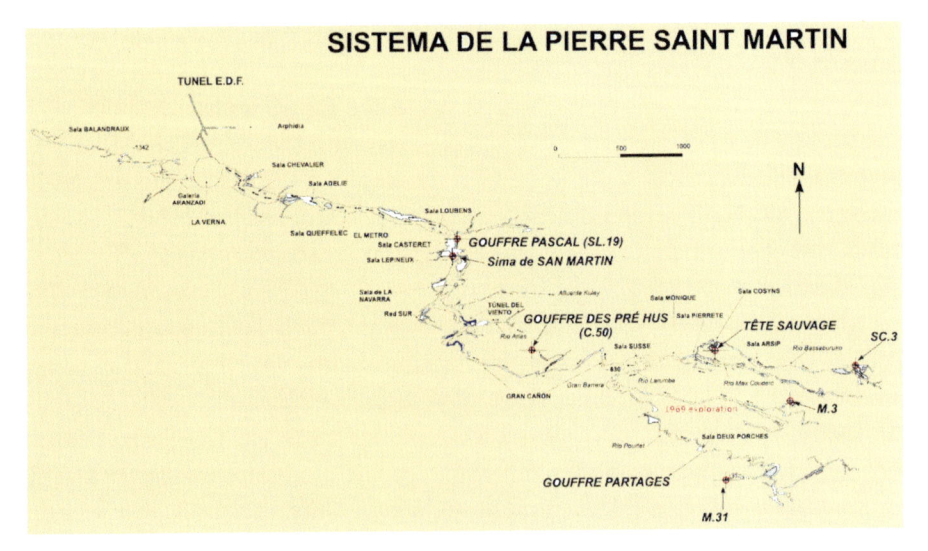

Plan survey of the Gouffre de la Pierre St. Martin.

On the way through Kent, Mike Boon was driving. It was important to prevent the engine over heating by keeping the speed down to 40 miles per hour as every half hour we had to stop and top up the leaking radiator with water. Mike drove fast while the three of us slept and the poor engine finally gave up the ghost. Mike, Richard and Mike Wooding grabbed their personal belongings and deserted the field, leaving me stranded with a smashed-up car and a load of expedition equipment.

I remembered that Bruce Bedford, then the editor of the cavers' magazine Descent, lived in Kent. I found a telephone box and rang him. Bruce very kindly drove through Kent and picked me up along with all the expedition equipment which was then stored at his house. I returned by bus to Derbyshire after falling asleep at Victoria bus station in London and missing the first bus of the day. I had to wait 12 hours for the next one and with empty pockets I was pretty hungry. The boss of the car hire company was not a happy chap and I made sure I never asked him again if I could hire another car.

I did a few interviews for BBC as the voice over for Sid's film, The Deepest Hole in the World, and a few months later received a phone call from the producer. 'We are short of a shot,' he explained, referring to the story of the crows flying out of the shaft as the French cave explorer Lépineux sat on a rock throwing stones. This was an important part of the history of the Pierre Saint-Martin as it led to the discovery of the 300 metre deep Lépineux shaft, leading into the main cave system. 'Can you find me a hole that looks like the Lépineux shaft in Derbyshire, somewhere we can drive to?' he asked. 'It's £10 for the day.' Rather a tall order but I needed the ten quid and thought anything with a limestone cliff and a small hole would suffice so I took them to Stanley Moor in Derbyshire. Here they could drive their cars along the track with all their filming equipment close to a few small caves with remnants of small limestone cliffs.

Sid Perou, the producer and a large group of sound recording engineers, lighting technicians, cameramen and clapper-board men turned up on Stanley Moor. The producer opened the boot of his car to reveal two sacks with things wriggling inside.

'What have you got there?' I asked.

'Crows,' said the producer. He had managed to persuade the game keeper at Chatsworth Estates, Derbyshire to capture for him two sacks of crows. This was a resourceful man I thought.

Sid hid just inside the hole, wearing a helmet, with his two sacks of crows, out of sight of the cameras. I sat on a rock pretending to be the great man Lépineux. I threw a stone at Sid's helmet and when – or if – it hit, he was then supposed to grab a couple of crows out of the bag and release them to fly up, up and away back to Chatsworth. The first stone scored a direct hit and Sid released his crows, they coughed and collapsed on the grass then wandered off dazed.

'Cut!' shouted the producer.

After about six attempts, we finally managed to get two crows to fly away. Sid and I were in hysterics laughing but I got my ten quid.

This little episode, lasting no more than a few seconds, probably cost more than Sid received for three months of very hard work making the complete film.

The final version of the film was received well but Sid was very disappointed with the editing, which had been out of his hands, so he only viewed it once. Many years went by before Sid saw the film again, this time by accident as he was attending a caving film festival in France. A man came up to him and asked if Sid remembered him, then he introduced himself as Ruben Gomez. They talked about the film and Ruben said he had an old copy that he used for showing to cavers visiting the PSM. He sent Sid a copy and on looking at it again all these years later he realised that it was nowhere near as bad as he originally thought. In fact, considering the immense difficulties with the severity of the undertaking, the unforgiving nature of the cave and, in those days, lighting and film stock, the film was something of a classic and an important piece of historical archive material. He eventually obtained another better copy and transferred it to DVD.

PSM Base Camp. Photo: David Gill

Sid made many caving films that depicted real people, not the jumped up, overpaid, false actors and TV presenters who have featured in a few films inside caves and elsewhere in recent years. 'This is absolutely amazing,' seems to be the favourite line, when it actually comes across to the viewer that they dislike caves and would much prefer to be in the sun on a beach somewhere and not down a dark wet cave far beneath the earth and an awfully long way from daylight. They do not come across as good actors. Sid's films had no actors, just rough and ready unpaid cave explorers, warts and all. His films come across as the real thing, which in fact is exactly what they were.

9

Gouffre de la Pierre Saint-Martin Expedition, 1973

'Life is either a daring adventure or nothing'

Helen Keller

After Sid's film there was a growing interest in the caving community about the Gouffre de la Pierre Saint-Martin explorations and it was not long before I was yet again involved in another expedition. This time anyone could turn up and enjoy the fun. As with the last one there was no leader as such, just a group of like-minded friends out to explore one of the greatest cave systems on earth.

We had a large contingent from the Mendip region of England, including Tony Jarratt, Mike Wooding, Mike Jeanmaire, all three sadly no longer with us, and Nigel Taylor from the Bristol Exploration Club, the BEC. Ken James and Aubrey Newport from the Wessex Cave Club and a large group from ULSA involved in the last expedition were also there. I organised the Eldon team which included George Cooper, Paul Deakin, John Levan, Steve Dickinson, Richard Townsend, Gordon Parkin, Bill Whitehouse and Wayne Rickert.

It's surprising what a TV film could do as previously I'd had great trouble trying to recruit team members. From the Derbyshire Caving Club, Alan Gamble also joined me along with John New and Albi Sole from the Lancaster University Caving Club. Even Peter B Smith turned up along with Bob Cockeram from the Northern Caving Club and Chris Pugsley from Sheffield University Speleological Society. The place was heaving with friends. It was described as the PSM circus at the time as every man and his dog seemed to turn up at some time or other throughout the expedition time period. Ruben Gomez, the ARSIP coordinator, had his work cut out to try and control it all.

We travelled down in George Cooper's Land Rover and, driving fast in the dead of night, got the Land Rover stuck between two stone walls of the narrow track to the Sainte-Engrâce camp site. George managed to free it and drove into the camp making lots of noise, as the Eldon often do. As it was about midnight, a guy came out of his tent dressed in pyjamas and started to scold the noisy Eldon. This was Bill Brookes from the Westminster Speleological Group who was here with a group of his caving friends from Poland, most attached to the Wroclaw University. From that day forward he became known to all as Pyjama Bill.

One of the projects I was interested in involved the investigation of a stream passage just near the start of the Arphidia the cave just off the EDF tunnel we had attempted to explore in 1971. This was just marked and described as a wet shaft containing the main Arphidia stream, leading to an uncertain end. For convenience we just called it the Wet Way as it did not seem to possess a French name.

On Monday 6th August 1973, Alan Gamble, Chris Pugsley, Spike and myself began fixing electron ladders down the series of shafts in the Wet Way. The first pitch of 16 metres could be laddered in the dry, avoiding the stream, followed by a steep descent along the stream. A traverse to a large block again avoided a wet decent down the second pitch of 15 metres. The third pitch of nine metres was in the stream, there was no way we could avoid it and at the base of the shaft we found the remnants of an old winch. A short two metre pitch followed and a steep eight metre descent which we rigged with a ladder. By this time, we had run out of equipment as another deep looking pitch followed almost immediately.

Meanwhile, a large group were enjoying a tourist trip into the big main passages of the PSM and Paul Deakin produced his magic multi flash bulb black and white image of the Salle Verna. No one had attempted to photograph this immense chamber previously as it was just too big.

Pyjama Bill and eight Polish cavers busied themselves exploring the main Arphidia cave while the ULSA team concentrated on the passage seen in the Puit Sauron, climbing up to the black space across the pitch I had seen on the last expedition. Disappointingly, it proved to be a rock bridge and led to a dead end.

Also kicking around was a team from Bulgaria making a film. Things were certainly very chaotic, to say the least.

On Tuesday 7th August, I received a message from Ruben asking me to meet him, it said 6.30. I presumed wrongly it was pm. I missed him as he meant 0630 hours. A team descended the Wet Way and took more ladders and ropes down the cave, also fixing a rock anchor bolt above the fifth pitch to obtain a dry descent.

On Wednesday 8th August, we completed the descent of the Wet Way with a team consisting of Spike, Gordon Parkin, Tony Jarratt and myself later joined by George and Alan. The fifth pitch was a nice descent of 40 metres followed by the sixth pitch of 26 metres. We arrived at a deep pool of water followed by only 20 metres of well-decorated passage to two small sumps, deep green holes in the floor full of water. We mapped the cave and it came to little more than 130 metres in depth. Disappointed, we retreated, there was no way on.

The same day it transpired that five Polish cavers had decided to attempt the though trip from the Tête Sauvage to the EDF tunnel descending on Monday 6th August, the day after our arrival. We knew nothing about this and presumed when informed that they had cleared their trip with ARSIP. The five had not reappeared at the EDF tunnel and they had now been missing for three days, so Bill Brookes with members of the Eldon team and John New went all the way as far as the Tunnel de Vent to search for the lost Polish group but they were nowhere to be seen. When the search party returned, it was decided to bivouac on the plateau the night and then to descend the Tête Sauvage the following day as they were most probably stranded at the bottom of the shafts. The story came to light that they intended to abseil down the shafts on their ropes, pulling them down via a pull through technique, thus retrieving their ropes but cutting off their means of retreat to the surface via the shafts. In later years, this technique became quite common for tourist trips through caves with a lower entrance, known as a through trip. It was of course essential that the team were capable of the traverse and that the exit from the lower entrance could be guaranteed, otherwise they would be stranded.

It was around this time that cavers from many countries started experimenting with the use of good strong ropes to descend pitches rather than using electron ladders. This technique would make the exploration of caves much easier, without the need to carry large amounts of ladders, plus life-line ropes. This was called, Single Rope Techniques or SRT for short. Various pieces of equipment for SRT had started to appear on the market. The device for descending, simply called a descender at that time, consisted of a Figure of Eight, made by a climbing hardware company called Clog, in Wales. This was a lump of aluminium through which a climber's karabiner could be attached to a continuous sling of strong nylon tape, threaded around the legs and waist. By threading the rope through the device, it acted with friction so the descent could be controlled but losing control by not holding the rope could be fatal. Due to friction, the device also got hot. This technique was known as abseiling and had been used by climbers for many years, in the old days just by threading the rope around the back and beneath the crutch to obtain friction; this method was often rather painful, as can be imagined.

For ascending, another clever device had just appeared on the caving and climbing scene, again simply called an Ascender. This was of aluminium construction with a spring-loaded cam with small teeth through which the rope passed. The device went up the rope but not down, as the cam trapped the rope from moving in the downward direction. With a pair of these, the first one attached to a sling as above and the second one on a tape loop for the feet, it was possible to ascend a single rope, climbing monkey-like. Over the years, these techniques were perfected along with static ropes which unlike climbers' dynamic ropes did not stretch. There were many trial and errors, some with fatal consequences. We did not fully understand the properties of ropes and abseiled sometimes on polypropylene which melted due to the heat transmitted to the Descender via friction. Static caving ropes were gradually developed with a plaited outer covering called the sheath and a core of multi-cored nylon fibre within. Also, waist harness and chest harnesses were introduced. These were far preferable to tape slings and much more comfortable.

We bivouacked the night on the plateau and the following day prepared to descend the Tête Sauvage. The Speleological Club of Paris were also camped up on the plateau and one of our team, when asked what we were doing, let it slip about the predicament of the Polish cavers. They of course informed ARSIP as they knew that the Poles did not have the required permit to descend. Access for expeditions to the Pierre Saint-Martin and surrounding areas was strictly controlled as it was essential that there was co-ordination of all the different groups from various parts of the world, including exploration and research. Rather like the access permits to climb Mount Everest and other major peaks.

Ruben Gomez arrived and was adamant that we could not descend the Tête Sauvage and rescue the Polish cavers. The French rescue teams would be called out, the Speleo Secours. I was equally adamant that we were going down to get them out as this was now the fourth day. He threatened us with police action if we descended so to keep the peace I relented. Ruben had a valid reason as all cave rescues are the direct responsibility of the Speleo Secours.

The reason he had been searching for me was that Ruben had another serious project he wanted us to look at. This was a deep series of shafts provisionally named FR3. As there are thousands of shafts in this area, all new explorations of surface shafts are designated with a number to avoid confusion and marked with red paint. A name had now been allotted for this cave, the Puit de la Bordelaise. It had been measured at 420 metres in depth to a river passage containing a small stream.

The French had a small camp close to the entrance called Bordeaux, with a water supply from a fast diminishing block of melting snow. The entrance was a long way across the lapiaz-riddled limestone mountain and at a much higher altitude than the Tête Sauvage. If a way on could be found,

The author at the Tête Sauvage entrance to the PSM.. Photo: Jim Cunningham

this cave could become much deeper than the PSM as it was presumed the stream at the bottom resurged into daylight at the same resurgence as the Pierre Saint-Martin, the Anialara. Ruben considered that British cave explorers were more adept at exploring the more difficult sections of caves. The brief was, we were to rig the cave to the bottom, install a telephone cable part of the way, place 14 kilograms of fluorescein dye in the stream and explore downstream. It sounded like a good project and the team was up for it.

We returned back to Sainte-Engrâce and hiked back up the mountain track to the EDF tunnel to collect our equipment. Tony and Spike picked up the fluorescein and telephone cable and set off over the mountains for the Bordeaux camp, but returned late at night as they had been unable to find it.

On Friday 10th August the police asked me to wait for Ruben and Max Coysns as they were on their way to see me. They met me at Sainte-Engrâce and again explained the situation with the rescue of the Polish cavers; on no account were we to go down the Tête Sauvage, they could handle it without our assistance. The Speleo Club of Paris had descended the Tête Sauvage to conduct a search, but it would help if a small team could wait at the Tunnel de Vent with food and sleeping bags as it was planned to bring the Polish cavers out of the EDF tunnel. We agreed and Dave Yeandle, Bill Brookes, Alan Gamble, John New, George Cooper, Aubrey Newport, Spike and Ken James set off for a possible long stay.

My team consisted of Ken James, Nigel Taylor, Albi Sole, Bob Cockeram, Richard Townsend, Wayne Rickert, Steve Dickenson, Gordon Parkin, Tony Jarratt, Chris Pugsley, John Levan and myself, a team of twelve good men in all. We departed for the plateau but were considerably delayed when heavy rain swamped the Speleo Club of Paris tents and we dug ditches to try to drain the water. We set off across the mountain with our personal equipment. Soon it went dark and we were probably only half way there. We set up camp in heavy rain and no one wanted to hold the metal tent poles as lightning flashed all around, spectacular but unnerving.

Very early the following morning, 11th August, we reached the Bordeaux camp, dumped our gear and returned back to Sainte-Engrâce for more loads of caving equipment. We received the news that the Polish cavers had been found, one with a broken arm, and were being evacuated via the Tête Sauvage as the canals had flooded due to the heavy rain. It appears they had lost their light batteries in the canals when a dinghy overturned and were unable to continue with little light; also, being cut off from their retreat via the Tete Sauvage, they had decided wisely to sit it out and wait for rescue.

Sunday 12th August saw us all back at camp Bordeaux accompanied by a French caver called Gerald from the Bordeaux caving club. Ken and Tony were still in Sainte-Engrâce and arranged to join us later. The cave was rigged with ladders and ropes except for the first 54 metre deep pitch a short way inside the entrance. This was only rigged with a 12 mm climbing rope; being dynamic it was akin to abseiling on an elastic band. Ruben asked us to completely de-rig the cave bringing all the tackle back to the surface. By mid-day, we were all on our way to the bottom with the fluorescein dye and laying the telephone cable as we went. A fine series of pitches followed, twelve in all, with some deep drops of over 60 metres. By 4 pm, we had all congregated at the bottom and, after a brew, set off to explore and dump the dye in the stream. Downstream was completely flooded in a small passage with a side passage merely looping round to join the sump. We deposited the dye at 7.30 pm and explored upstream. This was far more complex with a number of side loops and low passages, but all degenerated into tiny squeezes, too small to follow. Ken and Tony turned up at 8 pm in the main passage after descending around 5.30 pm. They intended to sleep below ground and then begin de-rigging the cave.

It was around midnight when we all set off on the long climb out, the last man out was me, reaching daylight at around 10 am the following morning. My philosophy has always been to make sure all my team are out of the cave and safe before I leave. It had been a good trip but rather disappointing. Ken and Tony Jarratt remained down below.

On Tuesday 14th August at around 10.30 am to mid-day we were all back down the cave and met up with Ken and Tony at the base of the eight pitch, 55 metres deep, at 4.30 pm. They had de-rigged the bottom three pitches and left the ropes and ladders at the base of the ninth pitch, 10 metres deep, ready to be hauled out.

We began the strenuous job of hauling the tackle up the pitch when suddenly our ears popped. Chris and Bob received a slight electric shock as they descended the ladders. Within minutes a deluge of water poured down the shaft and the team dived for safety beneath a small overhang only a metre from the by now roaring waterfall. Chris and Bob managed to escape by seconds and joined us. The noise was deafening, and the spray lashed our already wet bodies. We huddled together trying to keep out of the waterfall, perched on a small ledge above the roaring cataract of the ninth pitch. We were not going anywhere; to attempt to climb out would amount to certain suicide, we had no alternative but to sit it out until the flood subsided.

Switching off the water supply for our carbide lamps in order to save our dwindling supplies of calcium carbide, our life-line to daylight, we told stories, sang songs and laughed to keep our waning spirits up.

Sixteen hours later, the water at last started to recede. Cold, hungry and tired, we made our way slowly to the surface. Tony Jarratt's light gave out as he had been underground for almost three days so he used a camping gas stove for lighting. I have no idea how he managed to climb the ladders holding a gas stove at the same time, as you need both hands, but he did. Of course, being in a sorry state we had no alternative but to abandon the ropes and ladders, we left them safely stashed to prevent them being washed away.

We were all safely on the surface by 5 pm on Wednesday 15th August. I was the last one out and as we only had a 12 mm climbing rope on the first and final pitch to daylight, we had to use a primitive form of single rope techniques (SRT) in order to climb it. Our problem was we only had a few tape slings and ascenders so each man when he reached the top slid his ascenders and slings down the rope attached to a karabiner for the next man to follow.

Alone at the base of the pitch and falling asleep, my two descenders and tape slings came down the rope but unfortunately the wrong ones. The ascender I received was only designed for a 10 mm diameter rope and refused to move in an upward direction, becoming jammed. Tired and in frustration I tried many times but failed. After about 30 minutes Tony popped his head over the shaft edge wondering if I had dozed off and kindly sent his ascenders down which worked. It had been a long trip. Exhausted we evacuated the surface camp and returned to Sainte-Engrâce.

Ruben and Max were very glad to see us alive as the thunderstorm had caused a great deal of flooding and as they had not heard anything from us for a few days, we were presumed dead and they dreaded organising another major rescue.

It is worth recapping the epic acted out in the rescue of the Polish cavers over the few days we were sitting out the flood in the Puits de la Bordelaise. This is their version of the story.

The party that entered the EDF tunnel on Friday 10th August with food a dinghy and sleeping bags arrived at the Tunnel de Vent and Alan, John, Bill and Dave proceeded through the low windy section of the tunnel with a dinghy and a couple of lilos, arriving at the far side at about 6 pm and proceeded upstream to the start of the long canals. Two French cavers arrived and informed them that the Polish cavers had been found and would exit the cave via the EDF tunnel. They were to wait and assist in the evacuation. The French cavers had a rubber dinghy and were on their way back to the surface via the EDF tunnel as they did not seem interested in helping Alan's team. There was no need for a dinghy in order to exit via the EDF tunnel so Alan set off back with the two French cavers in order to bring back the dinghy which would be needed for the five Polish boys. On reaching the Tunnel de Vent it was obvious that the tunnel was rapidly filling with water as unknown to them the thunderstorm was raging on the surface. These small light weight rubber dinghies will not carry more than two at a time, so normally one person ferries one other across these freezing cold lakes and canals, then returns for the next man, or if possible a rope can be fixed to the dinghy and used to pull it across. The two French guys went through on their dinghy saying one would return for Alan so he could paddle the dinghy back. The French guys did not return.

On arriving at the other side of the Tunnel de Vent, George was informed by the French cavers of Alan's predicament. Ken James made a brave attempt to reach the stranded Alan but failed as the water had risen to within four inches of the roof. Alan saw Ken and swam for it just making it just in time before the tunnel closed off. The rest his team were cut off on the far side realising that the cave was flooding. For some unknown reason Bill took the only dinghy and went upstream in the canals probably to see if he could make contact with the rescue team but returned sometime later with a torn dinghy and no explanation.

At about 7 am the following morning the water had receded enough for Bill to get through on a rubber inner tube he had found lying around. George and Ken returned to the surface while Alan went back into the tunnel with a dinghy and the inner tube in order to bring John and Dave out. At 11 am, three French cavers arrived and informed Alan's team that because of the flooding, the Polish cavers would be evacuated via the EDF tunnel. They had started to move the Polish lads through the canals but when they realised the cave was flooding, retreated back to the underground camp, staying another night before getting evacuated via the Tête Sauvage. Alan's team returned to the surface arriving at 4 pm after a long stay.

The flood had caused havoc and Andy Eavis along with another ULSA team member also sat out the flood for two days shivering at the bottom of the Puit Parment.

Two of the major problems on expeditions will always be transport and food. Most cavers had cars by this time, some clapped out, some not and so most expedition members could make their own way the 900 miles to the Pyrenees. Expeditions to European caves did not present too much of a problem with regard to transport. Food supplies, though, were always a headache, with some success we tried the first freeze dried products to appear commercially on the market, light in weight and easy to transport. Vegetables, soups and soya bean dehydrated meat could be purchased. The trouble with dehydrated soya was it had to be soaked in water for a week for it to reconstitute. We did not have that length of time so if used in a stew on arriving in the gut, it started to swell. We often thought it may be possible to levitate up a pitch using wind alone.

Travelling rations while underground were essential items as many exploration trips lasted over 24 hours. Light weight but nutritional food was required as we had little time for cooking. Tins of sardines, peanuts and chocolate bars were popular. On this expedition I purchased Amazing Raisin Bars, which were soon devoured. Alan Gamble in his indomitable style thought that, 'The British Speleological Expedition to the Gouffre de la Pierre Saint-Martin, France, 1973' was far too long winded. He gave it a new name and it stuck, it was always referred to in the years to come as, 'The Amazing Raisin Show'.

Although the expedition had only lasted two weeks, it seemed like a few months. The PSM expeditions were indeed becoming a circus; it was time for new horizons.

In retrospect our four expeditions to the Gouffre Pierre Saint-Martin had been a huge success and we had made great discoveries becoming a part of the history of exploration of this world classic cave system.

10

Tatra Mountains Expedition, Poland, 1974

'It is not the going out of port, but the coming in, that determines the success of a voyage.'

Henry Ward Beecher

After our run in with Bill Brooks and the Polish cavers, we were invited to join them to explore caves in the Tatra Mountains. It was suggested that the deepest cave in Poland, the Jaskinia Wielka Sniezna, would be worth a look. At 814 metres in depth with two entrances, we could descend the higher altitude entrance, Nad Kotlinami, and return via the main Sniezna entrance. The underground river in the cave emerged into daylight way down the mountain at Lodowe Zrodlo. It sounded interesting with many good caves in the high mountains that they asked us to look at.

Bill Brookes had an old ex-Royal Navy ambulance that he claimed would get us to Poland and back. This was in the days when Eastern Europe was still behind the Iron Curtain and Poland was still a communist country, but we obtained visas without too much trouble.

This was going to be a family holiday as our respective wives and girlfriends had decided that enough was enough, they wanted a holiday too. From Derbyshire, I had some of my friends from the last expedition to the Pierre Saint-Martin: Alan Gamble and his wife Anne plus their little girl Melanie, Steve Dickinson, Albi Sole and John 'Bulmers' Benson, along with Andy Ive and his sister Sarah, Bill and his wife and my wife Patricia plus my little boy, Mark. Another caving friend and his wife from Sheffield also joined up. With eight cavers in all, it was quite a crowd.

We paid Bill a deposit up front and on Saturday 31st August we drove down to his house in London but on arriving we found a Polish friend of Bill's and his girlfriend were to join us on the trip to Poland. Fifteen adults and two little children, plus all our caving equipment meant the ambulance was going to be a little cramped. After sorting out the deposit money which Bill seemed to have lost, I took charge of the finances and we set off for

Ramsgate and the ferry across the channel. It started off on a bad footing on the road to Ramsgate when a tyre burst, the first of many. The weight was just too much for the tyres to stand and anyway they were pretty well worn down to the canvas to start off with. My friend and his wife from Sheffield came to the conclusion that this trip was going to be a shambles and this clapped out ambulance would not get us to Poland in one piece. They opted out and started hitch hiking back to Sheffield which made our transport a little lighter.

We managed to reach Calais and camped for the night somewhere in Belgium then, driving on through the day and night, passed through Holland and into West Germany. On Tuesday 3rd September, we had another tyre blow out on the autobahn at 6.30 am. The whole wheel was in a pretty bad way. The jack-booted police arrived and threatened to tow us to a scrap yard at great expense, but the British Army came to our rescue and towed the ambulance to their base where we spent a nice day in the NAAFI. Our boys once more saved the day. Our Navy ambulance was finally repaired, and we drove on to the East German border.

The border crossing at night was not pleasant with watch towers manned with machine guns, barbed wire a plenty and the sullen faces of the guards. Amazingly, they let our motley crew through and stamped our passports. We resembled a large family of gypsies. Once again, we drove through the night and on into Wednesday 4th September. East Germany at 6 am just as the sun was rising was a depressing site. Dreary looking buildings and people on their way to work, trudging along in the mist. We crossed the Polish border and stayed in Wroclaw for the night. We spent a nice day in this historic city and moved off on Friday 6th September, arriving in Zakopane late at night. Zakopane is one of the major tourist towns of Poland, at an altitude of 900 metres and in 1973 had a population of 27,000. It had taken a week for us to get this far. The monotony on the long drive was only broken by the constant playing on a tape recorder of Pink Floyd's, Dark Side of the Moon, probably the greatest album of all time. After that I was to become a lifelong fan.

On the way through Poland we passed by the infamous concentration camp at Auschwitz where so many innocent men, women and children were murdered. No one felt like visiting this depressing sad reminder of the horrors of World War Two, so we drove on. The Polish cavers had arranged for a wooden chalet for us to stay, situated in a small village called Gronik, overlooking high above the impressive mountain range of the Tatras.

Some of us set up our tents as the small chalet was also occupied by the elderly owner and his wife. It appeared this was the Polish caving club hut, rather different, I thought, to the grubby Eldon Pothole Club Hostel near Spring Gardens, Buxton.

The Tatra Mountains, Poland. Photo: David Gill.

    The Tatra Mountains covers an area of approximately 750 square kilometres and is the largest range in the Carpathians and, after the Alps, the second highest group in Central Europe with granite peaks rising to 2,660 metres. Ten peaks rise to over 2,600 metres. There are no glaciers, but eternal snows are present. They are relatively young in geological terms and rigorous erosion is evident with steep-sided valleys, grazing meadows and post-glacial cirques. The lower forest belt reaches an altitude of 1,250 metres with upper forest up to 1,550 metres and beautiful grazing meadows. There are three major groups of mountains, the Belanske Tatra group to the east being mostly Triassic limestone with the highest peak, Hauran, at 2,154 metres above sea level. The frontier lies along the crest between Poland and what was then Czechoslovakia, now Slovakia. At that time the mountain range had two protected areas classified as nature reserves, the Polish Tatrzanski Park Narodowy or in English the Tatra National Park and the Slovak Tatranský Národný Park. The area is spectacular with outstanding natural beauty; we were warned to be careful of the bears that roamed the forests.

We spent a pleasant day sightseeing in the lovely town of Zakopane on the Saturday, and on Sunday set off with our Polish friends on a mammoth hike across the western range of mountains in order to get us acclimatised to the high altitude. It was important that we became conversant with the area and the relative position of the cave entrances in case we exited from a cave at night; this was not a place to get lost. It was possible to jump on a passing bus going part way up the long massive valley towards the mountains, but none came so we walked all the way. The weather was superb as we hiked up the Dolina Malej Laki to Wielka Turnia and located the entrance to Poland's deepest cave, the Jaskinia Wielka Sniezna, and the higher entrance, Nan Kotlina, a very long walk from our base camp down in the valley. From there we hiked over to Dolina Mietusia and the entrances to Mietusia cave with magnificent views of the tiny alpine like villages far below.

On Monday 9th September, the caving started with a vengeance, with a visit to Czarna cave. The entrance is high up on the steep sided cliff face of the Dolina Koscieliska. There was a nice little café situated at Hala Pisana at 1,015 metres altitude along the walk in. Bill and Andy set off first, rigging the cave but Bill fell off a climb and badly damaged his arm. Luckily it was not broken but later it went a nice shade black and blue, a warning of things to come. We had some difficulty route finding but eventually found the way forward and arrived at a ridiculous traverse across a deep lake of freezing cold water. For the tall members of the team this was not too much trouble, but to short arses like myself it was a matter of stretching out to an almost horizontal position with arms and legs outstretched, pushing against both walls in order to gain some friction and shuffling forwards inches at a time. We reached the end at about 6.30 pm, was a blocked continuation that needed digging. We had no shovels so beat a retreat de-rigging the ropes and ladders on the way, arriving back to the surface at 10.30 pm. The last bus had long gone so we hiked the long trail back to camp arriving at 1 am the following day.

It was Thursday 12th September before we got going again. Bill was still nursing his badly damaged arm so the team along with the girls and kids set off on a nice walk up the Dolina Malaj Laki to the café at Przystop Mietusia. We left the girls and children here to make their own way back and set out on a pleasant walk along Dolina Mietusia and up through the woods to the entrance of Jaskinia Mietusia cave. This time the team was down to eight: Alan, Steve, Andy, John and I plus three Polish cavers. We rigged a 4 metre pitch down to a short siphon but I can't remember there being much water, it probably filled to the roof in the wet season. A steep slope of 80 metres followed, rigged with ropes and then two 30 metre pitches, one immediately following the first. A very narrow passage followed to the final 30 metre pitch at 230 metres below the entrance. At the base of the shaft, the cave reached a dead end that was probably a sump in wet weather. The Polish cavers elected to de-rig the cave so we had a nice easy trip out arriving back at camp by 10 pm. The Polish boys arrived at 2 am the following morning.

The evenings could be boring in the hut except for consuming large amounts of Russian vodka but this was not usually strong enough for our Polish hosts so they fortified it with pure Polish spirit, which was definitely fire water. I think the elderly owner of the house probably brewed it himself, I suspected he had an illicit still somewhere. The outside toilet was primitive, just a hole in the ground and with much use began to fill up. We spent many hours having competitions to see how many flies we could swat in one evening. The walls were eventually covered in black blotches.

The evenings were usually quite rowdy and one drunken evening the old lady of the house burst through the front door waving an axe, shouting in Polish which no one understood and spitting over the frightened crowd now cowering in corners, it was obvious what she was trying to convey. An approximate translation from the Polish is 'Shut the fuck up or I will chop your bleeding heads off with this axe!' Bill grabbed her from behind as he was hiding behind the door and stopped the agitated lady from doing us permanent damage to life and limb. I suspect we calmed down a little after this life-threatening incident.

Two of the team, who shall remain nameless, picked up two nice looking East German girls one night, but we had to tell them that the girls were most probably spies for the Ministry of State Security, better known as STASI out to obtain some compromising photographs for the purpose of blackmail.

On Monday 16th September, the real serious work began with the descent of the deepest cave in Poland. The original plan was to have two separate teams, a mixture of Polish and British cavers, descending at different times as the bivouac site was very small and could only accommodate a few sleeping bags at a time. The main entrance to Sniezna had already been rigged with Polish nylon caving ropes so single rope techniques (SRT) would be used to climb the ropes. My opinion was that the ropes were suspect having a lose weave on the sheath covering and easy to wear through if rigged over a sharp flake of rock. We had now progressed with this technique and had climbing harnesses, chest harness and USA made ascenders called Jumars. We still used the simple figure of eight descenders made by Clog in Wales. The Polish karabiners were Russian, made of titanium which the Russians had plenty of, but the gate springs were not to the usual British standard and the hinge became loose after a short period.

The first team of Alan, Dicky and Albi along with a group of Polish cavers would rig the Nad Kotlinami entrance to the system and then sleep at the bivouac site after their trip to the bottom of the cave. They descended at around 2 pm and arrived at the small underground camp at 3 am the following morning. They progressed only a short way down beyond the camp as they were short of the calculated ladders and ropes. They were also surprised to find the camp crowded with a few more Polish visitors than expected, including two young ladies and one male novice with little food supplies.

The second party consisting of Bill, Andy, John, three Polish cavers and I descended the Nan Kotlina around 8 pm after a long time stumbling around in the fast fading light trying to locate the entrance. The cave consisted of nine spacious pitches varying in depth from 80 metres to 15 metres and one long steeply sloping passage down to a depth of 400 metres at the underground camp site.

On the way down at each pitch head, the last two men in the team, which was one of the Polish lads and I, lowered the ladders down to those below. It was then possible for us to abseiled down on a double length of rope. We achieved this by tying a loop of rope around a boulder and threading one end of the rope through the loop. Pulling an equal length through the loop we then had a double rope tied together forming a continuous loop. We then threw this down the pitch to those below who indicated that the knot joining the two ends of rope had reached the bottom. We could then abseil down on the double rope. This was nerve racking as the rope went over many sharp edges of rock and the rope was of poor Polish construction to start off with. When we reached the base of the pitch, we then untied the knot and pulled one end of rope enabling the free end to run up through the loop. When the free end passed through the loop at the top of the pitch it then come whipping down to the bottom, thus with luck we retrieved all our ropes from every pitch. Of course we knew there was another way out of the cave via the main entrance, which was already – we hoped – rigged with ropes. This was probably the first attempts at pull through descents, now used extensively in through trips in caves from one entrance to another, but of course now with well-constructed modern ropes

We arrived at the camp site at 6 am to find the first team trying to grab a few hours' sleep in very cramped conditions. One of the Polish boys was ill and Bill had forgotten to bring the spare batteries for the Polish cavers' lamps. There were five more pitches to rig with ropes down to the bottom, the last pitch being 50 metres in depth. We hung around for hours getting very cold while waiting for the Polish cavers to get out of bed. After much protracted discussion it was decided that only the British team would attempt a descent to the bottom of the cave.

We set off after having had little or no sleep at about 6 pm on Tuesday 17th September and progressed downstream in wet uninspiring passage. On the way we collected the rope for the fifth and final pitch to discover it was only 40 metres long. As the fifth pitch was 50 metres deep, a decision was made to abandon the attempt, as there was no way we could reach the bottom as we were ten metres short of rope. We returned to the miserable underground camp site and got our heads down for five minutes in wet cloths and wet sleeping bags, after collecting all the ropes which had been left at the base of the Nad Kotlinami series of pitches.

Before retreating back to the surface via the main entrance, our Polish friends insisted we wait for three more Polish cavers to join us to help in carrying out all the equipment. It was a long wait, so it was not until early morning of Wednesday 18th September that we began the long and arduous trip back to the surface with a mountain of equipment. We remember little of the retreat as most of us were falling asleep but I remember being stationed at the top of the first 50 metre deep pitch virtually in sight of day light, hauling bag after bag of very heavy equipment up the shaft. To gain the entrance, a final ice slope had to be climbed and it was 3 pm before we arrived back at base camp, three days after descending. With only a few hours of snatched sleep and not much food, to put it mildly, we were a little worn out.

On the way back home, we stayed for a few days with our Polish friend just outside the capital city of Warsaw. The old town area, which during the war became known as the Warsaw Ghetto, had been completely rebuilt stone by stone after its destruction by the Germans during the uprising. What was surprising to us was the lack of elderly people out on the streets, most seemed in their 20s and 30s, an indication of the large numbers of Polish citizens killed during the war. The ladies seemed particularly good looking. The Palace of the People built by Stalin was not to the liking of the Warsaw population, so they built their Christian cathedral right next door.

We were told not to ask them questions about the political structure in public as the walls had ears but up on a mountain where no one could hear the Polish certainly expressed their dissatisfaction with the communist system. In a bar one night, one of our Polish friends a little worse for wear after consuming large quantities of vodka had to be gagged by his colleagues and taken outside as it appeared there were informers everywhere. Two men arrived at the house one day ostensibly to check the phone line; our friend said they had been sent by the Polish Secret Service better known as Security Service of the Ministry of Internal Affairs, Służba Bezpieczeństwa to check up on us.

I felt for the Polish people as it seemed to me they had all been betrayed by the allies as after all, we did declare war on Germany because these people had been invaded but then left them to their own fate.

A large proportion of my caving friends around this time were left wing, including myself. Some had Marxist views but our experiences in Poland and East Germany gave us a firsthand viewpoint of the impossibility of a true socialist system operating with impartiality. Humanity is not like the ant colonies as we are driven by greed, we always want more than we have. If we did not possess this inherent genetic trait we would still be living in caves, rather than going back to explore them.

It took a Polish electrician from the shipyards at Gdansk, Lech Walesa and his organisation, Solidarity, the first independent Polish trade union, to set the ball rolling which eventually brought the whole pack of cards falling to the ground. Lech finished up as the President of Poland between 1990 and 1995.

The long drive back to the UK throughout the day and night was relatively uneventful except for a stop at a sleazy West German bar showing porno films from an old projector on the bar.

The expedition had not achieved any completely new discoveries but it had not been a complete waste of time. To visit caves behind the Iron Curtain was something of a first for western speleologists, and the so called Iron Curtain was not made entirely of iron, wire cutters were not needed in order to penetrate through the wire and negotiate the mine fields, a legitimate way was revealed. It was all about having the right contacts.

We had made an impression on our Polish friends. They had made contact with speleologists working in the USSR through their respective universities and had been invited to participate on the exploration of caves in Russia. Attempting to cross the border without the required complex permission, they had been arrested and deported but seemed sure that through the universities, permission would now be granted. They invited us to join them on a Russian, Polish, British expedition to the Pamir Mountains, a great expanse of unexplored limestone mountains bordering a few communist controlled countries. At high altitudes the mountains had the possibility of a deeper cave than the Pierre Saint-Martin in France, this opportunity was too strong to resist as no British cave explorers had ever visited the area.

On returning to the UK I began work on this project against a backdrop of little enthusiasm from the British caving hierarchy as they considered it to be impossible to achieve. A Polish caver came to the UK to stay with me for a while to discuss the plans. It was then that disaster struck.

11

Félix Trombe, France, 1975 and 76

'Whether it's the best of times or the worst of times, it's the only time we've got.'

Art Buchwald

I had a steady contract working as an installation and maintenance engineer at a factory in Birch Vale, Derbyshire, an old mill with sandstone walls. Most of my time, I seemed to be perched at the top of a long ladder somewhere in the roof.

On this fateful day I was only about twelve feet up, drilling holes in the hard stone wall in order to clip electrical cables. To gain some force on the drill bit I held on to a water pipe when suddenly I received a severe electric shock. I had no idea straight away what was happening, just the intense pain but I soon realised that the drill's metal casing must have shorted out to a live terminal and I was completing the circuit by holding on to the perfect earth, a water pipe. Alternating current paralyses the muscles so the drill stuck to my hand and I was unable to release it, the same went for the water pipe. The pain was excruciating but I could still think clearly and tried desperately to release my fingers and drop the drill. It became obvious that this was impossible so I tried to let go of the pipe by taking my feet off the ladder but I still hung there with one hand. I tried to shout for help, but no sound came as the current passing through my body also paralysed my voice. Being an electrician, I knew the dangers of electric shock, the heart goes into spasms after a very short while and stops. There seemed no way out so I prayed for death to come quick as the pain was far too much to stand. I then thought, no, I still have things to do, a wife and two boys, there must be some way to release my hand from the water pipe. If I could do this, the current passing through my body would cease to flow. The current was passing from one hand to the next so I placed both feet on the wall as I could move my legs, pushing with all the strength I had left I went shooting backwards through the air like superman tearing my hand away from the pipe and landed with a crunch.

This small act saved my life and I now know why electrocution is used as a very effective means of torture. The whole incident probably only lasted seconds but it seemed like an eternity as I hung there slowly dying. My whole life did not pass before me as some people claim as I was far too busy trying to figure out how to save it. Maybe a large quantity of adrenaline was produced that gave me the strength to save my own life or fate had other things in store.

The end result was a broken nose and a shattered heel, I was very lucky as I was not wearing a helmet and could have fractured my skull. I found out later that someone had run over my extension cable to the drill with a fork lift truck and fractured the earth wire, as if it had been intact the drill would have just exploded in a flash and the fuse would have blown rupturing the flow of electricity.

They took me to hospital where many nurses came to look at a completely shattered heel bone, but I was left in incredible pain with it shooting up my leg all night without even an aspirin. The following morning after an x-ray, a physiotherapist came to look at my by now black leg and grabbing the foot yanked it. When I recovered from the pain, she received something of a mouth full of Anglo-Saxon words straight off a building site. She explained after I apologised that there was nothing they could do, the bone was in a thousand pieces, like sand with a few bigger bits, there was no way they could stick it back together. The heel bone (*calcaneus* or in those days referred to as the *os calcis*) is one of the largest complete bones in the body because it is designed to hold all our weight. It would heal and knit back together naturally given time, a long time. The Achilles tendon would eventually reattach itself to the heel bone, but the main problem was swelling and blood clots that prevented the ankle from moving. I was told I would have a permanently stiff ankle with little movement and my caving days were over, but they underestimated my determination to get some movement back and continue exploring caves.

The owner of the factory, considering it was their fault, said that their insurance would cover me so advised me to see a solicitor, which I did. After a protracted correspondence, doctor's appointments with the insurance company consultants, interviews with the Health and Safety Executive and engineers' reports on the drill, the Royal Insurance Company refused to pay a penny as they said that the factory owner had negated his contract with them by accepting liability. I, of course, had to pay my own solicitor's invoice. I am sure in today's litigation mad society I would have been in for a few thousand for permanent disability, but I was determined, no way was it going to be permanent.

Back home on crutches, I attended physiotherapy sessions and bought a football moving my foot backwards and forwards for hours on end each time obtaining a little more movement, it was a painful exercise but worth it. Being self-employed meant no work, no pay and with a family to support I went to work on crutches getting lifts in a friend's car as I could not drive. I wired things up crawling along the floor dragging a gammy foot behind me and even managed a complete electrical installation of a factory close by in an old barn which a good friend David Clucas had set up with his partner. Flowguard Ltd was to keep me in work for many years to come. A friend climbed the ladders while I did the ground work, perched on a stool with my crutches. It kept me going and helped to get movement back in the foot.

It took a year for the heel bone to completely knit back together but it was the wrong shape. The hospital offered to grind the bone down to the correct shape, but I declined as scar tissue would be a problem wearing caving boots. It was not long before I started caving again but on a long walk, I had to rest the leg for a while as it still tended to swell. Crawling along the caves in Lathkill Dale and digging, followed by my dog Pip, was no problem but walking was. My dog had the habit of following me down caves. After a couple of years I obtained 90% movement back in the ankle but even today it can give me some pain on a long walk or in the lousy British weather.

Unfortunately, the planned expedition to the USSR was a non-starter. I was forced to abandon the project so went for the easy option, holidays in the sun with the family and a bit of caving thrown in. The first British Expedition to Papua New Guinea was in the planning stage but with a knackered foot, no money and a family to support, for me it was out of the question so I went to see Pink Floyd instead playing Shine On You Crazy Diamond, Dark Side of the Moon and Echoes at Knebworth. A show that will forever remain ingrained in the memory when the spitfires flew above the massive crowd and the rocket ship hit the stage with the resounding explosion accompanied by fireworks. I also took up fishing.

In 1975, Paul Deakin, Ron Bridger and I plus, our respective spouses and my two boys had a nice holiday in Spain, driving all the way. We did get a chance to poke around the Limestone Mountains of Spain, but our main objective was a trip into the famous Cigalère cave in the Pyrenees, as Paul wanted to photograph it. This cave was originally explored by the great Norbert Casteret and recorded in his books. It contained a large river with many cascades that they climbed upwards using a maypole, a metal pole with a ladder attached to the end. The cave has a locked large steel door to prevent unauthorised entry as unique cave formations of aragonite and gypsum can be found within.

On arriving at Moulis, we found that our French caving friends had postponed their expedition to the Cigalère and as they had the key for the gate, we looked for alternatives close by.

The Reseau Félix Trombe cave system is again one of France's classic cave systems now over 100 kilometres in length with 45 entrances and 1,000 metres in depth. At this time, there was still much to explore in this mighty system. John Middleton and Clive Rowlands from the UK along with a team of French speleologists had made the first through traverse in 1972 in 28 hours from the high entrance, the Emile, to the Pène Blanque entrance, descending to a depth of 720 metres and then climbing up 200 metres to reach the Pène Blanque entrance.

We met up with our British caving friends and, with the late Ian Davidson, Harvey Lomas and John Conway, had a short trip down the Emile entrance of the Félix Trombe, we even met up with Emile who had discovered the entrance. Unlike the British, the French cavers have a habit of naming a cave after themselves. With the same team plus the late Peter B Smith we descended another entrance to the system called Pène Blanque, at 932 metres altitude. This short exploratory trip whetted our appetites for another trip to the same area.

Much interest was expressed by many cavers to join in the fun on the 1976 Expedition to the Félix Trombe. A large contingent from a number of Yorkshire based caving clubs, the Pegasus Caving Club, the Eldon Pothole club and various other Derbyshire based clubs along with our wives and children descended on the Forest of Arbas and a camp site at Prat in the Haute Garonne. The teams immediately began rigging ladders and ropes in the Pène Blanque entrance to the system. We were armed with the cave map produced by the French, but it had little detail to go on. The trip was long, and it was 3 am the following day before we surfaced. The next day, a large group descended and rigged a nice 40 metre pitch and a couple more 10 metre pitches, but we were unable to find any major unexplored cave, only small tight passages. One passage did look promising but after 120 metres it petered out in a boulder choke. The main mapped way through to the major system of the Félix Trombe could not be found.

We then turned our attention to the resurgence, the Goueil di Her where the underground river reached the surface. The intention was to dive the terminal sump where the continuing passage was flooded to the roof and carrying compressed air diving bottles we arrived after passing through the first siphon which was dry, at an unexpected 15 metre deep pitch. A few days later the pitch was rigged and a 30 metre roped traverse followed to the second siphon. This siphon had air space, so we swam through joining the main river on the other side. The river was followed to another siphon but above a low sandy passage could be followed which bypassed the siphon. The final sump, the fourth, was dived by the late Mike Jeanmaire and James Cobbett for 60 metres to a depth of 25 metres but the passage was still going deeper, too deep for the small amount of air carried by the divers. We found out later that this sump had been dived by the French for 153 metres down to a depth of 40 metres and was still going down at the furthest point reached. Mike was always known as Fish not just because he was a very competent cave diver but because he had webbed feet, or so rumour had it.

The cave had a strong wind indicating a higher entrance or extensive passages beyond the terminal sump. We spent some time climbing in the roof looking for a possible by-pass to the sump but only found six stream inlets in the main river passage which could not be reached without climbing aids.

To reach passages high in the walls or in the roof, cavers use rock anchors called expansion bolts normally 8 mm in diameter. A hole needs to be drilled in the rock and the bolt is then hammered home, it expands within the hole so becomes a firm anchor. The bolt has a screw thread so a ring or aluminium hanger can be screwed into the bolt and a rope attached via a karabiner. This technique is used extensively for hanging ropes down pitches if no natural anchor can be found as it's important for the rope to have a free hang without passing over sharp rock flakes or rub points where it could wear through.

I have mentioned Norbert Casteret in previous chapters as his translated books had inspired thousands of budding cave explorers throughout the world. Casteret was a professional cave explorer spending his time tracing, exploring and mapping underground rivers mainly for the French Water and Electricity Authorities as France contains huge areas of limestone with rivers disappearing underground and surfacing many kilometres away in large springs. These areas have little or no surface streams so the search for underground water supplies becomes an important factor. He used the caves as hideouts and munitions dumps for the French Resistance during the war.

One of his famous discoveries in 1923 involved free diving naked through icy cold water with a candle sealed in his rubber cap. Taking a deep

Transporting diving kit in the Goueil di Her. Photo: Paul Deakin.

breath he dived through and surfaced in a series of dry passages with archaeological remains from Stone Age man. The cave was called Caverne de Montespan and a dry entrance was eventually forced through to daylight.

We decided to take a look but had been informed that the entrance was gated and locked. We found the door open and on returning to our vehicles to change into caving gear a few cars drew up with an elderly gentleman and a load of young students.

'What are you doing?' the elderly gentleman asked in perfect English.

'Oh, just having a look at Montespan,' I replied.

'It's locked and you need a permit to enter, what are you doing in the Pyrenees?'

'We are just exploring the Félix Trombe cave system.'

'I am Félix Trombe,' he replied.

'Oh, hello Professor Trombe,' I replied with much embarrassment.

Professor Félix Trombe was another one of the great and famous French cave explorers I had the opportunity of meeting.

Further work in the Pène Blanque continued with a number of large teams and the main way on was eventually found. The system proved to be complex with difficult route finding. A further five of pitches were rigged with ropes and ladders, the fourth of 40 metres and the fifth a fine drop of 60 metres to a large chamber. Bob Toogood and the late Paul Nunn traversed across the first pitch to a further series of traverses and pitches leading to the main way on into the very extensive Felix Trombe cave system. The Pène Blanque River was finally reached but a sump prevented further progress in the downstream direction. A climb across the 40 metre pitch reached a small chamber with a further short six metre pitch leading to a nice passage with a sandy floor. A large chamber followed but petered out in tight crawl with no way on.

The cave was de-rigged and photographed and a few trips made into the highest entrance to the system, the Emile, which we had investigated in 1975. Four short pitches eventually led to the large passage called the Trou de Vent and the pitch down into the main cave.

Many years later, members of the Eldon Pothole Club finally completed the traverse of this complex French cave system.

We had failed to make any significant discoveries but became familiar with yet another one of the great classic cave systems in France. It became obvious that in a complex system like the Félix Trombe, little could be achieved unless a combined expedition was organised with the original French explorers who knew the system well.

The expedition was not over yet as we now had permission to look at another of Casteret's discoveries, the Cigalère, which we had tried to explore the year before. The ladies managed to get a lift up the mountain while we set of on the mammoth walk up to our planned camp site.

An old French mining site was situated close to the entrance but had started to collapse. The toilets were hanging over the edge of a cliff and with no doors gave magnificent views down the valley and also a disconcerting view to the bottom of the cliff, many hundreds of metres below, which could be of great help if suffering from constipation.

We had a few entertaining trips climbing up the numerous cascades which had been rigged with ladders, under very cold water. The team intended to dive the terminal sump and the late Rob Palmer plus a few others made the dive. Sadly, Rob lost his life some years later in a diving accident.

Many years later, Sid Perou, the British cave film maker, made a fantastic film of the Cigalère.

The Grand Cascade, Gouffre Berger, France. Photo: Robbie Shone.

12

Sima GESM, Spain 1981

'When one door of happiness closes, another opens; but often we look so long at the closed door that we do not see the one which has opened for us.'

Helen Keller

One of the favourite caving areas for several Mendip based cavers and the Pegasus Caving Club was County Clare on the west coast of Southern Ireland. Besides the pubs and the Guinness, the caves were good too. A combined Derbyshire Caving Club and Eldon Pothole Club group decided it was time to visit these great caves we had been told so much about.

We travelled not this time in an ex-Royal Navy ambulance but in John New's old truck as it was large enough to get us all in with wives, children and even my dog Pip. We camped on a farmer's field with un-mowed grass,

'No need to worry,' he said. 'Just help yourselves to potatoes in the garden and let me know how many pints of milk you need every day.'

It wasn't just the country and caves that we fell in love with, but the friendly people of Ireland as well. A pub landlord standing at the door to say goodbye and shake everyone's hand to us was unusual. Men in pubs insisting on giving my dog Pip a tin of salmon.

The caving was good as well as the evening's entertainment with magic mushrooms and smoking long cigarettes passed around the table. The evenings in O'Connor's Bar, Doolin can only be described as a wonderful experience with brilliant Irish musicians. A man would sit down with a fiddle and start to play, soon to be joined by someone with a penny whistle. Then someone with a harp would walk through the door and join in and so it went on all through the night and into the following morning with musician after musician joining the band. The place would be heaving, with Guinness flowing like water and the place rocking to the sound of the traditional Irish music. Music students came from all over the world to sit and study this unique music.

On one occasion, we asked the landlord if he could obtain any poteen, the original potato spirit brewed in the hills. One night, a car came screaming to a stop outside the pub, a man jumped out, opened the boot and thrust a couple of bottles into our hands, then tore off at great speed. No money changed hands; great stuff it was too.

A village close by had the distinction of having the most bars in any one town in the world. Even the undertaker's was a bar, you could sit on a coffin and have a pint of Guinness. I don't think there was anyone inside the coffins at the time.

When it was time to leave the farmer refused to take any money for the many pints of milk, the few sacks of spuds we had consumed, also the camping fee and flattening his mowing grass. We had no alternative but to stuff a load of cash in an envelope and push it through his front door before leaving.

The journey back was entertaining when John's van broke down in a small town somewhere in the border counties of Scotland. We parked up in a forecourt much to the annoyance of some rather stuck up lady who called the police.

We resembled a group of gypsies and the police officer gave us his orders. 'Get the hell out of my town or face arrest.'

As the van would not move, we asked, 'Do you want us to push it to Manchester?'

'I'll give you 24 hours then, I'll be back,' he replied.

Quite a difference from the friendly kind faces of the Southern Irish. We repaired it within the 24 hour deadline and got the hell out of town before being arrested by the sheriff.

The Sima GESM cave is situated in the magnificent limestone mountains of the Sierra de las Nieves, near Malaga, Spain, and had recently been explored to 1,098 metres in depth by the Grupo de Exploraciones Subterreneas de Malaga, hence the name GESM. The Derbyshire Caving Club always had an interest in descending any severe cave system that appeared to be ridiculously hard so fancied attempting a descent. Along with John New, Alan Gamble and the late Mike Jeanmaire and a few other caving friends we decided to take a look after making contact and arrangements with the Spanish explorers of the cave. It was arranged that they would also have a team to help de-rig the cave equipment at the end of the trip.

It was going to be a family holiday, so we rented a nice villa near the sea at Estepona and all made our own travel arrangements. Patricia, my two

Journeys beneath the Earth

boys and I travelled by coach to London through the night but on arriving found the capital full of tourists as Prince Charles was getting married to Lady Diana Spencer. We waited all day for a coach to Malaga and after a couple of days and nights arrived exhausted with little, if any, sleep on the bumpy ride to Spain. After hiring a car, we all congregated at the villa and had a nice few days relaxing in the sun before setting off into the mountains.

We had now developed single rope techniques with good hardware equipment and strong static ropes so ladders became obsolete in the exploration of deep caves. Fernand Petzl, the famous French cave explorer, had set up a highly successful business in Grenoble and developed high quality caving equipment that is now in standard use throughout the world.

Britain had by this time also gone over to the metric system so all measurements were now in metres. Personally, I still think the foot is a much nicer measurement for caves as a 1,000-foot-deep pitch sounds much more exciting than a pitch of 304.8 metres. Our trouble is we cannot make up our minds if we are Europeans or stubbornly British as we still love to use pounds per square inch, (PSI) for pressure measurements, ask a joiner's shop for a six foot length of three by two, distances on our roads are measured in miles, miles per hour on our cars and we ask 'How many miles does this car do to the gallon?'

We set off from the road head along a pleasant trail across the mountains to our camp site close to the entrance and the descent soon got underway. The cave was a series of vertical descents, one after another with the La Gran Pozo at 115 metres in depth being spectacular.

Many pitches followed so basically, we were permanently hanging from ropes. The next of the deepest pitches in the cave was the Pozo Paco de la Torro at a ridiculous 145 metres straight down. After a long trip rigging and carrying sacks full of ropes, we exited the cave after about 20 hours for a rest before the next team descended to the bottom carrying the remainder of the ropes.

For some reason I found the cave boring and I also felt uneasy, there was something wrong, but I had no idea what it was, I was soon to find out. It seemed to me to be just a physical exercise of getting down and getting out alive, there was no time or intention to attempt any original exploration in the cave so I went exploring the surrounding mountains while the team descended to the bottom.

The de-rigging and carrying out of numerous tackle bags full of rope was entertaining along with our Spanish friends. Mike had lost a few of his fingers due to an accident in the Derbyshire Fluorspar Mine where he worked and had a few problems hanging 115 metres off the deck with the fiddly ascenders at the top of the La Gran Pozo, but managed it eventually.

We were soon all in the luxury of our villa and had a swim in the sea. Before the long coach ride home we had a trip to Tangier across the straights and resisted the offers of a few camels for the ladies. On reaching home, we got divorced but I finished up with the house and my dog.

The late Paul Deakin and I took our dogs caving, usually along old abandoned mine workings where they could trot safely along and follow us, they seemed to enjoy it. We of course made sure they never pooped in a cave. I often thought of kitting my dog Pip out with a light and helmet as she seemed to love caves, the trouble was I could never get the helmet to stick on her head. She followed me once down the long crawl of Critchlow Cave in Lathkill Dale, we were digging and trying to enlarge the passage at the furthest point. Pip followed me but became bored and headed off out, how she found her way in the total darkness I have no idea. I found her many hours later sleeping under my Minivan; she just followed her tracks back up the dale to find her transport. A similar thing happened in Wales when, as usual, ammunition was thrown on the bonfire. She hated the loud bangs and probably thought she might stop a flying bullet. I found her the following morning again under my van which was over a mile back up the valley from where we were camping. She always recognised my car and even recognised the noise of the engine as I pulled up outside my door.

Another great stroke of luck happened when my outbuilding burnt down to the ground with all my caving and camping equipment inside. My main worry was not just the loss of my equipment. The late Henry Mares while walking along a beach noticed that the sea was washing away an old abandoned cemetery and he picked up a very old human skull passing it on to me. I had it on the mantel piece above the fireplace but it gave Patricia the willies so I put it in the outbuilding. I was just hoping the fire brigade did not find a human skull in the ashes; luckily, they didn't as it was a case of ashes to ashes, dust to dust.

Around the same time, I met Ken Kelly once again. I had not seen him for many years and in the intervening time he had become a respected businessman and also owned a night club in Buxton, The Gas Light Club. This became one of my favourite haunts with late night drinking. At the age of 40 I was gradually returning to my teenage years.

Ken had led the expeditions to a massive deep hole in Greece called Provatina in the 60s. Jim Eyre, the famous cave explorer from Lancaster, had joined one of Ken's expeditions to Provatina but in his book The Cave Explorers, Jim was critical of Ken's style of leadership and called him a conman. Ken took exception to this and sued him. This was a mistake as you can't get money out of a stone and Jim had little of it. The injunction to prevent sales of the book bankrupted the publisher. Jim eventually got the injunction lifted but too late to prevent the publisher from going broke. The publisher also produced a high-quality magazine devoted to cave exploration throughout the world which came to an untimely end.

Jim approached me in a pub in Ingleton, Yorkshire, and asked if I could talk to Ken which of course I did. I tried to get the two talking to discuss this ridiculous situation as cavers do not sue one another. Ken dropped the impending court case and an agreement was reached. The agreement was no business of mine, but I know Ken finished up with a load of Jim's books which he burnt, and a few of Jim's original cartoon drawings. After Ken's death I passed these on to the Ghar Parau Foundation, an organisation that raised money for caving expeditions hoping they could auction them off and raise a little more money.

Ken was something of an adrenalin junky and was a brilliant skier. Along with Alan Gamble and Sonia, Ken's partner, we went skiing together. He could ski backwards down a steep mountain while we slid down on our posteriors. We went diving and parachuting along with Alan Gamble and the fearless Ken Pearce but jumping out of an aeroplane at 2,800 feet without being attached to a rope was not to my liking being a caver, although I was on a high for a week. We had many crazy adventures together, but Ken was a heavy drinker and smoker which killed him in the end as he developed emphysema.

In the years before his death, Ken moved to Spain where we spent many happy weeks together reminiscing, drinking and cooking good food. The quotation from Lady Caroline Lamb about Lord Byron comes to mind, 'He was mad, bad and dangerous to know.' But with Ken this was in a good way with his friends. He had few male friends as he found most people boring. Respect from Ken was hard to achieve as it had to be earned and earned the hard way. Just before he died while breathing from an oxygen bottle, he lit a cigarette. Propane gas and oxygen like one another and with a whoosh the lighter exploded engulfing him in flames and setting fire to the kitchen. He escaped by crawling on the floor towards the door.

Being single again seemed strange after being married for twelve years, also Patricia and I had been seeing each other before we were married for six years. Eighteen years together was a long time, so it was hard to become accustomed to a totally different lifestyle of living alone, but without a family living with me this presented a new opportunity as regards to caving expeditions.

Cavers from Yorkshire, Mendip and Derbyshire had been talking about a possible expedition to Mexico for some time. Explorers from the USA had systematically been finding world class cave systems and it was about time we joined in. Sid Perou had been making a series of caving films for Channel Four, The Realm of Darkness, and wanted to film an original exploration as it happened. This had not been attempted before as most of his films involved reconstruction of actual events. To be in the right place at the right time was almost impossible in cave filming and shooting good footage underground is difficult, so it has to be the hardest place in the world to make a film. I signed on but had a huge problem as the expedition was scheduled to run over a five-month period. Paying the child maintenance and a mortgage without any earnings seemed impossible, but the opportunity of exploring caves outside of Europe was too tempting to miss. I solved the problem by renting out my house as fully furnished but it took a few months before an estate agent found a tenant. I rented it on a short-term lease, less than one year so I could get it back and hoped I could find work once more on my return. Over the preceding years I had developed many good contacts in the electrical contracting business so felt certain I could pick up from where I had left off.

In the 1960s and 70s, cave exploring for the British was generally confined to Europe and the Near East as only the wealthy could afford the airline fares to far flung corners of the globe. In the 1980's with the advent of reasonable priced airline fares, the growth of the long-haul airline industry and competition between the various airlines, the world was now our oyster and could with careful planning become our playground. At last it was within our meagre budgets to scrape enough cash together and fly to exotic locations.

At the age of 40, a new chapter was about to begin which would lead me to countries I could only dream about 20 years previously.

13

Chiapas, Mexico, 1982 to 1983

'The most beautiful thing we can experience is the mysterious. It is the source of all true art and science.'

Albert Einstein

A reconnaissance of the Chiapas area of Mexico indicated it had potential for large cave systems, so the plan was to set up a base camp at San Cristobal de las Casas and explore the surrounding limestone mountains for caves.

We had a large team who were all making their own way there, but it was important that we had transport in order to move various cavers to different areas.

My ex-wife Patricia agreed to look after my dog Pip and she did have the children to play with, although by this time she was getting old. It was hard to say goodbye to my boys and the dog.

Dick Ellis, Terry Whitaker and I set off to Los Angeles on a Pan Am flight and with clear skies had fantastic views over the USA. We were to drive two vehicles through the southern states and into Chiapas, Mexico. We stayed with one of our expatriate caving friends, Jeff Morgan, now married and settled 250 miles out of Los Angeles. He had a van which we could hire and he purchased on our behalf a Chrysler pickup truck, ideal for transporting men and equipment across the mountain roads.

We set off on the long drive passing through California, New Mexico, Arizona and Texas. We were only stopped once by the police who were searching cars for *wet backs* their term for illegal immigrants from Mexico swimming across the river. We were starved and asked if there were any towns around where we could eat. With a smile, the police directed us to the next small town. A dusty road led us to a small sleepy looking town; the only place we could see with lights on was a bar. It reminded me of a movie as we walked in through the door. The juke box was playing with a few dancers on the floor who virtually stopped what they were doing and looked at the three strangers entering their domain.

The place went silent as we sauntered over to the bar and ordered beer and steak sandwiches. A large sign over the bar announced: 'No guns allowed in the bar.' As we did not have any it was not a problem. Before long, a cowboy started to ask questions, when he discovered we were British he invited us to his ranch to hunt coyotes on horseback. His main topic of conversation was about all the different guns he had. After a while he went outside, returned and placed a few on the bar and began to wave them around. No one seemed to bother.

At Eagle Pass, Maverick County, Texas, we passed over the Rio Grande and into Mexico but were held up at the Mexican Immigration and Customs for a few hours as the van was full of ten boxes of new USA made caving rope. He wanted a few thousand dollars import duty, but we explained it was all coming back in five months' time. After waiting a long time, I noticed that every car had to open its boot and a hand went out to collect some cash from the driver. The collector probably shared the cash out at the end of the day. We made a deal and offered him ten dollars per box which he accepted and away we went.

After only a few miles, a Mexican policeman stepped out by the side of the road and waved us down, by the time I noticed him in my rear view mirror, I was a long way beyond as he was hiding behind a bush. As he seemed to be jumping up and down, I thought the best bet was to turn around and apologise for not stopping. After inspecting our documents, he did not seem to want to let us depart and finally came out with it, telling how little wages they received. I got the message and passed him 20 US dollars, we were away once more.

A great journey followed all the way to Mexico City where we met up with the Schenkers Shipping representative as they had agreed to transport most of our equipment to Veracruz.

We halted our journey at Veracruz as there we were to hire a large truck to transport our equipment to San Cristobal but the ship had not yet arrived. Considering most of the team were now waiting for us to arrive at San Cristobal with no equipment Dick set off in the van alone with the ropes. Terry and I waited for another few days in Veracruz.

One night we went to a bar for a beer, again this reminded me of something out of an Italian spaghetti western with swinging doors. Like two gunfighters we pushed open the doors and walked in, the place went completely silent with all heads looking our way. We ordered our Cerveza and sat down feeling slightly uneasy. A big man came over and asked if we were *gringos,* their derogatory term for Americans, when we explained we were British the whole atmosphere changed. The main conversation turned to football and as Terry could speak Spanish, we soon made friends and he invited us back to his house to meet his two sons who turned out to be two lovely young daughters. I think he was trying to get us married off as they were beauties. We spent a nice few days with him and his family while waiting for our boat to come in. Sadly, we had to leave when the equipment arrived and we drove on to San Cristobel.

We had a large collection of some of Britain's best cave explorers with my friend John New, Howard and Debbie Limbert, Steve Foster, Gail Searby, John Thorpe, Tony Jarratt to name a few and a strong contingent from the Mendip area including Bob Cork and Dany Bradshaw. Sid and Allison Perou arrived along with his filming team to start his film The Hidden Caves of Mexico and work soon got underway. The first thing was a thorough investigation of a cave open to tourists at San Cristobal. This was a huge system with fantastic cave formations, but little more unexplored cave was found. Attention turned to the mountains with numerous shafts, some deep with multiple entrances but none developed into the hoped-for large cave systems which we expected to find.

One such descent developed into an epic when on descending the entrance pitch the last man down noticed the rope being pulled up. He could just hear lots of shouting at the top telling them all to come out of the cave. They all ascended to find themselves surrounded by very agitated villagers waving machetes. The group were marched off at machete point and imprisoned in the school building. The headman of the village gave them his demands as they were accused of trying to steal the Mayan gold.

Most of the population in the hills belonged to various Mayan groups and legends had it that their ancestors hid their treasure from the Spanish Conquistadors in the caves. The demand was an extortionate ransom and after protracted negotiations a figure was agreed upon. One of the team, a Spanish speaking lady was dispatched back to camp to bring back a load of American dollars.

By Christmas, things were looking desperate and we were finding little of importance. A sojourn to a karst area close to the Guatemalan border looked promising and we camped in a farmer's field near his small wooden house. Large groups of Guatemalans had managed to escape the carnage going on at the time in Guatemala and he, along with many others, had crossed the border. The civil war from 1960 up to 1996 was a leftist uprising mainly composed of Mayan and Ladino peasants fighting against the government, which was heavily supported by the CIA. The Guatemala government were engaged in trying to get them to go back but he was still in fear for his life and wanted to stay put.

We discovered and mapped quite a few good caves in this area. John New and I entered a nice roomy entrance to a wide series of well-decorated passages with a hole in the floor. We rigged the pitch with rope and descended but disappointedly the passage below ran into boulder chokes with no way on. A very promising cave with a series of pitches and with a nice stream looked like this was the one we had been searching for but after less than 200 metres it hit a sump. Yet another nice cave entrance with a stream passage descending steeply down a series of slopes was explored and mapped to a chamber but once again it hit a flooded section. The sump was crystal clear and blue, so I attempted a free dive but the ongoing passage below water level was far too deep to dive with one lung full of air.

In the new year of 1983, we continued searching but were finding little on the plateau and the surrounding mountains near the town of San Cristobal de las Casas. The town was susceptible to flooding during the rainy season, so a tunnel had been constructed through the mountain to drain the water. I decided to take a small team down into the valley to search for possible risings as the streams sinking in the mountains and going through the tunnel had to come out somewhere.

I drove a small group down into the valley and we hired a house for £10 per month in a small village called San Lucas situated at the base of the mountain where it was presumed the streams sinking emerged into daylight.

The house was a delight to sleep in. First came the hour of the donkey, when every donkey in the village seemed to want to chat to each other and there were plenty of donkeys. Then came the hour of the dogs, followed by the hour of the cockerels and finally the ladies next door making their tortillas by slapping them on the stone slabs at five in the morning and chattering away ten to the dozen.

We did find the main resurgence with its associated cave close to the village, the river emerging from the cave being the village water supply. Because of the tunnel construction this river was now polluted as most of the sewage from San Cristobel was channelled through the tunnel instead of natural drainage which would in effect filter the water. We figured that the polluted water must be sinking again in the limestone somewhere after passing through the tunnel.

The cave proved extreme fun to explore and map. Progress could only be made with a hand guarding the face from thousands of frantic bats continually colliding with the explorers; we were invaders into their territory and not supposed to be there. Little could be seen except for the floor which seemed to be covered in red paint. It was soon realised that the red paint was in fact blotches of blood, the droppings from the feared little vampire bats that inhabited the cave. The hand guard was essential protection as these little creatures carried rabies. Fortunately, the cave terminated in breakdown after a few hundred metres with no way on for the team as the river just emerged from boulders.

Attention was then directed at an obvious dried out riverbed which seemed to terminate high up on the cliffs, which the villagers called Veshtucoc. It was obvious that a large river resurged into daylight during the wet season as there was no vegetation in the riverbed. Easy climbing found Gail Searby and I at a small insignificant looking cave entrance with a deep but short lake just inside, there seemed to be no way on with solid rock walls all around. I had an electric rechargeable head lamp so I swam across attached to a thin nylon line and felt with my feet to see if I could detect a passage under water. A way on could be felt, so I took a deep breath and dived below. Sure enough the passage continued and within a second I surfaced in a good sized passage with a small stream flowing into this short and easy sump. Tying the diving line to a rock, Gail dived through and we explored upstream in a nice spacious passage.

A short way along the passage became larger with the stream flowing over gravel banks. Most of the water flow vanished down a small crack in the side of the passage and we entered a massive chamber with fallen boulders and large stalagmites looming up into the roof far above. We eventually arrived at a vertical drop down which could not be descended without a rope or electron ladder, another large chamber could be made out below extending into darkness and we could hear water flowing some distance away.

We returned to daylight jubilant, at last we had found a good and most probably extensive cave after months of searching. It was decided to act dumb on arriving back at the house and tell the rest of the team we had found nothing. There was much celebration when we told them the truth with much drinking of Mezcal, the Mexican fire water with the worm in the bottom of the bottle.

The following day we were back to Veshtucoc along with more team members and the pitch was rigged with an electron ladder. It was only short and I landed in a large chamber which we later named Schenkers Chamber, after our shipping company. The stream emerged from a lake with solid rock walls all around. I circumnavigated the chamber but found no way on. Only one alternative that remained was the lake. Gail joined me and once more I attached a thin nylon cord to my waist belt and swam across to the far wall. A way on could be felt underwater and as the first siphon had succumbed to a free dive, I gave it a go. Again, I was using an electric lamp and not the flame of the standard expedition carbide light so I could see where I was going. Taking a deep breath, I swam underwater with my helmet scraping the roof and popped up after a short and roomy dive into the continuing passage. I checked the passage out to see if it was continuing in good style and as it looked very promising, returning after tying the diving line on a rock so others could follow. We all retreated and drove back to camp to get Sid Perou as I knew he would want to film some original exploration as it happened, and this was the ideal opportunity.

There was some excitement back at camp and a few more members of the team came back to San Lucas with us. The house was now a little crowded and a few days later we started filming with Sid. One of the team had picked up a nice Danish lady tourist and he took her to Veshtucoc. The problem was she insisted on stripping off starkers at the cave entrance to get changed into caving clothes, much to the consternation of the rest of the sex-starved male team members. In tribute to the lady and the show, we called a side passage in Veshtucoc, Danish Pastry Passage.

The original explorers of a previously unexplored passage have the privilege of naming it. As we never name passages after ourselves, we decided on song titles from a tape that we constantly played of Dire Straits, so the main passage became known as The Tunnel of Love. We spent a few days filming the short free dives and the big chambers and then moved on into the unknown.

Diving through the second siphon we explored and filmed beyond, arriving at a large river passage followed by a mass of boulders blocking the passage with the river pouring through. There appeared to be no way on but a climb up on the right led to the continuation and yet another sump. Sid filmed it all and set the camera rolling as I swam across a large deep pool. Looking for another underwater passage I searched all the walls and finally found the way on, but it was about six feet under the water and without a diving mask it was impossible to see where I was going. Sid was pleased with the results; at last he had managed to shoot good footage of an original exploration of a cave that no one had ever seen before. The urge to run off and explore, leaving Sid behind, was great, but we stuck by it for the sake of the film. We named the last section of river passage Dire Straits. Dick Ellis and I explored a side passage a few days later terminating in a blockage of rocks. We called it Telegraph Road after another Dire Straits song.

In the Mendip caving region of England many of the caves have sumps which can be free-dived. We were lucky to have some of the Mendip cavers with the team who were well experienced in diving through flooded passages. The problem was, we had no compressed air bottles but Bob Cork had a diving mask and managed to free dive through this final sump. Laying a diving line under water the other members of the team were able to follow and the team discovered a great deal more magnificent cave passage in the weeks to come. Veshtucoc proved to be many kilometres long and a great discovery for the team, in fact the only major discovery of note.

In the meantime another significant cave entrance had been found, named Borovitz, not far from the village of San Lucas. After we had completed the explorations and filming in Veshtucoc, attention switched for a time to Borovitz.

A large entrance beckoned, decorated with hanging stalactites and with multi-coloured flags adorning the entrance. The cave descended steeply in steps over numerous beautiful calcite dams, to a level area at the base of the entrance slope. This flat area was bathed in sun beams shining through the trees at the entrance and looking up it resembled a huge Roman amphitheatre. The sunbeams circumnavigated the base as the sun moved across the heavens, an imposing site which made for a nice time lapsed sequence in Sid's film of the expedition, Hidden Caves of Mexico. To the left and right were two low descending passages, both blocked with clay and collapse after a short distance. Broken bottles, jars, burnt offerings and dried flowers were much in evidence. Just a few metres down the calcite covered slope from the entrance a Christian cross and holy urn was found. The urn was completely encrusted in calcite and collected water from a drip high in the roof, it had obviously been there for a very long time.

Every few days our Spanish speakers reported our activities to the San Lucas village president. On one occasion our interpreter mentioned Borovitz and an old lady prostrated herself on the floor, shouting that we were all cursed; crossing herself with the sign of the cross, praying and in obvious distress. The president explained that Borovitz was a holy cave. Every year in April all the residents of the village prayed at the cave entrance for rain and it never failed. It always rained in May, of course, as it is the end of the dry season. Those venturing to the bottom of the slope must first pray at the cross, drink and anoint themselves with water from the holy urn and dodge the sunbeams. Failure to do so would invoke the Curse of Borovitz, a fate worse than death. The left-hand passage was used for the worship of God;

the right-hand passage was Satanic. We had all been down both and no doubt been hit by numerous sunbeams. We were all doomed and our fates sealed.

A short while later another fine resurgence came to light. The Nasimiento del Rio Salado, a deep blue lake with an enticing dry cave entrance on the far side just above the lake. I swam across and attached a Tyrolean rope across to a tree growing in the entrance so filming equipment could be moved across without getting it wet. Again, the cave was full of bats with a dry guano covered floor and the cave terminated a short distance in at a high circular chamber. Filmed by Sid, Steve Foster fixed expansion bolts in the rock walls and climbed to the top but it proved to be a dead end, the bats were just flying around having been disturbed.

The base of the Amphitheatre, Borovich, with the cursed sunbeams.
Photo: Stephen Wood.

Ten days later back at our base camp at San Cristobal nine of us started to feel sick with high temperatures, fever, headaches, coughing and finding it hard to breathe. We took the usual tablets thinking it may be just another case of Montezuma's Revenge but they had no effect and our illness became worse. We consulted a local doctor who took x-rays but although we had spots on our lungs, he had no idea what was wrong with us. Talking to Tony Jarratt later, Tony said he had suffered similar symptoms while caving in

Africa and it turned out to be histoplasmosis, a fungal disease of the lungs from bat guano. I checked my notes and realised that the nine sick cavers had all been in the Nacimiento del Rio Salado at the same time, which was full of bats and bat droppings.

The symptoms increased in intensity, so it was decided to head off back to Mexico City to a private hospital where they took great delight in sticking needles into us. There was no cure except for anti-fungal drugs which seemed to have little effect and according to the hospital other cases of reported histoplasmosis in Mexico had been fatal. It is quite possible that this was one of the causes of premature death of Howard Carter's archaeologists working on the Egyptian tombs, The Mummy's Curse, or the Curse of Tutankhamun.

We were extremely sick and many nights I refused to go to sleep, just in case I did not wake up in the morning. The fungal spores contained in the bat droppings are microscopic, so we'd had no idea we were breathing them into our lungs. The spores stick to the lining of the lungs and antibodies are naturally produced by the body to combat the infection as the spore is a foreign body. Eventually calcium is formed around the spore to isolate it, thus the tiny spots seen in the x-rays. The antibodies can be detected in the blood, but it normally takes many weeks before they can be detected successfully.

After three weeks we slowly began to recover and we made our way back to the UK. On arriving back, I weighed in at just over six stone.

The film had been completed and turned out well. Luckily, we all survived although it took many months to recover.

I wonder, if we ever went back to the village, would they think that a miracle had occurred and we had all risen from the dead?

On arriving back, I made my way to my parents' house in Droylsden, Manchester and presented my x-rays and medical report to a local doctor. He took one look and referred me to Monsall Isolation Unit in Manchester. Within a few hours the consultant for the hospital was knocking at the door.

'Would you mind coming into the hospital for a few days as this is the first case of histoplasmosis we have ever seen?'

I agreed and he sent a taxi.

I became a curiosity with students coming into my isolation ward and asking questions. Of course, they were only told the symptoms not the disease. No one got it correct as histoplasmosis is thankfully extremely rare and very few doctors had ever heard of it, especially in the UK where it does not occur. As a favour to the consultant I stayed for a few nights and he seemed to want to empty my body of blood as I gave lots of it.

I slowly recovered thanks to my parents and a few months later received a phone call from the consultant. He asked if I could attend a conference of doctors at the Manchester Royal Infirmary and he would send a taxi to pick me up. Every three months he presented a few cases of strange diseases to the assembled doctors and as mine was strange I agreed to attend.

Sat on a chair on a large stage in front of a few hundred eminent physicians was daunting as the consultant explained the symptoms and showed the audience the x-rays on a projector to a hushed and shocked audience. When he had finished it was their turn to ask me questions, my instructions being not to tell them the name of the disease. The questions came thick and fast and when asked where I started to feel sick, a very audible sigh of relief swept the room when I said Mexico. When asked what I was doing in Mexico one very smart doctor added the question, were there any bats in the caves. He remembered reading about a disease associated with bats but could not remember the name. One doctor asked if I would go caving again considering the risks and the assembled doctors seemed surprised when the answer was yes.

In 1985, Dave Arveschoug, one of my team members on an expedition to Papua New Guinea caught malaria and finished up in Monsall Isolation Unit.

The consultant asked, 'What were you doing in Papua New Guinea then?'

'Oh exploring caves,' said Dave.

'I had a caver in the unit some years previously called Dave Gill with histoplasmosis, do you know him?'

'Yes I was with him at the time.'

'I might have known,' said the consultant.

After an expedition to China, Paul Seddon one of our team members caught histoplasmosis and finished up in the same hospital.

'You're the second case we have had, the first one was a caver called Dave Gill, do you know him?'

'I was with him at the time,' replied Paul.

'I might have known,' said the consultant.

It seemed that I had gained a reputation for supplying the hospital with exotic diseases.

My house in Chinley was rented out to a lady and her small boy and I had no intention of asking them to leave, so I rented a room at Des and Carol Marshall's house in Buxton where I stayed for a couple of years.

Unfortunately, I had to leave my dog Pip with Patricia my ex-wife as Carol had a cat. Living there was handy as the Gas Light Club was just around the corner. Late night drinking sessions with Ken Kelly were common and no problem as Carol's cat would wait for me outside the Gas Light and show me the way to Carol's door.

Pip died while I was living at Des and Carol's and I was not told until after they had taken her to the vet's so I was unable to say goodbye. The utter devotion from a dog is hard to explain. She had been like a best friend for 13 years. I think about her often, as losing her was rather like losing one of my children.

The lady living in my house was the ex-partner of a friend in Buxton and seemed to be looking after my house OK and she paid the rent that paid for my mortgage. She later became interested in Buddhism and one night while I was drinking in the Chinley Conservative Club just opposite my house, the landlady asked me about the lady.

'There is something funny going on in your house,' she said. 'That lady has an altar in her bedroom with candles burning, I can see it from the snooker room,'

'Oh, don't worry,' said I. 'She practices witchcraft.'

It wasn't long before the whole village knew there was a witch living in my house, The Black Witch of Chinley. I told the lady but I was not sure if she appreciated the joke. My lodger later became a Buddhist nun.

14

V3 Tunnels, Hitler's Terror Weapon, 1983

'War does not determine who is right – only who is left.'

Bertrand Russell

The late Ken Kelly was something of a World War Two historian and had studied Hitler's vengeance weapons. The infamous and well known V1 and V2 had been well documented but there was another one, the V3 which few people had ever even heard of and was little known.

It was described as a high-pressure pump gun designated by the German's as HDP and, as a subterfuge, referred to as Busy Lizzie which could fire a projectile hundreds of miles. The idea was to flatten London. The barrels themselves had the codename the Millipede as it resembled one. The weapon was said to be buried in tunnels near Mimoyecques in France overlooking the English Channel where 5,000 slave labourers were said to be entombed. The farmer who owned the land claimed that during the war he saw the workers inside the tunnels, but he never saw them leave. Ken had found the site but was unable to enter as the entrance to the railway tunnels leading into the emplacements had collapsed but he thought there may well be a way in through the gun barrel inclines which were described as being 130 metres long and sloping down at an angle of 50 degrees below the surface. These inclines should lead into the underground workings, so we decided to take a look. The small team consisted of the late Ken Kelly, the late Ken Pearce of Berger fame and Alan Gamble; I was to do the mapping if we could gain access.

The story leading up to the development of this weapon is a fascinating one beginning with the discovery of a French patent for a long range gun found after the fall of France in June 1940 by August Conders, the chief engineer of the Rochling Stahlwerk plant in Wetzlar, Germany. The problem with long range artillery was that the explosive charge needed to propel a projectile for tens of kilometres destroyed the barrel of the gun. Conders thought that a series of charges spread along the barrel would solve the problem as each charge would increase the velocity of the shell and the first tests seemed to be encouraging using electrical activated charges to propel the shell to a high velocity.

Hermann Rochling obtained the support of the Ministry of Arms under Albert Speer for a series of cannons capable of firing on London from the coast of the Pas-de-Calais. The project intended to use two batteries to crush London under a barrage of 600 shells per hour with shells weighing 140 kilograms with an explosive charge of 25 kilograms, but the project hit problems by the end of 1943 with shell design. The trials at Hillersleben near Magdeburg only reached a muzzle velocity of 1,000 metres per second which was not fast enough to reach London from the coast of France as a velocity of 1,500 metres per second was required but it was still decided to build a full size gun with a 130 metre barrel at Misdoy on the Baltic island of Wolin near Peenemunde.

By March 1944, the Weapon Procurement Office took charge of the project and Conders along with many other engineers worked on the problems of projectile design and ignition of the charges. The problem with shell design was solved in May of 1944 with a 150 mm diameter shell 1.8 metres in length which had fins and was designed to be aerodynamic rather than gyroscopic. The smoothbore barrel was designed with pairs of firing tubes at an angle all the way along the length of the barrel and as the projectile passed, these would be fired using solid fuel rocket propellant rather than explosives, thus achieving the desired velocity, but timing had to be perfect. The trials at Misdroy only achieved a range of 93 kilometres and the barrel burst after eight rounds were fired. To reach London, the shell would need to travel 153 kilometres. Germany's top metallurgists worked on the barrel and finally perfected it.

Under orders from Hitler, construction started in September of 1943 on the proposed site at Mimoyecques, behind Cap Gris Nez, very close to the French end of the present day Channel Tunnel. This was only 8 kilometres from the coast and the geology of the area was limestone and chalk, which could be mined without too much of a problem. The site was identified by Major Bock of Festung Pioneer-Stab 27, the fortification regiment of LVII Corps, Fifteenth Army. The gun tubes would be located in inclined tunnels with supplies located in adjacent tunnels at 30 metres depth. An underground railway tunnel would serve the emplacements manned by 1,000 troops and underground ammunition storage areas constructed along with connecting tunnels and elevator shafts 100 metres below the surface. The guns would be immovable and would be permanently aimed at London 153 kilometres away. There were to be two gun emplacements one kilometre apart with five inclined shafts which would each hold a cluster of five gun tubes. The project was code named Wiese and the railway line was under construction by September 1943 and excavation of the gun shafts in October. The 50-degree inclined shafts exited the hillside through concrete slabs 30 metres wide by 5.5 metres in thickness with steel plates protecting the openings. Artillerie Abteilung 705 had been organised by January 1944 under Oberstleutnant Georg Borttscheller to operate the Wiese gun complex.

The bomb crater, V3 gun site, France. Photo: David Gill.

It was planned to have the first battery of five shafts each containing five separate gun tubes ready for March 1944, which would be capable of firing one shell at London every 12 seconds but following the failure at Misdroy the project was cut back to three drifts, which would be fifteen separate guns. Thankfully the site never went operational as on 6th July 1944, under the code name Operation Crossbow, RAF Bomber Command in the form of 617 Squadron, the Dam Busters attacked with Barnes Wallis 5,400 kilogram bombs, the Tallboy deep penetration bomb. A direct hit was scored on one of the inclined shafts, but the others remained intact. Collapse had occurred in the tunnel complex rendering areas unsafe.

The story was not yet over as the complex was captured by the Canadians in August of 1944 and Winston Churchill gave orders to have it destroyed as there was some opposition from the French who wanted to keep it intact. Churchill voiced his opinion saying, 'It would be intolerable if the French insisted on maintaining installations directly menacing our safety after we have shed so much blood in the liberation of their country.'

It was not until the 9th May 1945 that the Royal Engineers exploded ten tons of bombs in the railway entrance to the tunnel but failed to seal it. Five days later 25 tons of TNT was exploded at both ends of the railway tunnel finally sealing it, but the rest of the installation still remained intact.

If the metallurgists and aerodynamic specialised had been called in sooner with the design of the V3, there is no doubt that it would have become operational sooner with the inevitable consequences, the destruction of London.

We set off in Ken Pearce's car and found a ploughed field to sleep on for the night somewhere in France. The following morning at dawn we arrived at the site and, as suspected, the railway tunnel entrance was completely blocked. Climbing the hill, we searched over and around the many surface bomb craters and found large blocks of shattered concrete and one of the inclined shafts where the Tallboy had hit, true to the reports. It was just about open, and a steep descent down loose rubble led us to an open tunnel at about 30 metres depth with the ramifications leading onwards in various directions. The continuation of the inclined shaft down to the 100 metre level was completely blocked with rubble, presumably due to the intense bombing. I began mapping and exploring blocked sections of tunnel that had most probably collapsed even at this depth of 30 metres below the surface due to the massive explosions caused by the Tallboy. Some areas were still in good condition and the main railway tunnel was entered with tunnels leading off towards the inclined shafts. Both ends of the railway tunnel were completely blocked due to the explosive charges set off in 1945 by the Royal Engineers. A few small unfinished shafts led upwards, climbed by Alan, one mysteriously blocked with concrete. These were most probably the intended ventilation shafts for the complex. All the other inclined shafts had collapsed and did not reach the surface, but no gun tubes could be found or ammunition and the lower 100 metre depth sections could not be found. One of the intended lift shafts was found and descended on our wire electron ladders by Alan but it proved to be completely blocked after 20 metres. It began to appear that the lower sections had not been completed unless they had been sealed entombing the reported slave labourers. I mapped all the open tunnels within the complex and sure enough the inclined shafts were according to my compass bearing all pointing directly at London.

It is not known if the gun tubes or any ammunition was ever stored at the site but the USA Army did capture the Rochling works and shipped back the tubes and ammunition to the United States where it was reported as being scrapped in 1948.

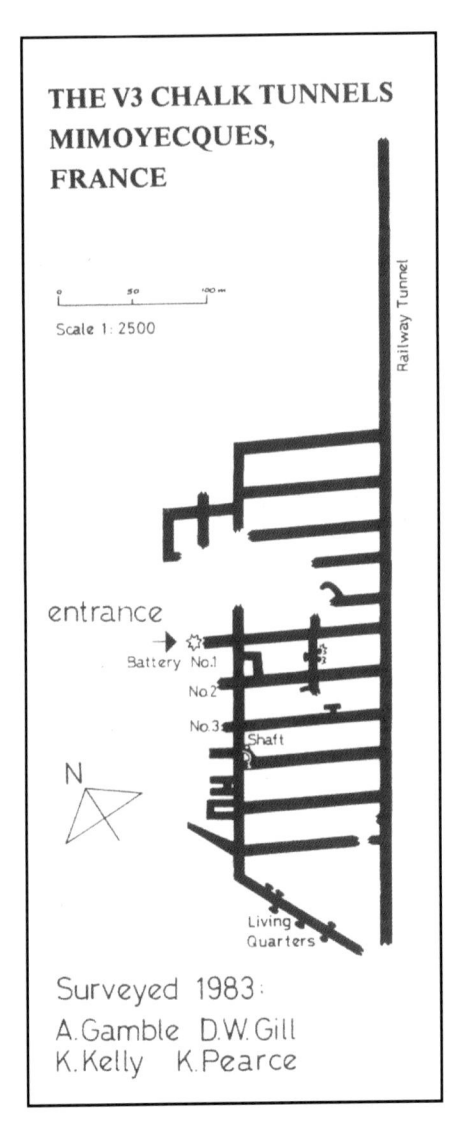

THE V3 CHALK TUNNELS MIMOYECQUES, FRANCE

Scale 1:2500

entrance
Battery No.1
No.2
No.3
Shaft

N

Living Quarters

Railway Tunnel

Surveyed 1983:
A. Gamble D.W. Gill
K. Kelly   K. Pearce

Plan of the V3 gun emplacement tunnels, Mimoyecques, France.

While in this part of France, we decided to visit the recorded sites of the V2s, the Dome at Wizernes and the Watten Bunker again both bombed by the Barnes Wallis Tallboy.

Wizernes had been heavily bombed and was surrounded by hundreds of craters and the site was overgrown but tunnels around the edges of the dome could still be entered. It had been captured by the Allies in September of 1944 and partially destroyed under Churchill's orders. It had been designed to have seven kilometres of tunnels, but it appeared the many of the tunnels had not been fully excavated but we managed to explore most of the site, around two kilometres. It was twice the size for a standard V2 and was suspected as being the launch pad for a super vengeance weapon capable of firing a missile as far as New York as it was aligned in that direction.

The Watten site was a different matter; again, it had been badly damaged by a direct hit from a Tallboy but otherwise was intact except for a barb wire fence with a sign saying, 'No Admittance, Keep Out'.

The site was completely deserted and we wondered about a possible minefield or guard dogs so sent Ken Pearce over the barbed wire first as he would frighten the hell out of a dog and he was impervious to minefields and as nothing attacked him and he was not blown up, we followed. The cathedral-like structure was impressive and again much larger than the area required for a V2 missile. We could see little except for a flame in the centre of the structure.

Alan called out to me, 'You're an electrician, find a light switch,' so I did. The problem was it was the gas tap for the eternal flame, and it went out. I relit it fast as I could as I did not fancy being cursed once more, this time for extinguishing the sacred eternal flame.

Areas had been set aside for the production of liquid oxygen but again these reinforced concrete structures had not been designed to withstand such bombs as the RAF had dropped on them.

We travelled back to the UK in Pearce's car but when Ken Kelly went for a pee; Pearce drove on to the ferry stranding Ken in Calais.

'He's a resourceful man, he will find his own way back', said Pearce, which he did without a passport, catching the next ferry.

Pearce spent the journey on the ferry lusting after a very huge lady. 'I like them big,' said Ken, after all he was the wonderful Big Black Pearce that we all loved and admired.

When I first wrote a report about this exploration way back in 1984 for Descent Magazine I said, 'These megaliths of concrete cannot be destroyed, they will merely become overgrown and will stand for all time as a permanent reminder of man's ingenuity and amazing inhumanity towards man in the service of mass destruction.'

I was wrong on one point as they have now become, I am glad to say, major tourist attractions. The Wizernes site, La Coupole or The Dome lay derelict until the 1990s but has been renovated and made safe, the base re-excavated and concreting of tunnels finished off. A museum has been built and £7.5 million spent on the project in total. In 2011, it received 120,000 visitors. The Watten Bunker has also been developed and opened as a tourist attraction and is designated as a French National Monument. I have no idea if the eternal flame is still lit. The V3 Tunnels are also open to the public with a monument to the slave labourers and Allied Airman that died during its construction and destruction; you can even watch a video of the site on YouTube.com.

Back in Buxton one day in August 1983 there was a knock on the door. It was none other than Mike Boon. I had not seen him for some time since the Pierre Saint-Martin expedition in 1972 as he was living in Canada and, like the good explorer that he was, he had managed to track me down.

Mike had a proposal; he was interested in organising an expedition to the Nare cave in the Nakanai Mountains of East New Britain, Papua New Guinea and wanted me to join his team. I suppose this was a compliment as I was the only man in Britain he came to see.

The Nare entrance is a huge hole, 320 metres in depth by 150 metres in diameter with the largest known underground river in the world at 20 tons of water a second flowing across the base of the shaft and into a large tunnel. This was the preserve of the French explorers who had organised a number of highly successful expeditions to this remote tropical island but in the Nare Cave they had turned back after two kilometres at a massive rapid they christened Apocalypse Now, after the well-known film. I had seen an advertisement for prospective cavers to join Mike's expedition in a caving magazine but thought his proposal impossible to achieve. He did not have a team, his budget was far too high for any caver in the UK and it was one year out of date. As the Nare was considered the greatest caving challenge in the world it was too hard to resist but Mike had only managed to recruit two cavers I did not know. One was called Steph Gough and the other Tim Allen, both with little experience of major expeditions.

I gave it some careful consideration for a couple of weeks and thought it possible with a good team, lots of hard work and lots of luck.

15

The Untamed River Expedition, New Britain, 1984–1985

'Men often become what they believe themselves to be. If I believe I cannot do something, it makes me incapable of doing it. But when I believe I can, then I acquire the ability to do it even if I didn't have it in the beginning.'

Mahatma Gandhi

New Britain is a tropical island paradise situated off the mainland coast of Papua New Guinea covered for the most part in primary rain forest, surrounded by coral reefs. It's a fairly large island that few people have ever even heard of, 477 kilometres in length with a maximum width of 80 kilometres and an area of 36,520 square kilometres. The island is dominated by active volcanoes along its northern coastline as it's situated along a boundary plate known as a subduction zone so is prone to earthquakes. The New Britain Trench, known as Planet Deep, runs along the southern coast and the sea here reaches an incredible depth of 9.1 kilometres. It can be something of a shock when swimming under water in crystal clear visibility in the shallows, when all of a sudden one swims over a cliff descending thousands of metres straight down. Vertigo sets in and the tendency is to swim back thinking that you are going to fall off the edge of the cliff.

New Britain was discovered in 1700 by an English adventurer-come-pirate called William Dampier who gave the island its name and it became a German Protectorate up until the outbreak of the First World War in 1914 when it was occupied by the Australians. In 1942 it was occupied by the Japanese and Rabaul became their major naval base which was heavily bombed during the last war by the US Air Force. After the war Papua New Guinea was handed back to Australia as a Mandated Territory, eventually to gain its independence in 1975. New Britain has two provinces, East and West, with the Nakanai Mountains being largely in the Eastern Province. In 1984, remains of crashed aeroplanes could still be found hidden in the remote rain forests, some with the remains of the aircrew, which were classified as US war graves.

In 1984, New Britain had a population of only 250,000 with many tribes living in small isolated villages in the mountainous jungle. The population to date is over 500,000. These communities practice subsistance farming growing taro and sweat potatoes, while coastal communities exist on fishing and growing cash crops including coconuts for copra, cocoa and palm oil. Many of the small mountain villagers had little or no contact with Europeans in 1984 and some areas were unexplored as the maps had blank areas which just said, 'Obscured by Clouds.' The fascination of Papua New Guinea can be found in the phrase 'the last unknown' as it is still considered as a mysterious land.

Tribal warfare was common throughout Papua but has now thankfully been largely eradicated but occasionally disputes on land tenure can flare up as all land is held under common traditional rites and is not owned by the state as is the case in most countries.

The Cargo Cult was still practised by a few in some areas as it was not until the 1930s that large numbers of people were found living in the Highlands of Papua New Guinea who had had no previous contact with Europeans. At first the native groups who were still basically living in the Stone Age thought the white men were gods arriving from the sky in flying machines and asking Joe for the cargo to be flown in using strange radios and transmitters. Cargo magically arrived and it was soon realised that these were just men but where did all the cargo come from? A cult developed and spread throughout the mainland and islands with native groups imitating the white man by building run ways and talking into tin cans tied to a piece of string and attached to a pole, asking Joe to send the cargo, but the cargo never came.

Language is another problem as many of the native groups are completely isolated from each other so 770 different languages have evolved. Melanesian Pidgin English gradually became the second common language. The culture is a fascinating subject and needs to be understood by foreign expeditions before venturing into this fantastic country as failure to do so can spell disaster. The pay back system is still practised by many, which basically is an eye for an eye and a tooth for a tooth, so great care and diplomacy needs to be taken when dealing with native groups. There are still animistic and black magic beliefs so missionaries can be found everywhere attempting to convert the people into Christians and get them to wear clothes.

This story really starts in the 1960s when a reconnaissance flight across the Nakanai Mountains of East New Britain observed enormous holes in the jungle with large rivers running along the base of the shafts. These holes could be seen on the aerial photographs made during the war and today can be plainly seen on satellite photographs, the black holes resembling giant craters. The first cave exploration expeditions took place in the 1970s by Australians to be followed by the French. In 1979, a Swiss expedition lost a man trying to cross the underground river in a cave called Kavakuna, which indicated the severity of these white-water underground rivers. A new approach was required in the exploration of these caves with the development of techniques to progress along the rivers in comparative safety. The enormous shaft of the Nare was first descended by a French expedition in 1978 but they were unable to explore up or down stream due to the massive river of 20 cubic metres a second or, put another way, 20 tons of water a second pouring with a deafening roar from the upstream portal and down the 100 metre high tunnel. The French returned in 1980 and succeeded in exploring upstream for 1.8 kilometres to a siphon and downstream to a wide white-water rapid which they called Apocalypse Now after a distance of two kilometres. It had been necessary to climb along the walls fixing ropes and cross the river on Tyrolean ropes eight times, they had used almost two kilometres of ropes in the exploration and the huge passage continued beyond the rapids and into the darkness.

When Mike Boon came to see me in August 1983 about his proposal to try to reach the end of the Nare, I was sceptical to say the least. This was French territory but from the French reports it did appear that they had no intention of returning.

It took me two weeks to decide as the problems were immense. We had no experience with this type of exploration and it was on the other side of the world, on a remote island in the middle of a jungle. Jean-Francoise Pernette the leader of the French expedition wrote in 1981 that he thought it was not worth the risks, his final quote said: 'Are we then faced with a new stage in underground exploration? History will tell us. For now there is no doubt that we are confronted with new problems which go beyond the scope of classical cave exploration. No doubt in the near future these lines will make us smile.'

So the gauntlet had been thrown down and it was far too hard for me to resist picking it up but this was going to be the greatest challenge I had ever attempted or, as history turned out, ever likely to attempt in the future.

As explained in previous chapters there has to be a logical progression to organise such a complex venture beginning with place and objectives, research, budget, team, dates, transport, equipment and food. There was one other headache, developing and practising new white-water caving techniques. The place and objectives had already been decided and the research was not too difficult as we had the French reports. The snail mail could be used to obtain the maps and I worked out a budget which came to a staggering £39,000. Where we were going to get this from was going to be a major problem.

The 300 metre deep doline entrance to the Nare River Cave, New Britain.
Photo: David Gill.

The team was the next problem to solve as the objectives could only be described as suicidal and few could afford months off work so it was important that the team were a group of friends who could work together and live together in total isolation from the outside world for months on end in difficult and often dangerous circumstances. I decided that considering the difficulties that the team faced and the remoteness of the Nare, five to six months would be a reasonable time frame for the expedition. Members of the team with permanent jobs would need to resign or obtain special dispensation and those with commitments would have zero earnings for possibly six months.

Mike disappeared back to Canada and left me with it but wanted to remain in control. Alan Gamble was keen and we met up with Steph Gough and Tim Allen who had both met Mike Boon but realised that his critical path analysis for his planned expedition was two years out of date and he had failed to raise a team. We discussed the expedition logistics and a formidable draft list of equipment drawn up by Mike and I for a six month stay in the jungle. On Mike's original list was a few nondescript items, one of them being seeds. We presumed considering we would be living in the jungle for a long period that Mike wanted to construct a garden and grow fresh vegetables. Steph wondered if we should take some garden gnomes for his garden and build a pond with a fountain.

Steph was a teacher living in Sheffield which was not too far away from Buxton so became my right-hand man for organising this venture. The first thing to do was to obtain as much media publicity as possible in order to gain sponsorship from suppliers of equipment as we were starting off from rock bottom with nothing. A catchy name for the expedition was required and we decided on The Untamed River Expedition. We produced a nice concise letter on headed notepaper explaining the project along with a photograph of the Nare shaft with a French explorer dangling 300 metres above the river on a rope. Steph posted it off to newspapers and it did the trick. The media became fascinated with this hair-raising venture to explore the largest underground river in the world which had beaten the French, at the bottom of a 320 metre deep hole in the middle of a jungle, on a remote island that no one had ever even heard of. Over the next year we had many reports printed in newspapers and TV news channels took an interest, so we made quite a few appearances on local and national news.

I contacted the French cave explorers and they agreed that I could have the Nare as their next expedition at the approximate same time as mine would concentrate on another huge shaft with a massive underground river, called

Minye. Pierre Bergerone, one of the French expedition, came to Buxton to see me and we agreed on mutual co-operation.

I started to recruit a team as it was obvious that five members was nowhere near sufficient to tackle this mammoth project as I considered that ten to twelve lunatics would be the minimum for a six month expedition. I needed at least one year to organise this, so the dates were set for October 1984 to March 1985 which coincided with the dry season in the Nakanai Mountains. Steph in his correspondence with Mike in Canada happened to mention that I was recruiting a team. Mike's reply was a little disconcerting and he told me to stop charging around like a little tank out of control, but as I was already committed to this expedition I started to believe it may just be possible to pull it off but there was no way this could happen with Mike in control as Mike's input from thousands of miles away was zero. The expedition could only be organised entirely from the UK, to succeed I needed a complete free hand as in 1983 we only had snail mail; the internet had not yet been invented so communication was difficult. I explained the situation to Mike, and he agreed, but sadly he became ill while in Canada and had to drop out but the expedition owes a lot to his original conception. Without his enthusiasm I would not have picked up the French gauntlet and the expedition would not have taken place.

As publicity grew, more interest was shown by members of the Eldon Pothole Club and other friends from the Buxton region. I was still living at Des and Carol Marshall's house in Buxton and Des asked if he could join the team and I needed a competent climber. I had tried to recruit Ron Faucet, a famous Derbyshire based climber, who was described in the press as the Exocet Missile of the climbing world but he did not fancy climbing above a roaring white water river in the dark. Dave Sims, a highly resourceful man and a caver of long standing, asked if he could manage the base camp and I agreed to both requests. Dave Arveschoug was a teacher of Geography at Chapel-en-le-Frith and was keen to help with food which is one of the main problems for all expeditions to remote areas, he was also a very experienced caver so joined the team.

I desperately needed a cave photographer and tried to persuade Paul Deakin but with a family there was no way he could manage six months in the jungle with no earnings. Rod Leach, a photographer and journalist from Buxton, started to handle our publicity and made sure we had good coverage of the expedition in the newspapers and wanted to come with us. He had done little caving, but I agreed as this kind of expedition was a different ball game and he could join in our training sessions and take over as publicity officer.

Next were the problems of medical care for such a potentially dangerous project. Dr Steve Ray and Dr Hugh Kidd of Buxton gave much advice, but I could not persuade them to come. Hugh had been in the British Army Medical Core and had served in Borneo during the confrontations with the communist guerrillas and the Indonesians. He talked to his friend Lieutenant General Sir Alan Reay KBE from the Ministry of Defence who asked for a volunteer from the Medical Corps, a man who was a cave explorer as he thought this expedition would be good experience for a British Army doctor. I was lucky enough to get Captain John Salmon who joined the team and considering his totally different background fitted in well with the rest of the team. Steve Dickinson I knew well as we had caved together many times on past expeditions and Steve was a level-headed easy going man and nothing ever seemed to rile him so would be perfect for the team. Along with Ken Kelly and Jim Hook who was to be our geologist all three signed up to what Alan described to a TV news channel, 'the greatest adventure of a lifetime.'

I had caved with Alan Gamble for 20 years and, besides being a highly competent cave explorer, he had the kind of dry sense of humour that was needed in difficult situations. Steph Gough turned out to be a hard-working member and level-headed and we spent many months together organising the expedition with many journeys down to London on the train. There is little doubt we could not have succeeded in getting to New Britain without Steph's huge input. Tim Allen, although young, proved to be a highly competent caver, an expert on rope work with tremendous courage, daring and confidence in his own ability. Steph described him as a little like a steely-eyed SAS recruit.

I now had a team of twelve; all characters in their own right and all seemed willing to work together on obtaining equipment and accept the risks involved. Some arm twisting was used by Alan and Ken to invite the infamous Dr Ken Pearce who wanted to join us but this was furiously resisted by the other members of the team as his reputation preceded him.

We applied for recognition from Britain's prestigious Royal Geographical Society and received the British Sugar Award; also, the son of Ernest Shackleton agreed to be our patron, the Rt Hon Lord Shackleton, KG, PC, OBE. The expedition was becoming respectable considering that most of us were a little rough around the edges, in the building trade and had not attended Eaton.

At last the lady living in my house left so I could once more go home to

Chinley and convert my front room into an office. The work load became that great that I had to give up paid work and work on the project full time for five months, which was a terrible strain on my meagre finances.

We received grants from the Ghar Parau Foundation, the Sports Council and the Mount Everest Foundation, and started to receive calls from companies asking if they could supply us with their products. This was all due to the publicity in the papers and TV news appearances. Tim Allen's dear mother chipped in with a substantial amount and it was beginning to look like we might be able to pull this off.

Steph and I brokered a deal with the Sunday Express Colour Supplement Magazine for two stories, one before the expedition and one after and obtained sponsorship from British Airways to fly us out to Port Moresby free of charge. When we stood at the top of the British Airways head office in London gazing out over London and feeling elated, Steph asked, 'Where's the escalator?'

My reply was, 'We might as well jump out of the window as we are bound to land on our feet.'

Steph and I seemed to succeed in convincing companies to support us; many directors said that they would love to be able to come with us as this adventure was something they could only dream about.

The equipment started to mount up but one problem remained. How were we going to get tons of equipment halfway around the world? We received another stroke of luck via Tim Alan and managed to persuade Bank Line to give us a free container to ship our equipment to Rabaul in New Britain. There was now no turning back.

Regular training meets were organised on white water rivers in Wales to hone our skills in traversing and Tyroleans. The French had thrown grapnel irons across the river hoping to obtain a firm anchor for a Tyrolean rope. This could then be tensioned and the first man across could then fix a firm anchor for the rest of the team to follow. The journalist covering the story for the Sunday Express had contacts at GQ Defence and we visited them to discuss the problem of launching a grapnel iron across a river. Their boffins supplied us with a compressed air launcher charged from a diving bottle and it resembled a mortar tube, a slightly different version was supplied to the SAS. The grapnel iron was attached to a rope and could be fired across the river. Wilkinson Sword, the maker of shaving blades, had their boffins designing and producing stainless steel grapnel irons for us. We scrounged R.F.D inflatable dinghies used in fighter jets and buoyancy aids from Crew Saver

Marine and Dave Sims and I spent weeks packing and compiling the shipping lists in Dr Hugh Kidd's garage.

We had been told that obtaining food supplies would be a problem in Papua New Guinea so we had scrounged huge quantities from British suppliers along with Beal Ropes and other caving hardware. The total value came to around £35,000 and it weighed in at 4.5 tons. Everything was now packed into wooden crates and blue plastic drums, so we borrowed a truck and drove up to Hull docks, loaded the container and said goodbye to one year of hard graft.

Using the air launcher, Nare River Cave, New Britain. Photo: Rod Leach.

Three months before we were due to leave at one of our regular meetings Tim and Alan proposed that we postpone the expedition for one year as Tim did not think we were prepared enough and the team was nowhere near strong enough to succeed. I explained that it was now too late, sponsorship had been obtained, our word and promises given, to postpone now would lead to a loss of face and enthusiasm which would lead to the expedition being abandoned, to put it in caving terms, it was shit or bust.

At the last minute a few British cavers attempted to jump on the band wagon now that all the work had been accomplished and the money had been raised which amounted to an amazing £11,000, but it was far too late considering the effort the team had put in to get this far, flights were booked, equipment for 12 men sorted, the answer had to be a resounding no, which made me unpopular in some caving circles.

We received many crazy suggestions from various journalists such as descending the Nare doline in a hot air balloon and kayaking or white water rafting down the underground river. It seemed hard to explain that the cave was pitch black and no one knew where the river went. It was presumed that the river emerged somewhere in the Essis Gorge or Iso Gorge but no one knew for sure. One amazing press story said that the river ran beneath the sea to emerge hundreds of miles away on a remote island, journalists seemed to be having a field day with the story but all publicity is good publicity so we just laughed at the strange press coverage.

I sat one day alone on a railway station platform in Birmingham after a meeting with the BBC who wanted to make a film of the expedition, wondering if I was just plotting my own death, later the BBC pulled out as they probably considered it far too dangerous.

On one of the last BBC TV interviews at the Royal Geographical Society before we left, the presenter said while showing a photograph of the Nare, 'A few builders from Buxton, bricklayers, teachers and an electrician are about to set off to a remote island at the other end of the world for six months to descend a 1,000 foot hole in the middle of a jungle and explore the largest underground river in the world, which goes god knows where. Surely this must be every little boy's dream.' Well it was not just a little boy's dream, but the dream of a few very eccentric individuals.

The journalist covering the story for the Sunday Express asked me what the secret was in welding such a crazy team of individuals together in order to tackle this suicidal mission. I answered altruism and a determination to bring them all back alive, but I do not think he fully understood the concept. The magazine was published a few weeks later which was well illustrated and written and best of all, we received our first payment which gave me almost enough money to see us through during our stay in the Nakanai Mountains.

I managed once more to rent out my house, which covered the mortgage payments and after all the work involved, it came as an anticlimax when Steph, Tim and I set off four weeks in advance on 3rd October 1984 on a sponsored British Airlines flight. It had taken over one year of hard work to get this far; the stage was set and the die was cast and British cavers wondered just how many of us would return.

Due to the publicity, we had made contact with Helen and Bryson Huddlestone, Australians living in Port Moresby, who were friends of Kevin and Diana Rutherford, living in Derbyshire. Diana had contacted me after reading reports in the press and we were able to stay with Helen and Bryson for a few days while we obtained our research permits and aerial photographs of the Nakanai Mountains. We visited His Excellency the British High Commissioner for Papua New Guinea at the British Embassy and signed the visitors' book a few pages after Prince Charles. We had also made contact with a man from Scotland called Lindsay Telfer, who was working in a logging camp at Gonaile on the south coast of East New Britain only ten kilometres from Pomio village. It had been suggested that we could set up a shore base here which was only 50 kilometres from our objective, the Nare doline.

By the 15th October, we were in Rabaul waiting for the Bank Line ship the Ivy Bank to arrive with our supplies and equipment and we were sleeping in a hut loaned to us by Gonaile Logging Company. Rabaul at that time was a beautiful provincial city with white painted wooden houses along tree-lined streets with the volcanoes dominating the city, belching smoke and rumbling away. A scare was on as seismic surveys indicated that the volcano could erupt at any time, but the red alert had not yet been issued. The deep water bay was the remnant of a huge volcanic crater with a bit sticking out in the middle.

We had many jobs to complete while in Rabaul and met up with friends of Mr and Mrs Rutherford, Danny and David Tan, two Chinese who owned a store called Tropicana. They kindly place a Land Cruiser at our disposal so we could travel around the city.

One particular man we made contact with was helpful with aerial photographs of the Nakanai Mountains; Brian Bennett had an interesting hobby of locating crashed planes from the Second World War and sometimes leading the American aircrew who survived back to their aircraft. He was married to a local lady and his garden was full of retrieved aircraft parts.

We paid courtesy visits to the Premier and Provincial Secretary of East New Britain and it was while in Rabaul we had an amazing stroke of luck. Cozinc Rio Australia had a helicopter for ferrying geologists into the Nakanai Mountains searching for gold deposits and we made contact with their chief geologist Frank Hughes. Frank was fascinated with our project and considering our patron was Lord Shackleton who just happened to be an executive director of Rio Tinto Zinc UK, he agreed that we could borrow his helicopter which was flying near Pomio. Depending on the weather it dropped off his geologists and returned empty then once more returned empty to pick them up later in the day. Our original plan had been to hire porters which would cost a fortune and take a very long period to ferry tons of equipment and supplies the 50 kilometres to the Nare doline.

On Saturday 20th October, the Ivy Bank arrived bang on time and our container was stored at the docks until we could find a boat to take us the 150 kilometres along the south coast to Gonaile Logging Camp situated in Jacquinot Bay. It was 28th October before we managed to charter a government launch, the Taurama. Unloading 4.5 tons of equipment from the container to a truck, then loading the launch in the scorching sun was back breaking work for just the three of us but we managed it in a day and 17 hours later, after a pleasant trip along the coast, saw us unloading it all at the Gonaile logging camp. We spent the day in pouring rain setting up a large marquee tent donated by Franklin Ltd and storing everything inside.

On Wednesday 31st October, we got our first sight of the Nare as we flew on a compass bearing over the Nare doline in the borrowed helicopter. An incredible sight greeted our eyes as we flew over this imposing hole in the jungle, which without doubt has to be the most awe inspiring shaft in the world. Perfectly symmetrical, as deep as the Eifel Tower is high, and steep sided with a huge white water river disappearing into a tunnel 100 metres in diameter. Our pilot Bill Wineburge decided he could fly his Hughes 500 down the hole. We gritted our teeth as he crazily hovered lower and lower down this huge 150 metre wide shaft but when rocks and trees began falling off the sides he thankfully gave it up. He said he could have landed but the down draught would have made take off impossible.

Bill landed us at a tiny clearing in the jungle near the closest village which was called Ire and we waited around until the villagers turned up from their fields. I asked them in broken English to clear the landing zone so I could drop off our equipment and explained that we wanted to explore the Nare, which was on their tribal land. I agreed to pay them for the work and they appeared to be enthusiastic. We then flew to Nutuve, the closest village with a school, church and clinic. Nutuve had a grass runway for light aircraft but the problem was the pigs kept digging it up so it had not been used for some time. Arrangements were made with Camillus Tati, the headmaster of the Nutuve School, for us to store some food supplies in the school hall. Things were going well as the weather was good so over the next few days, we dropped off one ton of supplies at Nutuve but then disaster stuck when Bill flew too close to some trees and broke his aerial.

A four day delay ensued, so we went exploring. I had brought along my outboard engine in the container, a compressor and diving bottles so we drove along the coast in a borrowed boat and looked at a fantastic waterfall just off a beautiful coral beach with a large river pouring out of a cave called Iowa, but it sumped after only 25 metres. No doubt there is a large cave system associated with this rising. Another rising of a river was looked at called Sibuli which was a deep blue lake, but no caves were found in the vicinity.

By November 7th, the helicopter was once more back in service so I flew back to Ire village to see if I could meet the headman. On landing I was surrounded by 50 villagers all talking at once. The head man was called Unaso and with broken English protracted negotiations began. I explained our project and he agreed to let us camp on their tribal land near the Nare providing we employed only his people. I promised to employ them as porters and fixed a rate of pay which they all seemed happy with as great cheering and dancing followed.

Accompanied by Unaso, I walked the two kilometres towards the Nare doline to find a good camping spot for our base camp and as I approached still 500 metres away I could hear a rumbling noise which grew louder and louder by the minute. The huge Nare shaft acted like a funnel amplifying the noise of the massive river which reverberated through the jungle. Looking through the undergrowth down the hole from the edge was at first a terrifying but an exhilarating experience. I found a section of flat ground where we could build a camp but no areas where we could land a helicopter so made arrangements for the Ire people to clear the intended camp site.

A long wave single side band radio link was available at Gonaile logging camp and I was able to contact the rest of our team who had at last arrived in Rabaul. They were in the process of arranging for a boat to sail to Gonaile.

Over the next few days, the villagers made the clearing larger at Ire and our equipment and food was dropped off by Bill in seven loads, all free of charge. Over an 11-day period the three of us had packed and sorted all the equipment and food for a seven week stay at the Nare base camp for 12 men with 1,100 kilograms as a reserve at Nutuve and 1,400 kilograms dropped off at Ire village.

Because of the language difficulties we decided to employ a local English-speaking man from the coastal region as a full-time helper and interpreter so held a few interviews. Camallus Lontania was 20-year-old from Pomio village and could speak the local dialect and seemed ideal. He was a little worried that the people from Ire belonged to the Kol tribe while he was a coastal Mengen so he would not be accepted, and they might place a black magic spell on him and make him blind. I assured him that this would not happen as I would tell them that he was our official Liaison Officer, so he agreed to stay with the expedition until the duration.

On Thursday 8th November, we were dropped off at Ire village where we slept the night in a hut where our equipment had been stored. It had taken the three of us five weeks to get this far.

A 6 am start the following morning saw 15 men carrying a total of 46 loads the two kilometres to our planned base and construction started. Tim and Steph stayed the night while I returned to pay the porters and arrange for the rest of the equipment to be carried in the following day. This time I employed every man, woman and child in the village to move everything in one fell swoop. Tins of fish and one cupful of rice were distributed and the well-loved long Spear cigarettes rolled in newspaper given out as a bonus. The villagers had few clothes so I had brought out a few bin liner bags full from an English jumble sale and gave them out. We were now very popular but the ladies had nowhere to put their cupful of rice so took their tops off. It made us smile thinking of giving a lady in England a cup full of rice, what a way to get a girl to take her blouse off.

Water supplies were something of a problem as the only source nearby was a muddy puddle. We set up a filtration system using Survival Aids $H_2 0k$ filtration units and blue plastic drums to divert rainwater from the tarpaulin roof of our camp and into the drums. This worked well providing it rained but as it rained most days this system provided us with enough water from a good downpour to last for three or four days.

Tim could not stand the lure of the Nare shaft for long and reconnoitred the best place to descend and the following day he completed the rigging with the 360 metre length of Beal rope especially made by the manufacturer for the job. The descent began on an 80 degree slope and there were plenty of small trees growing out from the sides of the shaft so the rope was tied off 13 times and offset as far as possible. This would prevent falling rocks from hitting any one below whom happened to be climbing at the time; also the descent and ascent would facilitate a number of men climbing at the same time. The last drop before hitting the bottom of the shaft was 126 metres and as this was vertical had no trees, so Tim placed four 8mm bolts into the rock to hang the rope from. At the base was a steep slope through jungle to the mighty river which looked decidedly ferocious.

Unaso the head man offered to guard the camp as there appeared to be some trouble with a nearby village who also claimed the Nare as their tribal land. I made it clear that I would be perfectly agreeable to employing men from this village in order to prevent any tribal warfare; after all it was my birthday.

I was now getting concerned about the rest of the team and made attempts to contact them on a Tait short wave radio transmitter I had managed to borrow from Rabaul but failed to get through. Climbing the hill at the back of the Base Camp, I had a much clearer bearing on a radio relay station on Mount Bunong and eventually succeeded in making contact. The good news was they were due to arrive in Gonaile on Wednesday 14th November. This did not prevent us from continuing with the work as Bill dropped off the last loads of equipment at Ire village and Camillus mobilised the porters on the Tuesday. We were now in a position to work our way along the downstream river passage as we had all the equipment required.

Traversing across the Nare, River Cave, New Britain. Photo: Rod Leach.

Steve Thornborrow worked at the logging camp and had actually by coincidence attended a public school in Buxton, Derbyshire. He had made a special request to descend the Nare shaft and to experience one of the wonders of the world and considering all the help we had received from the logging company staff could hardly refuse. A crash course in SRT techniques saw him at the bottom of the shaft along with Steph, Tim and I when we attempted our first river crossing on Wednesday 14th November.

Facing downstream the right-hand wall was a sheer cliff face but a bank of boulders could be seen on the far side of the river. A large boulder overhanging the river 100 metres inside the entrance porch offered the best chance of fixing a Tyrolean rope across the river with a waterfall just below.

I threw a grapnel iron across the river attached to a rope by swinging it in an arc to gain momentum and on the second attempt it caught behind some rocks and appeared firm. While Tim placed 8mm rock anchors in the large boulder I donned a buoyancy aid, grabbed hold of the rope and took a running jump into the river.

This technique we called the Trail Ferry and although potentially a dangerous manoeuvre is one of the best methods for crossing turbulent water which we had practised during our training sessions. Holding on to the end of the rope and life-lined from a point downstream, the force of the river pushes the swimmer pendulum-like to the far side where with luck he can grab hold of anything handy and drag himself onto dry land. If one gets into trouble the life liner can, again with luck and a great deal of strength, pull the swimmer back to shore, again utilising the force of the water as a pendulum which happened on this occasion. There of course needs to be a bank downstream to act as a recovery zone for the swimmer.

I became stranded in a standing wave and, bobbing up and down like a cork in a washing machine, was forced to release the rope or drown. I was swept towards the waterfall at great speed but Steph managed to pull me onto a nearby boulder, which I grabbed and managed to jump back to dry land.

Tim took up the challenge and wearing a couple of buoyancy aids and this time with two lifelines, one downstream and one up, took a flying jump and landed beyond the worst of the rapids. We held our breath as he was pushed across the river fast but the rocks on the far side were slippery and Tim failed to gain a hold but as he was swept downstream he managed to grab a protruding rock and scramble to comparative safety. We had learned our first lesson; this river was not going to be tamed without a fight.

Tim fixed more rock anchors on a boulder at the far side and we tensioned the rope using a series of clever tension knots, I crossed the 11 metre Tyrolean just four metres above the river while Steph and our visitor who was duly impressed started the long 240 metre climb out. The French had named the series of Tyroleans aptly after sunken ships and this one they called Poseidon.

We progressed along the left bank of the river to the next obstacle called Ledge Jo which was a ledge eight metres up and would require some climbing aids to reach. The French had attempted another river crossing at this point using a rubber dinghy but had lost it when it was swept away in the current never to be seen again, luckily there was no one in it at the time. We retreated after 12 hours feeling satisfied with the progress so far and without losing anyone. Climbing back out was painful and sweaty taking about one to one and a half hours of extreme effort.

We now realised what the French had said in their report about the noise of the river underground in the tunnel. Communication by shouting was impossible so we developed a system of hand signals, and flashing lights in order to indicate a basic means of instructions.

The following day our visitor Steve set off back to Gonaile and I managed to contact the rest of our team who at last had arrived at our Shore Base at the logging camp. Arrangements were made for Bill to fly Alan Gamble, Des Marshall and Steve Dickenson to Ire village with their personal equipment but the others would have to walk the 50 kilometres to our camp from Shore Base as the helicopter was vacating the area. The three arrived that day after an exciting flight over the Nare doline.

On Friday 16th November, Steph, Tim and I climbed up to Ledge Jo and fixed a traverse rope. Tim found a French climbing peg which had been hammered into the rock and a five metre abseil followed down to river level where a further six metre traverse led us to dry land. The left bank of the river could then be followed in this huge circular tunnel 30 to 40 metres in diameter with the thundering river flowing along rapids. The noise was amplified by the tunnel and resembled that of an express train. After fixing a few traverse ropes along the edge of the river we arrived after 200 metres at the next blank wall. The passage bent around to the right so the bank had run out on our left-hand wall but a large bank could be seen on the far side, this was the point of the second French crossing called Python. We retreated to the comparative silence of the jungle camp after about 13 hours of very exciting caving but once more having to sweat it out climbing the tedious 240 metres up to the surface.

It was nice to have a cool refreshing bath in the underground river but by the time we reached camp, we were once more stinking, dirty and very sweaty. We could not waste valuable water at camp by washing clothes and bodies so when it rained, we stripped off and had a shower.

The last of the equipment was dropped off by Bill before he left and 30 porters carried it to our camp while Des, Steve and Alan set off to attempt the Python river crossing carrying heavy bags of caving ropes and hardware. Alan donned two buoyancy aids and threw a grapnel iron across the river obtaining a firm anchor and successfully crossed using the same method, the

Trail Ferry Technique. He explored as far as the next obstacle, the Ledge Bosom so called because of its perfect breast shaped stalagmite handhold, complete with nipple. They returned after 13 hours. We now had 10 bags of equipment stashed at the far side of the Python Tyrolean.

That day. Tim and I went jungle bashing and Unaso showed us a large open shaft two kilometres south west of camp which he called Kille, after a little yellow bird that chirped away close by. This was considered as a good project for the future.

On Sunday 18th November, the remainder of the team arrived after a strenuous two day walk up the mountain. They had slept one night at Nutuve before setting off on the last leg. They set to work organising a kitchen, store, more sleeping accommodation, table and a toilet. Dave Sims constructed a clay oven so we could bake steak pies and bread mix, this was real luxury, hot bread in the middle of the jungle, problem was we did not have much of it and it disappeared in seconds. Dave Arveschoug started to produce some amazing meals by purchasing fresh vegetables from the Ire village ladies.

Captain John Salmon, our medic, started work on the bog. He dug a huge hole, covered it with solid branches with a hole for a toilet seat which someone had the foresight to stow in the container. For a little privacy, he constructed a small fence. Unfortunately, the toilet was constructed next to the path used by the Ire villagers on their daily visits to sell us fresh vegetables. so it was pleasant to say good morning and pass the time of day while sat on the throne. One day I had a nasty experience during one of the frequent earth tremors when the toilet structure began to shake violently. I had a premonition of an early death by drowning in deep shit. How the newspapers would have reported the accident back in England does not bear thinking about. 'Expedition leader drowns in poo in toilet collapse.' What an epitaph.

Before leaving the UK, we arranged a meeting with His Excellency the Papua New Guinea Ambassador to Great Britain. I asked him if there were items of our supplies we could not take into Papua New Guinea. His reply was just the usually things: guns, pornography and drugs. Our gun was the 50mm bazooka type air launcher, copies of Penthouse Magazines appeared at camp and as for drugs, well one of the team went diving and forgot to empty his pockets containing film canisters with no film inside. When he surfaced, he discovered that they were no longer there so spent hours searching the seabed without success, but there were an awful lot of very happy fish. Another member who shall remain nameless sweated in his shoes on going through Singapore customs with a large sign saying 'Penalty for drug trafficking is death.' When he arrived at Base Camp his shoe was emptied on the table, which was made of thin sticks, and whatever it was he had in his shoe fell through onto the muddy floor below. Being the same colour as the earth many days were spent searching in the mud below the table to no avail but again there appeared to be many very happy ants around.

Monday 19th November saw Des, Tim, Steve and I with a mountain of sacks full of equipment and a small camping gas stove and some food to keep us going. I also brought along my little 35 mm Rollei camera, some flash guns with bulbs to attempt a few photographs in these very wet and humid conditions. Des led off attached to a dynamic climbing rope along a steep calcite ledge gripping the bosom with delight and well above river level. but communication was still impossible. With flashing light signals he eventually indicated us to follow. Tim fixed a permanent traverse line and we ferried the equipment along the ledge clipping on the traverse line with karabiners. A climb up to a boulder pile followed and then a diagonal descent down to the river.

300 metres beyond, we hit the next obstacle; this was where the French had crossed the river for the third time which they had christened Andrea Doria. A blank wall presented itself but with a bank on the far side full of stalagmites. Our home-made grapnel irons had now disintegrated so we attempted to throw one of our specially made Wilkinson Sword irons across the river with the hope of hooking it behind the stalagmites, the problem was there was no room to swing the iron as we were situated right up against the wall of the tunnel. Many futile attempts only managed to get one iron stuck in mid river and it could not be recovered. We tied the rope off to keep it out of the way with the hope of retrieving it later. The other major problem was that the Trail Ferry Technique could not be used as there was no recovery zone for the lifelined swimmer. Two ropes were needed, both tensioned so one of us could climb commando style across using both ropes, a difficult and highly dangerous manoeuvre. This was a job for our heavy artillery, the GQ Defence Air Launcher, which could fire a grapnel iron using compressed air across the river. We retreated taking photographs and fixing a few more traverse lines along sections of the tunnel close to the white water just in case the river rose at times of rainy periods.

Because of the time and effort it took to climb out of the Nare shaft it was decided to bivouac down the cave, which would save many wasted hours as it took around three hours for six cavers to reach the surface from the base of the climb. It was important that we had communication with the surface, so Alan and Steph ran a telephone cable down from Base Camp to the bottom of the shaft as we had a few battery operated telephone sets.

It was also impossible to lower equipment down the shaft using the cave explorer's trade route because the first part was an 80 degree slope so Dave Sims constructed a hauling platform out of trees overhanging the shaft with a vertical drop of over 320 metres. Again. we had planned for this eventuality and had a single length of rope of 400 metres and a number of pulley blocks.

On Thursday 22nd November, Alan and I started construction of a bivouac camp in torrential rain at the base of the shaft digging out a flat area and with a polythene sheet cover, one of the strangest places on earth to camp. Tim, Des, Steve and Steph armed with the GQ Air Launcher returned to the Andrea Doria Crossing and successfully fired two Wilkinson Sword grapnel irons attached to ropes across the river using 600 psi of compressed air. The grapnel irons had to be fired from an aluminium tube with a plastic bung of 50mm, which slotted into the barrel of the gun. Dave Sims had constructed these, and we only had a few so it was important that we retrieved the tube to be used again so they were attached to the grapnel iron with a short piece of thin nylon cord. It was hoped the grapnels had lodged firmly at the back of the stalagmites and not the tube.

Both 10 mm static Beal ropes were tensioned and Tim crossed on one rope and clipped on to the second with his karabiner and was life-lined by the team just in case. He made it across and by luck had crossed on the rope attached to the grapnel iron jammed behind a stalagmite, the other one was jammed by the tube and the piece of string. The Tyrolean was fixed in place but was less than a metre above the rapids. Des attempted the crossing but is a heavy man and became entangled in the rope attached to the grapnel iron stuck in the middle of the river and became completely submerged. When crossing a Tyrolean we were always life-lined with a polypropylene floating rope just in case of problems. Gasping for air and spitting water, Des was pulled back to the bank by Steve and Steph. Steve braved the death trap next and succeeded in freeing the trapped grapnel stuck in mid-stream and reaching the far side safely.

Tim and Steve explored downstream passing huge cave formations to a traverse at river level where some French bolts were found hammered into the wall. Steve used these to rig a traverse rope and a short distance along they arrived at the next blank wall. This was the site of the fourth French river crossing which they had called Titanic. Here the roof was only four metres high and the noise of the river was completely deafening but it looked possible to fix traverse ropes at river level by wading in fast moving rapids along the left hand wall. If this could be achieved the fourth and fifth river crossings could be avoided. All four exited safely after a long hard trip to spend the night at the bivouac gazing up at the fireflies and stars from the bottom of the 300 metre deep shaft.

The next day saw Steph and Des organising the lowering of supplies from the hauling point with successful communication with the surface team via the installed telephone line. First, they had to cut a trail through the jungle at the base of the shaft and along a steep scree slope.

Meanwhile Steve, Tim, Alan and I returned to the next obstacle hoping to bypass the fourth and fifth French Tyroleans called the Titanic Crossing and Les Priapes. It looked possible, but the water was deep and moving fast. Tim led off held on a life-line that prevented him from being swept away and fixing runners for the rope. A couple of 8mm bolts were drilled in the wall and a few climbers' pitons used. After 100 metres Tim reached a bank of shingle, the other side of the fifth French Tyrolean. I followed, fixing a permanent rope in place. We had great fun clipped onto the rope and ferrying the bags along the traverse through huge rapids. We had succeeded in bypassing two Tyroleans so we called it The Dirty English Sneaky Bit.

Just 20 metres beyond we hit the next ridiculous looking obstacle which the French had called The Tuttering Hand. This looked impossible at first glance as it consisted of a virtually non-existent ledge only three metres above the largest standing wave we had seen so far. The passage here was much larger and turned to the east so it was impossible to see around the corner.

Alan led out attached to a rope and a locking device which would automatically lock holding him fast in the event of a fall. He found a French climber steel peg jammed into the rock which seemed very shattered and loose and after about eight metres, just as he approached the corner, a hold gave way and he plunged backwards into the standing wave only a few metres below him. The locking device held and as he bobbed up and down in the wave, we all pulled on the rope to no avail. The force of the water was akin to being hit by a bus and we were unable to pull him out of the river. Occasionally he surfaced above the wave and we could just hear him shouting above the appalling din of the river but had no idea what he was trying to communicate. Steve waded out as far as he dared and heard the word slack before Alan once more disappeared beneath the wave. I unlocked the device and gave him a slack rope and Alan was washed downstream to disappear from view. There was no light to be seen and no answer to our shouts but after what seemed an age a light appeared from around the corner. Alan by good fortune had been washed into a slack area of water and managed to pull himself ashore.

With Alan on the far side with the rope, we were able to rig the traverse with a couple of ropes attached to our 8mm anchors drilled firmly into the solid rock and after only 100 metres the next obstacle presented itself, which the French had called the Flying Dutchman. Alan returned back along the Tuttering Hand Traverse thankfully still alive and rolled an Old Holborn cigarette to calm his nerves as Gallaher International had kindly supplied me with a few kilograms of rolling tobacco. The Nare kept biting back and this had been the third close call.

A restless night was spent back at our bivouac camp at the bottom of the shaft but throughout the night we were bombarded by falling rocks. The kitchen was destroyed by an avalanche where Des was sleeping at the time and he found himself rolling down the slope towards the river. As everyone slept with earplugs due to the relentless noise of the river, it was sometime before we realised Des was in trouble. Luckily his injuries were not severe and that night we all slept wearing caving helmets.

The following day supplies were lowered down from the hauling platform and it was a pleasant surprise to receive letters delivered to us at the bottom of the shaft all the way from England. The mail from our wives, girlfriends, parents or children had been flown into a small landing strip near Gonaile and from there had been carried up the mountain to Nutuve by anyone who happened to be going that way. From Nutuve the letters had arrived via Ire village and Base Camp. The record was ten days from the UK to the bottom of the shaft, faster than many mail deliveries from London to Manchester.

We repaired our camp and rigged more polythene sheets to keep out the worst of the rain but as dusk fell another avalanche narrowly missed the camp. Des decided enough was enough and returned to the surface with shattered nerves.

I commented to Alan, 'We must be insane to be camping here with rocks falling all around.'

In typical Alan Gamble philosophical style, he replied, 'If we had the slightest intelligence we would not be here anyway.' He was as usual perfectly correct.

On Sunday 25th November, Steph and I decided that this camp was far too dangerous and had to be abandoned. We moved the camp across the first Poseidon Tyrolean 100 metres into the cave and extended the telephone cable; the noise was deafening but at least there were no avalanches to contend with.

Alan, Tim and Steve returned to the French Flying Dutchman crossing. A ledge could be seen high up at roof level on the far side of the river which the French had reached by following the left-hand wall to a climb up to a bridge of boulders spanning the river. By passing over the bridge the ledge could be reached 20 metres above the river and a long Tyrolean sloping at a steep angle down could be rigged. They followed the left-hand wall and rigged a traverse rope at river level, then climbed a 50 metre steep calcite covered slope to within 6 metres of the bridge but a smooth wall very exposed presented itself. They returned to our new Poseidon camp to consider the problem.

The following day, Tim, Alan and Steve returned to the surface for a well-earned rest while Steph and I mapped downstream as far as the second Tyrolean and climbed back to the surface later that night after an underground stay of five days. The surface party had been busy getting to grips with the exploration of Kille Cave and Ken Kelly had set off in his search for the resurgence of the Nare as it was unknown where the river re-emerged. Ken successfully located a small resurgence cave called Posongave 100 metres above the base off the Essis Gorge. Rod was back in Nutuve recovering from a badly cut hand but went cave hunting and found a nice dry cave called Tegelve which was mapped at a later date during the expedition by Tim, Camillus and I for 500 metres.

On Friday 30th November, it was decided for photographic purposes to rig the big drop which would give a 310 metre descent down the sheer side of the Nare shaft. This was rigged through the steep sided jungle by Tim. with Jim Hook directing from the other side of the shaft via Micman CB radios and prearranged signals so the correct position could be ascertained. Tim had a struggle with the bag containing a 360 metre length of specially made 10mm Beal caving rope but found a few good belays where he could tie the rope off to small trees. A 20 metre free hang led him to the edge of the shaft where a forked tree no more than 100 centimetres in diameter hung over the edge to give a completely 230 metre free hang down to the Nare river. The descent began a metre from the shattered rock wall but after 20 metres the wall receded further and further away to disappear into the roof of the downstream entrance porch. The small tree above with the rope attached resembled a fishing pole swaying up and down as Tim descended landing in the middle of the river. As the bag hanging beneath his feet was swept downstream Tim finished off walking on water just above the waves and Des managed to grab his leg and haul him on to dry land. The rope was tied off at the dry bank so others could follow without drowning in the river. This can only be described as a mind-blowing descent with magnificent views of the shaft, the up and downstream entrances with the white water river far below.

Des, Steve and John Salmon descended the trade route that day to spend the night at the Poseidon bivouac along with Ken Kelly and Alan. The following day the 1st December Alan took Ken on a tour as far as the Python crossing then Ken made his way back up the ropes to the surface while Alan went to the bottom of the hauling rope to collect three bags of supplies being lowered down. The bags landed on a steep bank of scree and as Alan attempted to retrieve the bags he slipped and fell all the way down to land in the river. He was quickly swept downstream but managed with a superhuman effort to reach a bank and haul himself out of the rapids; yet another near miss for the untamed river.

Tim joined Des, Steve and John and they set off to tackle the climb up to the rock bridge at the Flying Dutchman. Des led the climb and fixed a few runners as protection for his lifeline rope and a 10 metre climb reached the bridge. Tim followed and they traversed back across the rock bridge to the stalagmite covered ledge on the far side. Two ropes were fixed into place, one as a 30 metre long tight line and the other as a slack line as this Tyrolean was not horizontal but went steeply uphill from the left bank to the ledge high above. It was then possible to clip onto the tight line with a karabiner and prussic up the slack line so gradually moving in an uphill direction, a strenuous manoeuvre. The way back was a spectacular descent whipping through the air at speed 20 metres above the river.

The next day, the four were joined by Alan, Dave Sims and I but torrential rain turned the river into a thunderous mass of muddy foaming water and the river rose at least 50 centimetres over its entire width estimated at 5 tons of extra water flowing every second.

Steph decided enough was enough and decided that the Nare was not for him so he did not descend with us. This was a sad decision to make considering the enormous amount of work he had contributed towards getting us to this point but he felt very uneasy traversing this dangerous river and did not fancy a watery grave so it was completely understandable.

By Monday 3rd December, the river had returned to its normal ferocious self so Des, Tim and Alan set off to explore beyond the Flying Dutchman. Steve was nursing a badly cut hand and stayed at the bivouac while John, Dave and I began mapping the base of the shaft in order to find its exact dimensions and moving supplies to our Poseidon bivouac. Due to the storm the phones were once more out of action so communication with the surface was lost. The rest of the day was spent taking photographs and mapping downstream and by 9 pm, we met up with Des, Alan and Tim returning from a successful trip beyond the furthest point reached. They had de-rigged the climb up to the bridge and had continued along the ledge at roof level to a 10 metre roped descent back down to river level. An easy free climb followed up to a ledge 10 metres above the river which eventually petered out at a blank wall. Retracing their steps they climbed diagonally up for a further 20 metres where they fixed a rope for aid and followed a 50 metre ledge again fixed with ropes for protection against a fall. The ledge petered out to nothing so another abseil was installed down to a sloping calcite covered ledge just a few metres above the river. This ledge had many small stream inlets and had been named aptly by the French, The Howling Ledges. This sloping ledge eventually ran out so a descent was made to river level where another traverse along the edge of the river arrived at a small respite, a bank of shingle. Slack but deep water followed beyond the bank to where the holds gave out completely. The only route forward seemed to be up and a free-climb reached yet another ledge where more rope was fixed into place as protection. The cave was eating up rope fast but before long the ledge led the explorers to a large bank of rubble, the site of the seventh French Tyrolean river crossing named after another sunken ship, The Torrey Canyon.

They decided to follow the bank until the end to see if it was possible to bypass the seventh and eighth river crossings. Sure enough by wading out into the fast moving current a string of boulders could be reached and by boulder hopping for about five metres another ledge was spotted. By following this for 80 metres the three arrived at a large bank in a 50 metre diameter passage and Apocalypse Now, the final point reached by the French expedition. The river was over 20 metres wide at this point with monstrous looking rapids descending down steeply but with a large bank at the far side looming off into darkness. The seventh and eighth Tyrolean's had once more been bypassed so we called it Tim's Ledge.

The next day was a rest day for Tim, Des and Alan while Dave Sims, John and I spent our time taking photographs until all the flash guns ceased to function due to the continually wet conditions.

Wednesday 5th December dawned, the culmination of years of hard work, meticulous planning, huge personal expense and a great deal of good luck but the day did not get off to a good start. Des, Tim and Alan insisted on rushing off ahead to attempt a crossing of Apocalypse Now while the rest of the team followed on behind with supplies and equipment acting the role of porters. I could see no reason why all could not act as a team without egotistical behaviour from a few. A heated argument followed finally resolved when John and Dave gallantly offered to return to the surface to fix the telephone communications from Base Camp to Poseidon Bivouac and, a little disappointed, I consented.

Alan, Steve, Des, Tim and I set off for Apocalypse Now at 11.30 am armed with ropes, food supplies and our heavy artillery, the GQ Defence Air Launcher complete with grapnel irons and compressed air bottle. All crossed the crazy looking Flying Dutchman hanging way above the river and ferried many heavy bags of equipment across the Tyrolean. Tim and Alan picked up a few bags and went ahead while the rest of the team struggled forward. The Howling Ledges were howling and Steve who was carrying the Air Launcher lost his grip with his still painful hand and began to fall backwards towards a watery grave but somehow managed to grab a rock with the other hand and hang on eventually obtaining a grip on the slippery rock.

We trod forth with great care to arrive at the end point. We scanned the far bank with high powered Survival Aids Techna battery lights. There appeared to be three options, the first was to attempt a very dangerous stepping stone crossing which would entail jumping from boulder to boulder but the separation in the centre part of the river was more than three metres from one rock to the next. It would be impossible to retrieve a man if he did not make it to the next rock even if attached to a line. The second was to fire a grapnel iron across the 20 metre wide river which had worked well at the Andrea Doria crossing. The third option was chosen as it looked the simplest. Upstream was a narrow section of the river which with the huge amount of water resembled a water turbine but a sloping bank of solid looking rock could be seen on the far side about two metres away. It looked possible to carefully follow the river keeping close to the left-hand wall in order to reach the bank on the far side of Apocalypse Now.

Tim on a life-line took a running jump and a flying leap of faith downhill and successfully made it to the other side where he managed to cling on to the wall before he was swept away. We fixed a rope across and Alan followed traversing in deep fast-moving water by clinging hold of small rock projections to gain the large bank of scree and boulders at the far side of Apocalypse Now. The two explored new ground in a massive passage descending steeply to where the roof lowered to only two metres above the river and five metres in width. The noise and very fast-moving white water was horrendous but a small ledge could be seen along the left hand wall across rough water where the passage appeared to bend to the left. They returned and Alan traversed back to the crossing point just in time to prevent us from crossing. A rope was slung across the rapids back at Apocalypse

Now and a 23 metre long Tyrolean fixed in place. Although low in the water so everyone received a thorough soaking, we all assembled on the far side to tackle the next obstacle. As the English do in these circumstances, we put the kettle on a stove we had brought along for a brew and to collect our thoughts.

Tim once more volunteered and braved the white water by traversing along the left-hand wall on a life line. Occasionally he vanished beneath waves but fixed a line to the ledge so we all could follow. Although only a tiny ledge, we could walk along for 20 metres without too much trouble but the ledge was half submerged as the rapids lapped the edges. Communication was almost impossible due to the violence of the rapids. Here the passage reduced in size to only one metre high by two metres across with the waves continually hitting the roof of the passage. There was no way any man could pass beyond this point and survive. Even with our powerful electric lights we could see little beyond due to spray, waves and mist. Flood debris had been noticed 20 metres above river level near the Tyrolean indicating backing up of the river so it appears a flooded small section of passage lies beyond.

As I mapped back from the furthest point reached, the end of the tape fell into the river and the fibron measuring tape whipped off the reel at great speed cutting into my hand as the tape was pulled like a huge caught fish downstream. Reeling it back was akin to landing a shark the force of the river was that powerful.

There is no caving terminology to describe this place as no one had seen anything like it previously, so we called it Armageddon.

Steve and I surveyed back to our start point and we retreated disappointed but at the same time elated that we had reached the end, or as far as man can go without committing suicide, in what must be the world's most technically difficult cave to explore, probably the most dangerous and without doubt the most spectacular and exciting cave on planet earth.

By Thursday 6th December, after a gruelling six days underground, we were all back on the surface to the luxury of Base Camp in order to make preparations for the mammoth task of photography and de-tackling of the cave. Unlike the Himalayan peaks I was determined to leave this world wonder in the pristine condition that I had found it and make sure all equipment and rubbish was removed even though it was doubtful if anyone would ever return.

During the next few days, reconnaissance trips were undertaken looking for other caves which we could explore after Christmas. The surface team had been busy with the exploration of Kille Cave, which had been found by Tim and myself on 17th November. this open shaft being situated only 1.8

kilometres to the west of our Base Camp. Under the guidance of Dave Arveschoug along with Dave Sims, Jim Hook and John Salmon they rigged ten roomy water worn pitches down to a nice stream passage to a sump at a depth of 260 metres. The stream seemed to be heading towards the French explored passage in the upstream Nare, The Monogoue Affluent. Upstream was also flooded to the roof but contained some interesting blind white coloured crabs. The cave was mapped by Steph and I during our stay at Base Camp but flooding during periods of rain proved to be a problem. Steph and Dave found themselves trapped by flood water for two hours on the entrance pitches.

Over the next few days, John, Rod, Steve and I had to de-rig the cave as we needed all the ropes for our next exploration; two cave entrances which the four of us had found during our reconnaissance of the area. We had been guided by the headman of Ire village Unaso who pointed out the entrances to Gouvi Cave 700 metres northwest of Kille Cave and Pavie Cave situated two kilometres further to the northwest. Both looked very promising for finding the underground upper Nare River. The four of us had started exploration in Gouvi and had rigged the first pitch of 10 metres but had no more rope for the next pitch of 27 metres.

During this period, Alan, Steph and Dave Arveschoug spent a few pleasant days in the sun at Nutuve recuperating while Des, Tim, Dave Sims, Jim Hook and Camillus set off on a four-day trek to locate the Ora doline. This had been investigated during an Australian expedition in 1972 to 1973 but they had turned back at a whitewater river of about five cubic metres a second with no banks just sheer walls. The underground river was situated at the base of a 200 metre deep double doline. which could be descended via a steep slope on the north side without the need for ropes.

A ten-hour trek to the north along a well-worn track arrived at the remote and tiny village of Ora at the headwaters of the Iso River. The village seemed deserted, so they bivouacked out in the open for the night. Des and Dave Sims set off back to Base Camp the following day after reaching the Ora resurgence. The Ora River issued from a ten metre diameter cave opening and poured down the cliff for 60 metres as a beautiful waterfall but the entrance could not be reached without a serious climb using ropes.

Tim, Jim and Camillus climbed the mountain up to the plateau where they hacked a route through the jungle on a compass bearing and after 3 hours found the doline. A steep climb down arrived at the river and the upstream porch led to a short climb but reached a sump after a short distance. Downstream they were able to cross the river twice in low water conditions to the Australian end point by boulder hopping but could go no further without ropes and caving hardware. Retreating they descended back to some gardens where they spent the night in a small hut attempting to cut through the forest on a compass bearing back to camp the following day. This area of polygonal karst hills is all up and down with numerous blind valleys and after 11 hours they had failed to find the track so bivouacked for the night next to a small cave. The following morning they headed towards the Iso Gorge and found the track arriving back at camp after five days.

By 12th December all the preparations had been made for a prolonged stay at Poseidon Bivouac in order to de-rig the cave of all the caving equipment and ropes. Rod had serviced and dried out flash guns as it was essential we obtained some good photographs for the Sunday Express Colour Supplement Magazine in order to obtain our final payment which would hopefully pay off the bank overdraft.

John, Alan, Steve and Dave Arveschoug undertook a photographic and de-rigging trip to Armageddon but again they were reduced to one flash gun as the rest soon ceased to function due to the incredibly damp conditions. The Tyrolean across Apocalypse Now was de-rigged but this left Alan effectively stranded on the far side so he traversed back to the original crossing point, the turbine and life-lined by all three team members on three ropes made the dangerous jump back up hill and made it without mishap. They completed the de-tackling of the fixed ropes as far back as The Howling Ledges and returned to the bivouac at Camp Poseidon.

I surveyed the trade route down the shaft then joined Des to move all surplus equipment to the hauling rope ready for hauling up back to the surface. Unfortunately, Des decided at this point to leave for home and make his way back to Buxton as his financial situation was dire. I felt he was deserting the field before we had completed the de-rigging but could understand his predicament.

The following day, Rod joined us to start photographing but his box of tricks packed in a steel ammunition box parted company with the hauling rope and fell 1,000 feet to the bottom of the shaft destroying the box and the majority of its contents. We spent all day taking photographs with what equipment which still functioned and transporting more equipment to the base of the hauling rope.

Tim joined us on Sunday 15th December and set off with Alan and Steve to be joined later by John and me. We de-rigged the Flying Dutchman and took more photographs carrying all the bags of ropes and tackle back to Camp Poseidon. The following day, Dave Arveschoug returned to the surface and Jim Hook took his place to help with the work while Alan, Steve and I de rigged and photographed as far back as Ledge Bosom. Rod, Tim and John met up with us and we de-rigged to Ledge Jo. We now had masses of bags of equipment at camp which was going to be a hard back-breaking job for the surface hauling party.

On the 17th December, 14 more bags were hauled up to the surface but the pulley blocks they were using for the rope to run through were made for yachting and they had already melted three.

We finished taking the ropes off Ledge Jo while John, Rod and Jim returned to the surface to help with hauling up the last of the equipment. Steve, Tim, Alan and I spent our last night at Camp Poseidon and the next day, Tuesday 18th December, a dawn start saw Alan and Steve setting off back to the surface after transporting more bags to the hauling rope which was now showing some wear. Tim and I dismantled our bivouac camp, removed the telephone cable and de rigged the last Poseidon Tyrolean transporting the last of the bags, which now amounted to 33 to be hauled up the shaft. Tim and I had to stay below to attach the bags for hauling but by lunchtime Dave Sims communicated by phone that there was no way they could complete the work as most of the pulleys were now destroyed and the team was suffering from complete exhaustion. As Tim and I had no food or camping gear, I persuaded Dave that it was a case of all hands to the pumps as I wanted to leave the cave as I found it in pristine condition. By 3 pm, they had succeeded in a super human effort to haul all 33 bags to the surface so Tim and I said our goodbyes and thank you for not killing anyone to the Nare and began de-rigging the ropes and telephone cable.

We left the Nare as we had found her, except the Untamed River had been tamed, but not without a hard fight and four near fatalities.

The following day the hauling platform was dismantled while Dave Sims and Dave Arveschoug set off for the long walk back to Gonaile Logging Camp where we intended to spend Christmas and New Year before returning to continue exploration in other caves. Steph, John, Alan and I de-rigged the big drop after I descended, while Alan snapped a few reels of film off. After the de-rigging, we all returned back to camp except Alan who seemed to have disappeared. We searched around the shaft hoping he had just become disorientated and not fallen down the shaft but by dark there was no sign of Alan. We spent a worried night and at first light began once more to search for our lost friend. Unaso, the head man, joined us and thankfully found Alan who had lost the ill-defined track back to camp and had spent an uncomfortable night, hungry, thirsty and alone, lost in the jungle.

We employed Tume, another senior Ire village man to guard our camp and set off with 28 porters on Thursday 20th December for Nutuve where we hired a small hut to store food and equipment for the intended work in the New Year. The next day, along with 14 porters, we walked the long trail back to the tropical paradise of Gonaile Logging Camp where our friend Steve Thornborrow allowed us the use of a spare room in his house by the beach where we spent a great relaxing Christmas and New Year.

Steph decided to go back home, and I saw him off on a light aircraft that landed at a small grass runway near Pomio on the coast. I was sorry to see him leave as I considered the conquest of the Nare as a team effort and not the just the efforts of a few at the sharp end of exploration. Even though he did not reach the end, his contribution had been immense and indispensable and our success was his to share.

I was disappointed when Jim, Alan, Dave Sims, Dave Arveschoug and Ken decided that they did not fancy the rigours of the jungle once more and headed off back to the UK. I handed over the expedition reels of film to Alan to send off to the Sunday Express who would process the films and choose what they wanted to publish. On publication, the second payment would go into our bank account, hopefully paying off the overdraft and leaving enough spare funds to duplicate photographs for our sponsors.

This left only five of us to continue with the work for the next three months, but it was a good team of the highly dependable Steve Dickinson; the indomitable Tim Allen; the ultra-keen Rod Leach and of course our highly skilled Doctor John Salmon.

We spent the next few days packing and weighing supplies to last us three months which weighed in at 350 kilograms but all flights into Nutuve had once more been suspended due to the pigs digging up the grass runway. I managed to hire a Jet Ranger helicopter from Island Helicopter Services for £200, which was cheaper than hiring porters.

We set off for Nutuve with our supplies, meeting Camillus we hiked to Ire village and hired porters to carry our supplies to Base Camp. Tim, Rod and Steve flew in the hired chopper searching for the Nare resurgence but flew along the wrong river. On the way back, they spotted a huge doline with a 50 metre high entrance, noted for a future date. We settled back into our by now half empty Base Camp. Tim spent many happy hours devising methods to kill the jungle rats as they had now invaded the camp raiding our food supplies. The blue plastic drums with sealable lids proved indispensable.

We began the exploration of Bogalavi-Gouvi cave which had been found in December, but lack of rope had prevented further work.

The major danger facing us was that the cave completely flooded to the roof during heavy rain which was often. Great care was taken to monitor the weather. The pitches were rigged leading to a clean washed flood prone stream passage with four short drops. A fine series of pitches followed of 14 and 35 metres in depth to a streamway with a small stream inlet and two downstream sumps. The cave measured 1.2 kilometres in length and was 172 metres deep. As with Kille Cave, the downstream sumps lined up with the inlet passages of the Nare.

Approximately two kilometres northwest of our Base Camp, a canyon in the dense jungle had been found intersected by a 50 metre diameter doline. This was investigated on January 12th, and a short climb down into the canyon led to a series of pitches. After a Sin-Sing at Ire village when many pigs were slaughtered and many given away to a nearby village, we rigged the pitches to a large passage. Short climbs down and a 14 metre pitch arrived at what is known as a marmite. This is a huge hole in the floor formed by swirling water. It was possible to free-climb down and up the far side. Just beyond a deep rumbling noise could be heard. A 23 metre pitch led down into a massive river in a passage 15 metres in diameter. We had defiantly found the main upstream Nare River.

Upstream was sumped after 50 metres but downstream led through deep fast flowing water where we attached a traverse line for safety. A short Tyrolean was fixed from one rock in the river to another and on the following day two further river crossing were tackled by giant leaps from one boulder to another while life-lined. A broad ledge was then followed where the river narrowed to 10 metres and 30 metres high. Yet another river crossing presented itself with 500 metres of huge river passage now mapped and no end in sight.

Trying to find the way back to Base Camp at night was almost impossible so it was decided to set up a bivouac camp in the canyon. On the 19th January, John and Rod built a cosy camp relatively sheltered from the rain. Tim, Dicky and I set off to rig the fifth river crossing. We made good progress and reaching the fifth crossing, a stalagmite was lassoed on the far bank and a Tyrolean fixed into place. We named it Commando Crossing. An exposed traverse above a giant wave followed, which was rigged with fixed ropes to a 10 metre waterfall.

A short abseil down led us to a tiny ledge where a wide step over a chasm with the massive foaming river below gained a huge stone block. This had detached itself from the roof and divided the river into two narrow channels. A rope climb up the stone block gained the right hand channel where a bold step across the flow led to a delicate climb. By traversing to the right along a very tiny ledge situated just above the very turbulent combined river flow we fixed a traverse rope. The seventh river crossing now presented itself where a large scree bank could be seen 15 metres away on the other side of the fast moving deep water river. Crossing was going to be a problem as there was nowhere on the far bank where a grapnel iron could catch so the trail ferry technique could not be used as there was no recovery zone for the swimmer. The decision was that with the aid of a rubber dingy it might be possible to float a man across downstream attached to a line. Only 78 metres had been made that day with ropes fixed all the way. This was a serious cave to explore.

On Sunday 20th January, Tim and John set off back to Base Camp to bring in the navy, on the way John had a nasty accident in the jungle with a badly cut hand. Being a doctor, he stitched it himself. The remaining three surveyed the main river passage back to the 23 metre pitch and the entrance passages were also surveyed by Rod and me the day after. We returned to the relative civilisation of Base Camp but not for long as we now had the RFD inflatable dingy.

Crossing the river was fun once more as we pushed Tim out in the dingy on a life-line. He managed to reach the far side with some difficulty and fixed a rope diagonally across the river. The dingy was attached to a fixed line so it was possible to return by hauling on the line. That day we crossed the river a total of thirteen times mainly by massive leaps from one half submerged boulder to another. Life-lines were used for safety as slipping into the river was not an option. Many wall traverses through the deep ranging torrent reached the inevitable sump after two kilometres of magnificent huge river cave. We were back on the surface by 3 am the following day but there was still much to do.

Rod had to leave to get back to the UK, so the team was now down to four men. Over the next week surveying and photography proved to be epic. On one trip the river turned a murky brown colour and increased in ferocity. On returning to the surface 14 hours later our bivouac camp had been washed away with much of it floating in a lake at the base of the entrance doline. It was obvious that the entrance series of passages had flooded to the roof. Luckily, we were in the main river tunnel at the time and the increase in water flow did not make too much difference with regard to safety. Back on the surface, Dicky was in great pain after breaking a rib on one of the crazy jumps crossing the river.

We completely de-rigged the cave leaving nothing behind and our bivouac camp packed and moved back to Base Camp. Pavie must be regarded as one of the most ferocious and magnificent river caves on the planet but the interesting point of being a cave explorer is that it has only ever been seen by five men. It will probably stay that way as these caves are truly remote. In a way I find this sad, as this wonderful underground spectacle will remain hidden. This can only be regarded as exploration in the truest sense.

Over the next few days base camp was dismantled and all equipment and remaining food supplies ported to Nutuve where we had the use of a small hut.

We succeeded in finding and mapping a few more small caves in the vicinity. One, called Poson Gave, we found after a very steep and difficult climb down into the Iso Gorge using small trees as handholds. This led through a small passage to a river that sumped immediately up and down stream. Following the surface valley, led to a massive resurgence flowing from boulders into the Iso River. We thought that this could be the resurgence for the Nare but it appeared to be in the wrong place, much too far to the north.

Attempts to explore the Iso Gorge to find the probable resurgence to the south failed. Three hundred metre descents would be required into the gorge with little probability of exploring the white water rapids up or down stream.

While at our Nutuve Base, the French team had arrived on their long walk back to the coast and John spent some time stitching up injuries.

We had some food supplies left which although limited would last the four of us a few more months. The next major objective was the 50 metre wide entrance spotted from the helicopter to the north. We sent Camillus off to try to locate the entrance. After visiting a few villages, he succeeded and his description tallied with what was observed from the helicopter.

Dicky and Tim set off on 12th February with caving equipment and food for around seven days. A 'House Wind' was constructed of sticks and leaves in a torrential downpour and the exploration began. Two normally dry valleys converged to the entrance, 80 metres high and 25 metres wide. Only 30 metres into the porch the floor gave way to an immense shaft 40 metres in diameter and 100 metres in depth. Thirteen re-belays of the rope was required in order to keep some distance away from any flood water. The huge numbers of flying fox bats announced their displeasure about the disturbance and massive spiders lurked on the ledges. The crashing of the afternoon flood pulse was disturbing when they finally reached the boulder strewn floor. The way on was wide open but they returned to the grass hut before being washed away.

The following day, after an early start, another pitch of 27 metres was descended which arrived at a river of two cubic metres per second emerging from a small horizontal crack. After 150 metres the river passage reached another descent. Aqua Bat pitch was passed via a traverse along pure white calcite flowstone and an abseil down to a deep water plunge pool. Six hundred metres of passage was followed with numerous flowstone gour pool cascades to a formidable obstacle, Edge of the World Cascade. On the way out at the entrance porch a large passage could be seen high up the vertical wall. This could be an upstream continuation of the cave but attempts to reach it failed.

John joined the team and the Edge of the World was tackled by bolting the wall with anchors and lassoing a stalagmite to avoid the mass of water falling down the pitch. Cascades followed to a lowering of the roof in deep water. By swimming a head size opening, The Green Eye, could be negotiated to a thunderous plunge pool. The river cascaded over a dam to fall into a four metre deep hole, The Kraken. With water pouring down on all sides of the hole attempts to go further following the right-hand wall failed as the force of water pinned the explorer to the side wall. The left side was only a little easier but calmer water allowed The Kraken to be passed to dry land. Many violent cascades followed with beautiful glistening cave formations. On a later trip, when I joined the trio, I was swallowed by the force of water at the base of one of the cascades, which after a while spat me out at the far end.

The 'Duk Duk Ducks' followed with a low roof and the river flowing over calcite dams. The passage continued and was full of beautiful pure white calcite formations. Gradually the character of the passage changed with much breakdown probably due to the roof and walls collapsing, probably the effect of the numerous earthquakes. Passing a few inlets which were explored and mapped later, the flow of water had increased and was now over five cubic metres a second. Deep water was encountered and the passage was immense being 60 metres high and 45 metres wide. Over the final 300 metres, the roof lowered to the inevitable sump.

Over the next week the survey and photography was completed, the cave de-rigged of all the ropes and the House Wind on the surface vacated. The cave was mapped for six kilometres in length and reaching 478 metres in depth. Gamvo Cave can only be described as a classic Nakanai Mountains cave system with superb cave formations and river cascades, a beauty beyond words explored by a very small light weight team. As with the Nare, Pavia and Gamvo, who will ever see these caves again?

Gamvo Cave, New Britain. Photo Steve Dickinson.

    The rainy season was approaching fast, and food supplies were now very limited so the decision was made to head off home. I had the job of packing and transporting all our equipment to Shore Base so managed to flag down a passing helicopter. Alan Rohl, the pilot of Pacific Helicopters, had been hired by the French and he agreed for a price to transport our packed equipment to our Shore Base. I set off with him and we unloaded our equipment, but bad weather set in and Alan did not fancy his chances flying me back to Nutuve. He dropped me off at the French Shore Base at Pomio dressed in my shorts and sandals. I stayed there the night and Jean-Paul Sounier kindly gave me a tee-shirt and a pair of socks. The long 35 kilometre walk back to Nutuve was fun, all up hill. The heavenly part was to have a drink of water at the Kiane River.

    While Tim, Dicky and John were finishing off the photography and surveying of Gamvo, I had the job of hiring the last group of 16 porters from Nutuve. We set off walking back to Shore Base but on reaching the logging road I was amazed to find no trucks as they are usually travelling all day up and down the road. The porters refused to carry their loads a further 25 kilometres down the logging road to the shore. so I had no alternative but to set off alone on the long very hot trek to the coast. On arriving many hours later, I managed with great difficulty to obtain a truck and pick up the porters and equipment. The logging camp boss was not happy with the arrangement as the logging quota had been reached and all work stopped.

Three days later, the remaining three team members arrived back at the shore and we eventually hired a small very rocky boat for two days to take us and our equipment back to Rabaul. Getting our equipment back to the UK was fraught with many problems but we managed it eventually. John went home but Tim, Dicky and I flew to Hoskins and hired a helicopter to search the Whiteman Range of the mountains in the search for large collapsed dolines seen from aerial photographs. We succeeded but although huge and at least 200 metres deep, no caves or rivers could be seen at the base of these immense holes in the jungle.

Tim went home but Dicky and I had managed to obtain a free room in the house of a New Zealander but late one night around midnight he threw us out. We never found out why. A very kind local man gave us a room in his little wooden house when he saw us sleeping on the beach. A few days later the two of us sailed off in an old boat with a hundred others sleeping on the deck to Lai on the mainland of Papua New Guinea. There we borrowed a truck to deliver to Mount Hagen where we intended to search for Black Holes in the jungle but unfortunately ran out of money. We managed to get a free lift on a little plane and flew to Port Moresby. I set off back to the UK with reluctance as Dicky had appendicitis and finished up in hospital.

On the way back via the Philippians with a Polish caver who was a member of the French expedition, we walked along the road passing many bars with half-naked dancing ladies. A procession came along the road with a man dragging a huge cross on his shoulder. They were going to crucify him. Crazy said my Polish friend, absolutely crazy country.

There were many problems on reaching home not the least was paying back the bank loan. Some of the team members on returning gave news stories to the press and radio channels for free, which should not have happened until the completion of the expedition. I spent many months on a full-time basis sending letters of thank you and photographs to our sponsors.

I also finished up with malaria which curtailed my activities for a few weeks. I was certain it was malaria due to the recurring high temperatures then the following day I felt fine until around 3 pm when it started again. We had a new young doctor in town, so I told him I had malaria which he found hard to believe until I told him where I had been. He sent me off to hospital with a note to check my blood for malaria. They had a good laugh about this new doctor diagnosing malaria in Chapel en le Frith. They had a surprise when it turned out positive. His reputation went through the roof and from then on when I called for my immunisations, he always asked me to bring him back some exotic disease from the next strange country where I would be exploring caves.

This expedition had been the experience of a lifetime. The star was without doubt Tim Allen who went on to become a leader of expeditions in his own right and one of Britain's most respected cave explorers.

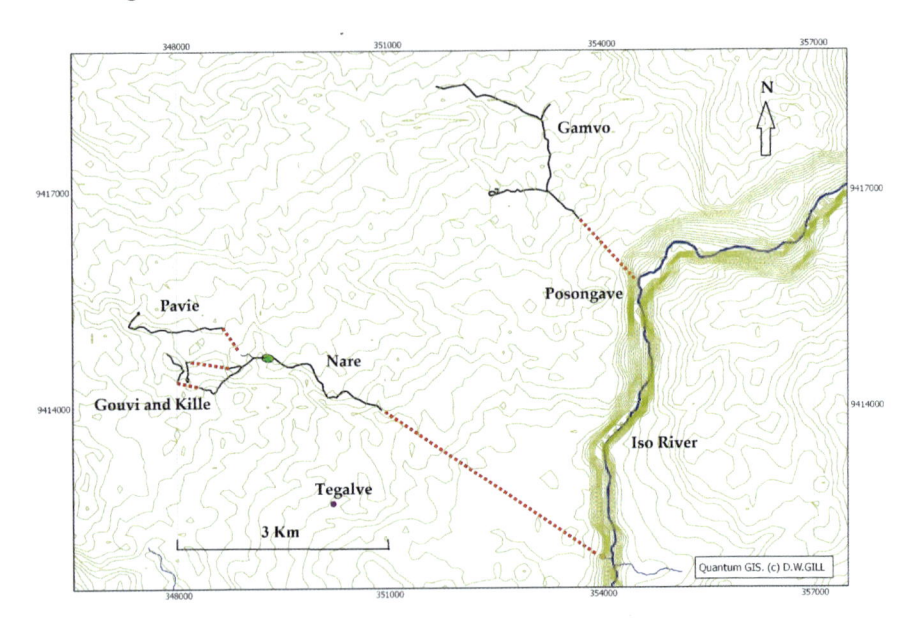

The Nare, Pavie and Gamvo cave Systems, Iso River, Nakanai, New Britain.

16

Tulakan Karst, Java. British Combined Forces Expedition, 1986

Life consists not in holding good cards, but in playing those you hold well.'

Josh Billings

My eldest son Mark was not happy at home with his mother and stepfather and wanted to live with me. This was difficult as I explained to him that I spent long periods abroad on expeditions. He was an independent lad and at the age of 13 could cook, wash and iron his own cloths and had his own interests in the Army Cadets. His mother agreed and I obtained custody. He moved in with me and looked after my house when I went on my regular excursions to foreign lands; it was nice to have one of my sons back home.

I had a succession of female friends but fell for a nice lady called Maggie. She worked as a teacher of children with severe special needs and as a teacher enjoyed the standard school holidays. She moved in and we were together for about five years.

I had written a chapter on transportation for expeditions for the conference on Expedition Planning held at the Royal Geographical Society, London. There I met Ian James, the secretary of the Army Caving Association, who was planning an expedition to Java, Indonesia. He asked me along as a cave surveyor along with a few other non-military persons. Paul Seddon, Graham Tutton and I jumped at the chance. A previous British Expedition had found many river caves in the Gunung Sewu karst area and Ian had an area lined up for investigation around the Tulakan karst on the south coast near a small town called Pacitan.

Maggie had never been to South East Asia and wanted to come. When asked by her fellow teachers where she was going for her holidays ,she replied 'The south coast.'

'Oh, are you going to Brighton?'

'No, Java.'

Her friends thought she was mad going with me on some crazy adventure to the other side of the world as most of my exploits had been reported in the local press and the general feeling was that I was something of an oddity.

We travelled out at the end of July via Singapore where we spent a few days, then finished up on the beautiful island of Tioman in Malaysia where the famous film South Pacific was made. Back in Singapore, we caught a flight to Jakarta and after a few days managed with some difficulty to get a train to Yogyakarta, which is a fascinating city where we spent a few days. A 40 minute bus ride took us to a beach at Parangtritis where, strolling along, we met up with an old man who claimed that he was a witch doctor and lived in a nearby sea cave. He could speak a little English and invited us into his cave where he demonstrated his strange rituals explaining that he had lived in this cave for 20 years, waiting to marry the lady of the sea, the legendary Goddess of the South China Sea, Queen Lara Kidul. We reckoned he would have a very long wait.

We also managed to visit the famous 9th century ruined Hindu Temple of Prambanan, the largest Hindu Temple in Indonesia. This is a UNESCO World Heritage site and at that time was undergoing a careful restoration project that had been going on since 1937. Much of the site had been rebuilt but a jigsaw puzzle of thousands of numbered stone blocks still lay scattered around the site.

We caught a bus to Pacitan via Wonogari and Butu, hoping to meet the rest of the team at the Bali Queen Hotel. The Pacitan Regency covers a huge area of 1,342 square kilometres, a large area to search for caves. Whenever anyone on the bus asked us where we were going, and we said Pacitan, they all started laughing; I think there was a lunatic asylum close by.

There was some delay as to carry out research in Indonesia a permit is required, and the exploration of caves is classified as research. This permit is a nightmare to obtain as numerous people need to be consulted, and occasionally bribed, before the right person is reached at the top of the tree. The permit had not come through so Paul Seddon had been sent back to Jakarta to sort the problem out. Ian had also arranged for a few Indonesian cavers to join us on the expedition. This would help with translations and talking to the villagers on the whereabouts of cave entrances. On an expedition of this nature local knowledge is essential as the villagers would know where the caves are located and just as importantly a foreign expedition needs to promote good community relations.

Maggie and I spent a nice day on the beach watching the baby turtles making their way towards the sea and trying to persuade the locals not to catch them. The local police officer wanted to know what we were doing in his small town where tourists never came and asked if I smoked dope as I was wearing a Hash House Harriers tee shirt.

In areas of karst, water supplies are a huge problem as the water sinks through fissures in the limestone and in many cases can be found underground in the caves. A villager may need to walk for many kilometres to obtain water from the closest stream when directly below the village is a cave with a flowing stream within. Shafts in the hills sometimes intersect these cave passages and it is then possible to install water pumps in the cave to pump the water to the surface. One of the objectives was to map the underground streams, which would help in the search for water supplies.

This kind of limestone terrain was known then as Cone Karst as the hills were conical in shape, rounded, with dolines and closed valleys between the hills rather like an egg box. The Chinese term of Fengcong Karst which can be translated as Peak Cluster is generally used today by geologists.

The team had already explored and surveyed a number of caves before Maggie and I arrived but none more than one kilometre in length so Ian decided we should concentrate our efforts around the Tulakan District, lying 52 kilometres from Pacitan. Ian had arranged for a couple of minibuses so the team could split up into various groups.

Paul Seddon had been busy teaching the children Yorkshire dialect, so everywhere we went we would hear the children shouting after us through the trees and across the rice fields, 'Ow art thee lad?'

'Rite as a bobbin,' we always replied in the same vein.

The first group descended a series of shafts, but all were blocked by boulders with no way on. The second group found a nice stream cave and mapped it for one kilometre in an upstream direction but unfortunately terminated in a boulder choke with no way through into the presumed passage beyond.

Maggie, Graham and I walked a short distance away and discovered another stream emerging from a low wet crawl. We hit a choke of boulders but a small passage on the right led to a totally different stream passage. Upstream terminated at another daylight entrance but downstream was explored for 800 metres to another entrance. A group of villagers were busy washing their cloths in the stream and informed us that another cave entrance, a *surapan*, which is their name for a stream sink, could be found one kilometre downstream. We followed the now soapy stream for well over one kilometre avoiding a huge snake but failed to find another entrance so retraced our steps to start the mapping of the cave we had just exited from.

The following day we completed the main survey of this fine two kilometre long stream cave which turned out to have five separate entrances. A number of small stream inlets and an extensive side passage was also explored and mapped where we found a shaft going up to daylight, a possible site for a water pump for the village above.

The following day, another stream cave was explored and mapped similar to the first, and many shafts descended. Most petered out in collapsed areas at little more than 130 metres in depth and some had bad air, a build-up of carbon dioxide. This became apparent when our carbide light flames faded to nothing and we surfaced breathless and with headaches. One nice shaft I descended led to a constriction, but I refused to go further as the continuation was guarded by a large aggressive snake barring the way on.

A number of these types of cave systems were explored over a ten day period and it began to become apparent that the limestone area was a succession of cone shaped low lying hills with streams passing through one hill, reappearing to flow on the surface only to disappear again down another cave. The main problem for the villages within the karst area was pollution of the streams as every village used the surface streams for drinking water and washing. By the time a stream had travelled a few tens of kilometres through the limestone terrain it was in a highly polluted state. Also one of the major problems with the installation of water pumps in the caves was maintenance, when the pump breaks down there are no engineers to repair them so some of the pumps installed in the past had been left abandoned and no longer function. Food production is of vital importance as Java has a very high population. All parts of the country are inhabited and there are millions of rice fields many on steep terraced slopes and with villages dotted around everywhere.

On Monday 18th August, the population celebrated their National Independence Day from the Japanese occupation ending in 1945 but we were back cave hunting and found one. After a two hour walk down into a gorge a large river of about five cubic metres a second resurged from a large cave entrance. The passage continued upstream measuring 20 metres in diameter passing a massive calcite column and some deep canals. A roaring of water could be heard beyond and the wind blew the flame of our carbide lights out. Beyond we could just make out a waterfall at the far side of a lake. We had no rope so I attached the end of the survey tape to my belt and swam towards the waterfall fighting the current, but the force of water swept me back to where Maggie waited. The falls looked around six metres high and did not look climbable without a rope so we mapped the cave on our way out. It later transpired the other team of explorers had found the sink where the river disappeared into the same cave but could only progress for 200 metres downstream without safety ropes as the river threatened to sweep them away.

We were now short on time as I had always wanted to visit the famous volcano of Krakatau on the east coast of Java, an opportunity not to be missed while in the country.

On Friday 22nd August, we managed to get a local rickety bus going to Carita via Jakarta, a nightmare bumpy 23 hour journey jammed together with our caving sacks on very small seats. We arrived at 9 am the following day exhausted and, after a couple of days to recuperate from the journey, arranged for a boat to take us to Anak (son of) Krakatau. This is the present active volcano that appeared having been thrust up from the sea in 1929. The main Krakatau Island exploded in 1883 with the equivalent of a few nuclear bombs demolishing the island only leaving three small fragments. The noise of the explosion was heard as far away as Australia. The resulting tsunami killed approximately 36,000 people and the shock wave was felt all over the earth. Where we were staying is the Bay of Carita, which means the Bay of Stories as many bodies were washed ashore at this spot.

Along with six other visitors we waded out from the beach at Luan trying to avoid the piles of human excreta as the beach is used as a toilet by the local population and boarded a small 30 foot boat which looked ready to sink. We landed after four hours slow going on the beach at Anak Krakatau and I climbed the mountain in sandals trying to get a grip on the hot cinders. Arriving at a crest, another hill presented itself and soon I arrived at the massive half mile diameter crater, blowing smoke from bright yellow sulphur holes all over the place. The smell of sulphur dioxide was overpowering and it looked like a scene from Dante's Inferno, real hell on earth. This volcano is still growing at about ten metres per year. We only had two hours on the island as the weather was turning bad, so I beat a hasty retreat and swam out to the boat. The wind began to blow hard and waves crashed over the boat on the way back, I enjoyed the exhilaration, but the rest of the tourists seemed very nervous as most were seasick. How this old boat managed to get back in one piece to Luan, I will never know but it did.

August 27th was the 103rd anniversary of the devastating eruption of Krakatau and on the following day we attempted to reach the remote National Park at Ujang Kulon. This is situated on an isolated part of east Java and the only route in is by sea. It was rumoured that a few white rhinos still survived in this park. Ten of us of various nationalities hired a small open boat from Labaun and preceded upriver, we were told it would be a ten hour journey. On reaching the estuary large waves came crashing towards us threatening to swamp the already overcrowded boat which was very low in the water. We all looked at each other and came to the same conclusion. Did the captain really think we could get there without sinking? We persuaded him to turn back before we were all presented with a watery grave. We attempted to hire a larger more seaworthy vessel without success so called it a day.

We had found some great river caves thanks to Ian's organisational ability and this was not to be my last expedition with members of Her Majesties Armed Forces. Ian was finally awarded the BEM.

17

Operation Paddington Bear, Peru Expedition, 1987

'The world belongs to the enthusiast who keeps cool.'

William McFee

Invitations to join expeditions started to arrive thick and fast and it was hard to choose but the invitation from Lieutenant Colonel Jack Sheldon was impossible to resist. The other attraction was that a few close friends not part of Her Majesty's Armed Forces had also been invited, Jerry Wooldridge, one of Briton's top cave photographers, and Ben Lyon. Captain John Salmon was also on the team, my doctor from the Untamed River Expedition, the late Ian Rolland, Rick Stanton, Ian Whaley representing the Royal Navy, and Ian James. There seemed to be all Ian's on this expedition, but it was a strong team with some good well established cave explorers.

The objectives were twofold. One team was to dive in Lake Titicaca, the highest major navigable lake in the world. The other objective, under the leadership of Jack, was an area of karst in the high Andes Mountains in the north of Peru, the longest mountain range in the world at 7,200 kilometres.

On Saturday 2nd May 1987, we all gathered at Heathrow Airport to catch our plane. The journey out was a long winded 26 hour roundabout route via, Paris, Milan, Caracas Venezuela, Bogotá Columbia and finally to Lima the capital of Peru.

Inflation was running riot at the time and US dollars were the currency of choice but it was good to have some cash in Peruvian currency so I changed 100 US dollars for 2.6 million soles, in the new revalued Peruvian currency this was still 2,650 intis, they had just knocked off three zeros.

Lima was a strange city as if a building was not complete, no taxes were payable, so most buildings seemed to be under construction. The troubles with the Maoist rebels, the Shining Path or Sendero Luminosa, was still in full swing as the capture of its leader Abimael Guzman did not occur until

September 12th 1992, so we were hoping not to fall into the hands of kidnappers as ransom money was in short supply.

After a trip to the mapping and geological office on Monday 4th May with Ian James and Ben, we set off in a hired coach along the west coast of South America. This long desert strip was a surprise to see so little vegetation with the desert stretching down to the Pacific Ocean but with the huge mountain range of the Andes rising majestically above the desert. Memorable were a few fishing villages with the overpowering stench of rotting fish. How the people lived with it on a daily basis I have no idea.

The coach struggled up the mountain roads with stunning views up into the main range with steep drops sometimes either side of the coach. We arrived at the famous historical city of Cajamarca in the north after a drive of 16 hours on Tuesday 5th May. Cajamarca is the site of many different cultures stretching over a period of 2,000 years and is also the site of the battle between the small 168 numbered Spanish force of Conquistadors under the leadership of Pizarro, and the Incan Emperor Atahualpa. Atahualpa was captured in the city under trickery and held to ransom. The El Cuarto del Rescate, or Ransom Room, was filled to the roof with gold and silver but Atahualpa was still garrotted.

From Cajamarca we hired an old banger of a bus and drove to a Peruvian army camp where the Lieutenant Colonel in charge assigned us two of his officers to accompany us for the duration of the expedition, it seemed that the British Armed Forces needed guarding. Being told not to take photographs, I sneaked a nice picture of his men, some of them marching in bare feet but was assured they had never lost a war.

A further three hours driving and we arrived at a small farm building at Aguas Coloradas, way up in the mountains. The driver refused to take his clapped-out bus any further to Celendin or Sorochuco along these dangerous, dirt and dusty mountain roads. The owner kindly allowed us to rent the building and camp on his field.

The following day, Ian James set off with five men for a four day reconnaissance up onto the plateau while I teamed up with Ian Rolland and went prospecting in the limestone hills only finding one small stream cave blocked after no more than 40 metres. We did find another promising looking hole in a field, but it required some excavation in order to squeeze though to a 10 metre pitch. As it appeared to have a draught but required further excavation, we left it for another day as there were plenty of blind valleys to investigate.

Next day we studied the maps and walked for three hours over the hills to a large doline and a large sink with a good size stream of about four cubic metres a second disappearing into boulders, a major digging exercise. After a visit to the village found at the end of a dry valley we went in search of a possible resurgence for the disappearing river. A 400 metre descent down into the valley along a track for about four kilometres in heavy rain revealed the resurgence, but no caves, all we found were rock shelters. Following the valley towards the town of Celendin we climbed back out of this steep sided valley to an extensive area of closed depressions, referred to as collapsed dolines in speleological terms. By 6.30 pm it was getting dark and my gammy foot and recent injury to my cartilage in the knee while parachuting started to give me jip. The pain was probably due to the damp and low barometric pressure as in the tropics I do not have too much of a problem. Exhausted with the high altitude and lack of food, I borrowed Ben Lyon's caving suit and a biscuit and crawled into my bivouac bag for an uncomfortable night's sleep in the pouring rain. Having had histoplasmosis and being a smoker, high altitude does present a problem and it normally takes me a week to become acclimatised. I set off at 6.30 am the following day as soon as dawn broke and reached base camp one hour later.

On Saturday, Ben and I, accompanied by our Peruvian guard Juvenal, travelled to Celendin with a plan to spend four days near a small town called Limon where caves had been reported. After four hours of waiting for transport we gave up and returned being told the next truck to come through would probably be on Sunday. There are few buses in these outlying mountain districts, so most people flag down passing trucks if they wish to travel from one town to the next, sometimes having to wait for a few days. Later in the afternoon I joined Ian Rolland who had managed to descend a couple more vertical drops of ten metres in our small cave that we had started to excavate a few days previously, but the way on proved to be too small for humans.

Ian James returned on Monday 11th May. It had taken his team two days to reach this remote region after having to hire mules but although the area looked promising all the shafts were blocked. One huge depression was estimated to be a mile long but with no caves. The main depression named Tragadero was also completely blocked. After running out of food supplies, Ian had no alternative to pull his men off the plateau. He described it as a miserable, cold, very wet and misty place.

On the same day Jack, Ben, Juvenal and I caught a bus going in the general direction of a karst area called Cuava Los Vergos where we had noticed on the map what looked like a large amount of water issuing from nowhere. This seemed to indicate a large resurgence and possible associated cave. We found the area without too much trouble but the resurgence was unfortunately only small with no associated cave but up on the plateau we found a series of shafts, one had a diameter of ten metres so looked promising for a return visit with ropes. Two other caves close by I managed to enter, one blocked by a roof collapse and the other became very narrow but the area did look promising for finding a major cave system.

The next day, Laurie, Jack and I went back to the area with the large doline. We walked some way beyond and did discover a large resurgence but the cave was completely flooded to the roof. We followed the water flowing out of the resurgence down a valley finding that it sank underground at the base of a small cliff. The stream sink was blocked with boulders, so we began removing them one by one but made little progress. Considering that this was the largest stream sink we had found so far, we intended to return at a later date if nothing else was discovered. A few days later another team continued excavating but the cave became far too narrow for further progress, yet another disappointment.

On the Wednesday we finally found transport to Limon on the back of a passing truck and camped among some small stunted trees. We had been told by some Peruvian Indians about possible caves down in the valley near a small town called Balza situated on the banks of the Rio Maranon, a major tributary to the Amazon, which is on the east side of the Andes Range. The Peruvian Indians assured us it was only a 15 minute walk to the village but two hours later we were still walking and the Rio Maranon still looked a long way down. Luckily, we flagged down a passing truck and arrived at the town crossing the bridge over the Maranon. We had descended down the east side of the Andes and the region now had a dry and desert type terrain, so different to the grass plains of the areas where we had been working which in many ways resembled our own karst areas in Briton, wet, windy and cold.

The local policeman took exception to our presence as we had no permit to be in Peru's Amazonian Province; he made it quite clear we should get out of town by sunrise and on no account were we to photograph the bridge as it was strategic. We got some nice photographs of it when he wasn't looking.

The rocks were all sandstone and as no limestone could be seen there was no chance of finding any caves. We camped by the river and waited all the next day in the town square for a truck but none came our way, so the policeman allowed us an extension of one more night. The next day a truck arrived at 5 am and we were dropped off back at our camp at Limon. The only other possibility was a gorge close by that we thought may offer some hope of finding caves, but we were unable to find a safe route down as the sides of the gorge crumbled away at the slightest touch.

The following day, Ian Rolland found a safe route down a gulley at the top end of the gorge and we both explored down through very rocky terrain to a narrow canyon where we rigged five short pitches. The steep sided canyon opened up but only a small spring of water was found issuing from boulders and no caves. We returned disappointed and packed up camp obtaining a truck back to Celendin, where we spent the night in a small hostel.

The following day at 5 am we set off back to our base camp at Aguas Colaradas and met up with Ben who had been suffering with tunnel vision, possibly due to the altitude. It had cleared up and he was now OK. He told us his remarkable story of attempting to reach the Inca ruins of Oxamarea. The following is my account with apologies to Ben Lyon and Stanley Holloway and his ditty, The Battle of 'astings.

Ben had hired a mule from a small village called Suere and had set off early with a guide along a steep mountain trail. The trail mainly followed a ridge with steep drops either side going down for thousands of feet to the valley far below. Reaching the top of the ridge after about eight hours, the guide informed him that the ruins were still three hours away. Having no camping gear and little food they headed back.

Ben on his mule wore his poncho, with his hat on his head. Riding on the back of a mule down a steep and narrow trail with huge drops either side was a little disconcerting. When it started to get dark, Ben got worried as he was afraid the mule would fall as obviously it could not see where it was going. Being the British agent for all Petzl caving equipment he switched on his Petzl head torch. The mule bolted and tried its best to throw him down the cliff. He had no alternative but to switch it off and hope the mule knew where it was going.

On arriving miraculously some hours later in a nervous condition at the base of the mountain the mule decided to go home as it appeared to have had enough of carrying Ben wearing his poncho with his hat on his head and wanted its dinner. Ben made a brave attempt to get the stubborn mule back on the right track but it was having nothing of it and proceeded to walk through the door into its owner's house with Ben still on its back, wearing his poncho with his hat on his head. What the Peruvian family thought when a white man came into their house while they were peacefully having dinner, on their mule wearing his poncho with his hat on his head cannot be described in the English language.

Journeys beneath the Earth

Ian James had taken a team back to Cuava Los Vergos where we had found the series of shafts; one was explored to a large chamber but with no way on into any further passages. Many more shafts were rigged and descended but again all proved to be blocked.

We had one last possibility in the regions to find caves; this was close to a town called Bambamarea situated around six hours away along these rough mountain roads. On Tuesday 19th May, we travelled to the thermal springs at Los Banyos as Juvenal needed to report back to his barracks and after a hot bath we proceeded onwards to Cajamarca by bus. An old Indian told us about caves near Minas Los Colorados, a mining region, near a small town called Hualgayoc. This area was on the way to our original planned destination at Bambamarea. The following day we were lucky to find a bus going our way and arrived at Hualgayoc after a five hour journey along some very rough and dangerous roads. We set up camp on a field just outside the town but felt like animals in a zoo as we were completely surrounded by what appeared to be all the people in the town watching our every move. It seemed obvious they had never seen foreigners before and were just curious, and it proved very embarrassing to go to the toilet as there was nowhere to hide.

To escape the crowds, a few of us set off walking up the steep mountain road to a range of limestone hills we had noticed on the way in from the grime covered bus windows. News must have travelled fast as I met a young Indian lady with a baby on her back in a papoose sack. She led me at great speed over the mountains pointing out holes in the limestone ground and indicated that there were many more. She spoke a little English so we could communicate with the odd words of Spanish thrown in and gestures. I headed back to camp and the crowds of onlookers and at an altitude of 3,500 metres it was a cold night's sleep.

The next day, a group followed a local man who led them up a 300 metre climb to some caves but they turned out to be old abandoned gold mines. I returned to try to find the lady I had met the day before and I came across a house made of turf with a thatched roof. It reminded me of a dwelling from Bronze Age Britain but inside with a fire going it seemed quite warm and cosy. This was where the lady named Carman lived with her two children, the baby of nine months called Hosea and his little sister Jessica aged three years. Carman's nine year old brother Wilme also lived there for most of the time, and we spent the day running around the hills noting many shafts that could potentially lead into caves. Carman's husband worked in the mines, so she stayed in her turf house as there was good grazing up in the hills for her horses, pigs and a few sheep and cows. Carman invited us to camp on her fields if we wanted to descend the various shafts around the area.

Back at camp the others had been attempting to explain that we were not interested in gold mines just looking for natural caves. A lady asked us to visit her house and it turned out she was the wife of the local police officer who had searched our tents during our absence possibly looking for mineral specimens as they presumed we were gold prospectors.

On Friday 22nd May, we moved camp as almost one hundred people now surrounded us just standing in groups and watching. A few of the town's people helped us carry our equipment to Carman's field but refused to go back to the town until Carman gave them a mouthful. We set up camp and immediately got to work descending six shafts, the deepest being 18 metres, one led into a large chamber but there was no way on, all the rest were either too tight or blocked with rocks. Jack, Laurie and Jerry Wooldridge managed to find us up on the hill and joined in the work. That night, Carman's mother invited us to dinner, the menu was guinea pig as the floor of Carman's turf house was crawling with these little furry creatures. We respectfully declined and made a curry.

The next day Jerry, Juvenal and I followed Wilme to investigate the karst on the other side of the valley, crossing the road and climbing up the far side Wilme led us to fourteen shafts requiring ropes in order to descend. Ian Rolland descended another few shafts on the hills beyond Carman's house but again all were too narrow.

Ten separate shafts were descended the following morning but again all were completely blocked with debris. That afternoon we walked down to the town with Carman as her mother had been injured when she interfered in an argument and got hit with a broom. There was quite a commotion in the town as a truck had come off the road and careered down the mountain killing six people mostly children and injuring a further eighteen. This seemed to be a common occurrence along these mountainous roads and a mother and her daughter from Hualgayoc lay dead in the church. We spent the rest of the day with Carman's family at her mother's house drinking the local distilled sugar cane fire water called Pisco and got rather drunk.

On Monday, Jack, Laurie and Juvenal caught a bus back to Cajamarca as the expedition was now drawing to a close and Jack needed to visit and pay his compliments to the Lieutenant Colonel at the Peruvian Army barracks.

I rode around the hills on Carman's horse then went walking up into the mountains to about 4,000 metres with some great views of steep-walled pointed mountains until the mist closed in, it was impossible to tell if they were limestone or just bleached sandstone.

Before I left for my walk, Ian Rolland borrowed another one of Carman's horses and rode into town dressed in his poncho looking for all the world like The Man with No Name, from A Fistful of Dollars. This has always remained with me as a valued memory of Ian who was a wonderful guy but was tragically killed in 1994 while diving the sump in Mexico's deepest cave.

The next day at 6 am we packed up camp and caught a bus back to Cajamarca, we left Carman with what little food we had left. The bus with the rest of the team were waiting for us at the bus station, they had made little more progress at Balza and Aguas Colaradas with, disappointingly, no major discoveries. Travelling through the night, we arrived back at Lima on Wednesday morning.

Before returning to the UK, we had a few days spare so flew to the amazing Inca city of Cuzon at 3,800 metres above sea level where we booked a train up the mountains to Machu Picchu at 2,430 metres altitude.

A three hour journey passing some of the most dramatic mountains I had ever seen to Aguas Calientis and a bus up the mountain brought us to this World Heritage Site scheduled in 1983 which is beyond description in its grandeur and magnificence. Overlooking the Sacred Valley and the Urubamba River, we wandered around for hours mesmerised by this 15th century Inca ruin and climbed the mountain which overlooks the ruins followed by a little white dog. Jerry was in his element and took some classic photographs but a two-dimensional photographs will never give Machu Picchu its true justice as it needs to be seen to be believed. It was discovered by Hiram Bingham in 1911 and voted as one of the new Seven Wonders of the World in 2007. We ran back down the hill and spent the night at Aguas Calientis making it back the following day to catch the plane back to the UK.

Considering the disappointments of the cave exploration in the Andes, this visit to Machu Picchu was one of the highlights of the trip. In retrospect, the expedition was a wonderful experience with a great group of cave explorers. Cave explorations to remote unknown areas are hit and miss. Sometimes successful, sometimes not but this is one of the great attractions of caving expeditions as no one knows what if anything will be found as caves cannot be seen. There is only one way to find out, go and take a look.

18

Guangxi Province, The China Caves Project, 1987 – 1988

'Your work is to discover your world and then with all your heart give yourself to it.'

Buddha

It was well known in caving circles that China had the world's largest expanse of limestone approaching two million square kilometres, more than all the karst regions in the word put together but the Bamboo Curtain prevented speleologists from visiting. British speleologists eventually, after a great deal of difficulty, developed contacts at the Chinese Academy of Geological Science and received an invite to explore and map China's caves. Their main contact was Professor Juan Dioxian and an expedition was in the offing. Everyone was familiar with the classic Chinese paintings of towers of limestone usually shrouded in mist and of course every man and his dog wanted an invite, including me.

Because China had such huge areas of limestone terrain, water supplies and irrigation was of great concern as regards to agriculture. A Karst Institute had been established at Guilin situated in the province of Guangxi to study and attempt to solve some of these problems. Guangxi Province had an area of 236,700 square kilometres with huge areas of limestone; the capital being the famous city of Nanning.

British speleologists convinced the Chinese that we could be of some help with exploring and mapping caves and it would cost them nothing as we would pay for all the logistics and would supply caving equipment not available in China at that time.

Sometime in 1986, I received a phone call from Tony Waltham asking for the contacts I had developed from the Untamed River Expedition in particular British Airways. Of course, I asked if there was room for me on the next expedition in return for my contact address list. With some embarrassment, the answer was no as the team had already been decided and numbers were limited. Tony was apologetic as he knew he was asking for trade secrets but as we are all friends and have the same passion for exploring caves and I had known Tony for almost 20 years, I supplied my contacts on the agreement I would be invited on the next trip, if any.

Tony was true to his word and the invitation arrived in 1987. The expedition was planned over the Christmas period from December 1987 to January 1988 with two objectives suggested by the Karst Institute, both in Guangxi Province. The first involved diving in flooded caves and mapping of other caves in Duan County situated 500 kilometres from Guilin; the second was an area of karst in Bama County with a river cave called Soulue with a 20 kilometre sink to rising distance. Bama was around 150 kilometres from Duan so was within striking distance.

It was important to send a two man reconnaissance ahead to smooth things over before the main team arrived and Tim Fogg, the deputy leader, and I landed the job.

We set off from Heathrow Airport on 19th December via a Pakistan International Airlines flight which was the cheapest one we could find and we arrived in Islamabad 11 hours later via Paris. The next leg to Beijing took another eight boring hours as there was not a drop to drink on board the non-alcoholic flight.

We were to meet Professor Juan at the airport but there was no sign of him and the ticket office was closed so we were unable to book our flights to Guilin. A taxi ride into the city to the Geological Academy also drew a blank as it was closed so we booked in a hotel for the night.

The following morning, we booked our tickets and caught a flight to Guilin where we were met by Hu Mengyu who spoke excellent English and would liaise with the British cave explorers and Zhu Xuewen from the Karst Institute. Zhu had been assigned to co-ordinate the expedition with Associate Professor Wang Xunyi as the leader.

Guilin is situated amidst some of the most impressive and dramatic karst terrain I had ever seen with massive steep sided limestone towers surrounded by flat alluvial plains with rice fields everywhere, just like the Chinese paintings. In geological terms this type of limestone terrain was normally referred to by Westerners as Tower Karst but the Chinese term Fenglin Karst, which can be translated as Peak Forest, is now predominantly used to describe these areas. My mouth watered with expectations of the cave explorations to come.

At the Institute we checked our equipment which had been shipped out but the compressed air bottles for the divers had not yet arrived although they were on their way.

It was arranged for some members of the team to carry out a reconnaissance at the end of the expedition to Longan, situated south west of Nanning in preparation for a future expedition, also much time was spent discussing the charges the Chinese wished to make. They had no intention of providing logistics on the cheap and asked for exorbitant amounts of US dollars. It was decided that Andy would sort the total costs out at the end of the expedition and sign the agreement as we had no control on expenditure. A jeep was arranged for us to travel to Liuzhou where we would spend the night before travelling on to Duan County. Seven Chinese from the Institute would join us and a further three from the Hydrology Unit at Liuzhou. Tim was to conduct a reconnaissance of the area around Mashan near Duan while I would proceed to Soleu Cave in Bama County.

Bama is a relatively small county by Chinese standards, of the 1,966 square kilometres, most of it is composed of limestone and it also has a reputation for longevity. More people are aged over 100 in this county than any other in China. There are various theories for this including the high concentrations of dissolved calcium in the water, which is derived from the limestone terrain. I was to discover another possible reason.

Bama is also considered a sacred land of revolution. In the 1920s and the early 1930s, Deng Xiaoping, Zhang Yunyi, Wei Baqun and many other older-generation proletarian revolutionists, organised and commanded the armed struggles here. From the Agrarian Revolution and the Anti-Japanese War, to the Liberation War, Bama was one of the important revolutionary base areas. It became obvious later on during the expedition that the caves were important refuges for revolutionary armies or in some instances used as hideouts for bandits. It is situated in the Administrative Division of Hechi and is classified as an Autonomous County because of its minority population of Yao people and is bordered by Fengshan and Donglan Counties.

The following day, we were introduced to the Director of the Karst Institute Dr Zhang Zhigan who welcomed us to China and hoped for long term co-operation in the future which was good to hear.

Tim gave the Chinese some basic lessons on the use of Single Rope Techniques by hanging a rope from the building as we had promised to supply the Institute with a variety of caving equipment and they needed to know how to use it in a safe manner.

The Chinese had also developed a few caves with paths and lights and had opened them to the public. These were very popular with thousands of visitors. A visit to Reed Flute Cave was an eye opener with fantastic formations but with multicoloured lights, it looked like a painted Aladdin's Cave. Trails had been carved out of the limestone towers, so it was possible to walk up these steep trails affording amazing views of the city and the surrounding karst formations.

On Thursday 24th December, we set off by jeep for the Liuzhou Hydrological Unit accompanied by a young enthusiastic student from the Karst Institute, Lian Yanging. Lian was to be my liaison on the planned reconnaissance to Bama County as he spoke good English.

We crossed the Lui River, a major tributary of the Pearl River, the Yu Jiang and arrived in Liuzhou where we were to spend the night. Later we met up with the three men who were to accompany us and I obtained a basic plan of the Soleu Cave.

On Christmas day we travelled along dusty roads for seven hours by jeep to the Duan Science and Technology Department. There we were treated to a very large Chinese banquet with some very nice beer, a sweet tasting wine and worst of all one of their favourite drinks called Touchu, distilled in Liuzhou, with an appalling taste and an equally appalling smell. Considering it was Christmas we retired and hit the bottle of Jameson's hidden in Tim's room to get rid of the taste of their fire water.

Having a hangover, we skipped breakfast the next day and started work on studying the maps. All I had was the 1-200,000 navigational charts which were of little use but Hu had some 1-100,000 maps which gave us a little more detail, but these were classified so we made some tracings.

On Sunday 27th December I set off by jeep with Lian, a copy of our official permit and the secret 1-100,000 maps of Bama County for a four day reconnaissance. The 150 kilometre journey along small dusty dirt roads passed through some stunning karst scenery and some famous land marks, the Tisu Cave Windows where huge caves passed through the limestone towers forming perfect arched natural bridges. We passed over a bridge across the Hong Shui He, marked on my map as the Li River where a dam was under construction arriving in Bama after an eight hour journey.

The accommodation was basic but clean. One of the ladies would bring in a bucket of hot water so I could wash off the mud and grime of the day. In the yard was a nice goat that I became quite friendly with. Unfortunately, a few days later the cook called me over to photograph him cutting its throat. That night goat was on the menu, but I did not feel much like eating.

In the evening, we both walked into town from our government quarters and accepted an invitation to join a Tea Workers party of a few hundred people where we were expected to sing along with the two Bama County Communist Party leaders. The people in this area generally belong to the minority group of Yao Chinese not the Han and singing seemed to be a tradition to obtain a female partner. As I did not want one, I politely declined the invitation.

I asked if Bama County had ever been visited before by Europeans and was surprised by the reply translated by Lian.

'Yes,' said the party leader.

'How long ago was that?' I asked.

'Hundreds of years ago,' he said.

'Who was that?' I asked in great curiosity.

'Marco Polo,' he replied.

If he was joking he said it with a straight face or it was Lian's idea of a joke but it became obvious that the people living in the region had never seen Europeans before so I became something of a curiosity.

The next day, while Lian presented our permit to the Bama County government, I studied a simple drawn map of the area hanging on a wall of the quarters. A large river called the Pan Yang He was shown coming to a dead stop near a small village called Poyue. It was an obvious rising of a river issuing from the Limestone Mountains. That day we drove along a road to the north which followed the boundary of the limestone and shale looking at stream sinks and risings marked on the 1-100,000 maps, finding a number of good possibilities. One nice cave descended to a lake, but it was obvious that extreme backing up of the streams occurred during the rainy season. Another one was a vertical maze requiring ropes to go further.

I had to keep asking Lian to tell the driver to stop the jeep at various places along the road at places I wished to look at. After a while he told me how to say *please stop the jeep* in Chinese. I tried the next time and they all fell about laughing.

'What are you laughing at?' I asked.

'You just asked the driver for a kiss.'

I gave it up as my pronunciation of Chinese was useless.

Tuesday 29th December can only be described as a great day. At Poyue I found two separate resurgences, the source of the Pan Yang River, one with the river boiling up from a lake. A massive cave entrance beckoned just beyond, in feverish haste we changed into caving gear and charged our carbide lamps and explored for about 200 metres to a large opening to the sky, a collapsed doline with some crops growing at the base. Any flat area in Bama County is cultivated so the cave was used as a pathway into the doline by the local villagers. The cave continued beyond at the other side of the doline and was explored for a further 100 metres with no end in sight. A strong wind blew through the cave indicating open extensive passages beyond and possibly another entrance.

Returning to the jeep elated we drove on to the north along a small dirt road again following the boundary between the shale outcrop and the limestone. Before long we came across a massive dry valley where the river could be seen once more flowing across the surface. In the distance was another huge cave entrance. The next dry valley to the north we decided to walk down and again this led us to yet another large cave entrance which Lian and I surveyed for 116 metres to a deep lake. The other side of the hill containing this cave revealed another large cave explored for 200 metres, when we asked villagers living close by they said it connected to the lake in the other cave and was called Tianping Dong. The first large cave we had explored near the resurgence of the Pan Yang River, they called Beimo Dong, Dong being the Chinese name for a cave. It looked like I had hit the jackpot.

The incredibly beautiful limestone terrain looked very extensive and seemed to extend as far as the eye could see. The topography appeared to be predominantly more like Cone Karst with rounded conical hills tightly grouped together and separated by closed valleys and closed depressions which we refer to as dolines. In modern geological terms these areas are now referred to as Fengcong, translated as Peak Cluster Karst, and a speleologist's dream world.

The main objective of my reconnaissance was to investigate the cave at Solue and sort out logistics for a possible exploration trip, so the following day we headed off in a south westerly direction from Bama along a very bad and dangerous road skirting along the side of a steep valley. At one point I noticed a very blue river which usually indicated dissolved limestone content but it suddenly stopped.

Lian and I climbed down the rubble strewn cliff into the valley to investigate, descending about 300 metres, and arrived at a huge cave entrance measuring 40 metres by 100 metres in diameter. At the bottom of a rocky slope which had presumably originated when the Chinese had blasted the road along the cliff edge above, was a deep blue lake with the cave passage disappearing into darkness, a job for a rubber dingy. This was the source of the blue river and presumably the river rising for the cave at Soleu, 20 kilometres away where a large river went underground. We mapped the entrance chamber and another short side passage and headed back up the steep climb to the jeep.

The next day we managed to find the main river sinking in the cave of Soleu, the road was still under construction and being built by pick and shovel. We arranged for accommodation at the Hydro Electric construction depot for six or seven people for six days if it was thought necessary. The cave was a Chinese giant of a river cave with a flow rate of three cubic metres of water a second and was supposed to be six kilometres in length; no one seemed to know what happened beyond the six kilometre mark but it was thought to end in a siphon. The engineers had built a few bridges to cross the underground river in order to explore the cave, but these had been washed away in a flood. It seemed important that the cave was fully explored due to the Hydro construction project. I only traversed the cave 30 metres above the river for about 500 metres to a deep water section then turned back having achieved the reconnaissance objective.

I took a quick look at a dry cave nearby called Yen Jain Dong which was supposed to connect to Soleu and then went on to the village of Soleu where a small boy led me to another village called Lalan. Nearby was yet another cave with the same name as the village which I explored along with the Head Man for around 600 metres. It appeared there were hundreds more caves in the area but none of them had been mapped. Most had been explored by local villagers probably searching for guano nitrate deposits used as fertiliser or for other minerals.

We travelled back to Duan the following day, this time by a different route to a ferry across the Hong Shui He close to the Hydro Electric construction site, arriving back in less than four hours.

The divers, Steve Jones and Gavin Newman, had arrived after a nightmare journey by train with the compressor for the diving tanks. They had to pay customs £800 import duty but would receive £400 back if re-exported back to the UK. Tim had investigated a cave at Mashan but the cave had been heavily damaged in the attempts to develop it as a show cave open to the public. Steve and Gavin had already completed a dive in one of the flooded shafts dotted around the region down to a depth of 85 metres with the cave continuing deeper, a Chinese cave diving record. They could not dive deeper just on compressed air and to go beyond would require mixed gas and lengthy decompression stops.

The Bama area seemed to be the best bet for cave exploration and I managed to get Ben Lyon, the proprietor of Britain's main supplier of caving equipment, Mike Meredith, who at that time was the development officer of the Gunung Mulu National Park in Sarawak, and our photographer Jerry Wooldridge to accompany me back to Bama County. Two Chinese journalists were also assigned to tag along and Zhang, a Mr Tan and Lian would also come with me. This time we had a small bus to transport us all with our equipment and on Saturday 2nd January we arrived back in Bama at our quarters where Lian had arranged for a few rooms.

Lian had also arranged for a jeep to run us to the caves, the problem was petrol as there was none left in the town, but we had just enough to get us to Beimo Dong and back where we began surveying. A side passage led down a muddy tunnel to a lake of deep slow-moving water probably connecting through to the resurgence. It times of wet weather this probably overflowed into the main passage.

Mike climbed up to a high level passage near the entrance which led to a sky light with old Chinese pottery; the cave had probably been used for habitation at some time in the distant past. The floor of this high level passage was a mass of pure white golf ball size cave pearls, calcite concretions formed in pools of water and all of this upper level contained huge stalagmites, stalactites and columns up to the roof, some of the finest pristine cave formations any of us had ever seen. A series of strange and unique stalagmites rose from the floor, shaped like Chinese fans, about two metres high by thirty centimetres wide. We had never seen anything quite like this before and it was considered that they were formed by the drips of water dropping from high in the roof and blowing from side to side as the direction of the wind blowing through the cave changed, depositing calcite and forming a narrow elongated formation.

The passage continued to drop down back into the doline but I was unable to descend without the aid of a rope. Ben and Mike continued with the survey while Jerry was in his element photographing this amazing place with help from Lian and me holding flash guns. Jerry then joined us and we continued across the doline into the cave entrance on the far side. We mapped the passage only for 270 metres as we entered a large chamber where the walls and roof were beyond the range of our lights and 60 metre high stalagmites rose majestically up to the roof some being over 20 metres in diameter. We decided that the best way was for two teams to map around each wall so we would have some idea of the total size of the place. Jerry produced a wonderful photograph of this chamber later; it was so large it had clouds in the roof, and it was produced by the China Caves Project as a poster later.

On arriving back and reporting our findings, the journalists wanted to tag along with us the next day so we kept the small bus as we only had one jeep which was too small for all of us. Petrol was now available, so we returned to Biemo Dong and Lian, Jerry and I completed the survey of the main cave and helped Jerry with his photographic work. Ben and Mike found a draughting muddy tunnel close to the entrance of the cave beyond the doline and mapped it for one kilometre to an entrance overlooking the large valley I had seen during my reconnaissance. They could see another massive entrance on the far side of the valley about one kilometre away with a river flowing across the valley and sinking against the limestone cliff below where they were standing.

*Beimo Dong 2 entrance chamber, Bama county, Guanxi China.
Photo: Jerry Wooldridge.*

That night I sent a message back with the bus driver asking Tim to send three more men as we obviously had a great deal of exploring and mapping to do.

We completed the mapping of the large chamber on Tuesday 5th January by surveying around the walls to another entrance again overlooking the valley. The chamber proved to be 160 metres at its widest point.

We descended down into the valley making towards the large entrance seen the day before. The entrance was indeed huge with dimensions of 30 to 40 metres and we mapped onwards to another large doline open to the sky with a small tunnel going off at the side leading to a large closed valley containing a small village. We helped Jerry take some impressive photographs of this long and straight cave. We found out later that the local villagers called the cave Qian Dong. We returned the way we came, back through Beimo Dong after taking a look at the river sink cave which required a rubber dingy in order to progress downstream.

I managed to get through by phone to Tim that evening and they had discovered a large chamber at Mashan but there was little the divers could do so he offered to send them over to Bama to look at Soleu along with more Chinese. I agreed as there was no problem in accommodating another seven people.

The following day Ben and Mike continued mapping from where we had left off and they could see daylight ahead. After 700 metres following this massive tunnel they arrived at yet another valley with a village on the opposite side.

Jerry and I, along with two of our Chinese colleagues, Tan and Zhang, mapped the cave to the north I had investigated during the reconnaissance which was one of the peripheral caves called Tianping Dong, the name given to it by the villagers. We surveyed down a steep mud slope overlooking a lake that we were unable to reach without ropes, there was a strong echo which seemed to indicate a large passage across the lake.

That evening Simon and Charlotte appeared from Duan to help us as there was little for them to explore in that area. I now had a team of six from the UK which would be of great help as we had so many other cave entrances that required investigation.

Ben and I thought it a good idea to take a look at the main resurgence so the following day we inflated the rubber dinghy much to the amusement of the villagers, who watched in fascination as we rowed across the blue lake dressed in all our caving equipment, looking like two intrepid great white explorers. The lake was a total dead end with no cave passage to be seen. We were back on dry land looking sheepish as they probably knew there was no open cave to find, the river just boiled up from depth.

After our embarrassment along with Zhang we continued mapping the large tunnel of Qian Dong towards the dry valley seen by Mike and Ben. Dressed in our high tech caving gear with our Petzl Expedition Carbide Lamps and helmets we felt a little foolish as a man passed by inside the cave riding a donkey. Then a group of children appeared on their way to school from the small village in the closed valley we had seen. It appeared that the villagers and the school children used this cave as a thoroughfare in order to reach the road from their village which otherwise would be completely isolated. The children walked through the cave then a steep walk of a few kilometres up to the road at the head of the dry valley and caught a school bus. If only British school children could see how these Chinese children managed to get to school, I thought.

We completed the mapping of the main tunnel except for a huge steep ramp going upwards into the blackness and we walked across the valley to the village. Right at the rear was another massive cave, this one at least 70 metres high. We asked if they had names for the caves, the one we had just emerged from they called Qian Dong and the one behind Hou Dong. We asked for a translation and Qian Dong was translated as, The Cave in Front while Hou Dong was just The Cave Behind. We could imagine the mothers telling their naughty children: 'shove off out of my way and go and play in the Cave Behind.'

The villagers told us that Hou Dong could be followed right through the mountain to an isolated village way up in the hills called Nongan and two men had made the traverse many years ago, it had taken them four days.

We commenced to map inwards passing a calcite column 75 metres high by about 40 metres in diameter, probably one of the world's largest cave formations, to a roped climb down into a lake with no way on. Climbing out up a mud slope to one side we entered a huge chamber and turned back after 500 metres with it still continuing into darkness. The only way back to the jeep was to reverse our route via Qian Dong across the valley and through Beimo Dong, a long way.

On Friday 8th January I returned to Hou Dong along with Mike and mapped a further 100 metres across a very dodgy looking traverse with a free climbable shaft below, unfortunately blocked with rocks at the base. Beyond the traverse there looked to be a way on but the traverse required ropes to protect the climber.

The main way on seemed to be a blank wall but a large passage could be seen way above and there was a good draught in the cave. Beds had been cut into the clay floor below the wall with dried grass as a mattress and many burnt sticks. Was this where the Chinese men from the village had slept for the night before carrying on? We could only imagine that they had brought into the cave bamboo poles in order to reach the high level passage if the story was indeed true.

Charlotte and Simon investigated the cave where the river reappeared close to the entrance of Qian Ban Dong but it hit a sump after 30 metres with no way on. They then turned their attention to the exploration and mapping of the huge ramp passage in Qian Dong which they mapped for 500 metres with no end in sight.

Jerry took the dinghy and explored for 250 metres down the sink in the valley where the river disappeared, again to a sump with no air space.

The next day while Charlotte and Simon continued work in the ramp passage we busied ourselves calculating the co-ordinates and drawing up the caves we had mapped so far; we needed information on where this system of massive caves was heading.

A picture started to appear of an active river cave system originating somewhere to the north but for the most part flowing below or just above the normal water table so the passages tended to be flooded. The river appeared in the various valleys from risings, then sinking once more underground to reappear once again in another valley. To the west streams flowed into the valleys from the impervious sandstone and shale rocks, sinking underground into caves when coming into contact with the limestone. These caves were much smaller in size than the huge dry tunnels of the main system and the underground streams found in these caves drained into the main resurgence at Poyue. The main massive tunnels were obvious fossil remnants from a much larger river, possibly the Hongshui River millions of years in the past formed these massive caves before being captured by its present course.

The whole region began to look like a cave explorers paradise and it appeared that the system of caves extended into the neighbouring counties of Fengshan and Donglan. Potentially it was considered that the system could be hundreds of kilometres in length but had been truncated over millions of years by numerous dolines and valleys, a jigsaw puzzle on a massive scale.

On 10th January, it was decided to have a change and visit the resurgence for the Soleu River Cave that Lian and I had found during the reconnaissance as it looked good for Jerry to photograph. There were some stunning shots of us floating along upstream in this massive blue coloured underground river in a rubber dingy. Mapping was difficult as there was nowhere we could get out of the boat; one person had to swim ahead with the end of the fibre tape measure while one stayed rocking in the dingy trying to obtain a compass bearing. After 600 metres we hit the inevitable sump and a nice beach where we could sit and have our lunch.

The survey of the ramp was completed by Charlotte and Simon and they reached another entrance after a distance of one kilometre. At the other side of a valley they could see yet another entrance but this proved to be blocked after only 30 metres.

Ben and Lian explored and mapped another passage just off the ramp which again reached daylight just above the main exit of Qian Dong.

Looking out to the middle doline from Quian Dong, Bama county, Guanxi, China. Photo: Jerry Wooldridge.

The next job on the list the following day, 11th January, was to investigate the second resurgence of the Pan Yang River but this was found to be the same as the first one and completely flooded to the roof. This seemed to drain a completely separate area of karst to the east so potentially would lead to a different cave system to the one we were working on. Jerry, Charlotte and I climbed above the rising and discovered two caves but both were short, the first, Goagin Dong, being only 120 metres in length and the second, Macang Dong, 140 metres, both blocked with no way on. Much effort would be required to penetrate into the mountainous area at the back of this rising and as we had plenty to go at this area was not revisited. As far as I know this drainage area still remains to be explored.

Ben and Mike mapped a nice cave called Jiabao above a small resurgence in the second valley near Hou Dong but there was no way on after 500 metres.

Next day, Tuesday 12th January, Ben and I were back to the blank wall in Hou Dong and Ben started to climb tied on a life-line rope. He managed to fix a few 6mm expansion bolts into the rock for protection so his life-line rope could run through a karabiner; if he fell I could hold him on the rope before he hit the deck. Ben retreated and I took over trying to fix another bolt, but the rock was a thin layer of calcite deposit with clay beneath. When a bolt was drilled in it could be pulled out by hand and the rock was slimy with mud and water impossible to obtain a good grip. The passage was a further 20 metres away so we retreated, this was a job for the climbers as Steve Jones, the late Rob Parker and Geoff Crossley were hopefully on their way to join my team at Bama.

A sink just up the valley from Hou Dong was explored by Charlotte and Simon for 500 metres called Limo Dong and was still going down stream and a cave opposite on the north side of the valley, Jue Jaiding was also mapped to a flooded section.

That night, Geoff, Rob and Steve at last arrived, they had completed a few more deep dives to minus 70 metres at Duan but there was little more for them to do. I now had a team of nine, increasing our chances of more discoveries.

On Wednesday 13th January, Steve, Geoff and Rob completed the traverse of the two major caves, Beimo and Qian Dong, and crossing the valley entered Hou Dong to the traverse left by Ben and I. They succeeded in passing this obstacle but, unfortunately, they arrived at a large lake with no way on. These lakes appeared to be the main river but all flowing below the water table and flooded to the roof.

Charlotte and Simon completed the mapping of Limo Dong for 1.5 kilometres to a doline that turned out to be the same closed depression containing the village where the school children lived that we had met in Qian Dong. Qian Ban Dong was explored at the other side of the doline which emerged in the first valley near the rising of the river.

We asked many local villagers where the village of Nongan was situated but no one seemed to know. How to find the lost village became a problem if we wanted to find caves beyond Hou Dong. On Thursday 14th January, Mike, Ben, Lian, Charlotte and I started a trek across the mountains intending to bivouac for a few nights determined to find the lost village. We eventually arrived at a small village called Long Wang situated in a large doline with three caves. One of the caves was used as a water supply and another pool as a bathtub for the ladies to wash their very long jet black hair.

Charlotte and I explored the first cave called Shui Dong to a pitch with a large chamber below. We fixed a rope and descended but the rope was too short to reach the base of the shaft so we finished up tying two ropes together in order to reach the bottom, this involved passing a knot on the way down and on the way back up. At the base we found a lake and Charlotte had a swim, unfortunately there was no way on as it proved to be a massive sump pool but the next cave, Bala, proved to be a good find with over 500 metres of passage ways. Mike descended Ming Guang to a very muddy section and a pitch. Later when the co-ordinates we calculated and we drew the maps, these caves were heading directly for Jiabao Dong explored by Mike and Ben on 11th January, the postulated connection between these caves being below the normal dry season water table.

While we were in Long Wang, Steve, Rob and Geoff tackled the climb in Hou Dong and Rob managed to reach the top. How he managed the steep mud covered climb in Wellington boots without sliding off I have no idea, but he did. A rope was fixed, and the others followed to explore a massive passage to a large chamber and down to a ramp, unfortunately leading to yet another lake with no way on.

On Friday 15th January, we found out the approximate location of the lost village of Nong Gan and we walked on skirting the sides of the mountains arriving at a strange hole in the side of a hill with steam issuing. It resembled a smoking chimney and a powerful wind blew out of the hole so strong it blew sticks into the air when thrown in. We had never before seen anything quite like this in all our year of cave exploring. I only had an eight metre rope so descended a steep slope to a deep shaft. Throwing a rock down it rumbled for 12 seconds before coming to a stop. This indicated that the shaft was more than 250 metres in depth. We had nowhere near enough rope to tackle this amazing hole so it would have to await a future expedition. The local villages of course called it Wind Cave, Feng Dong.

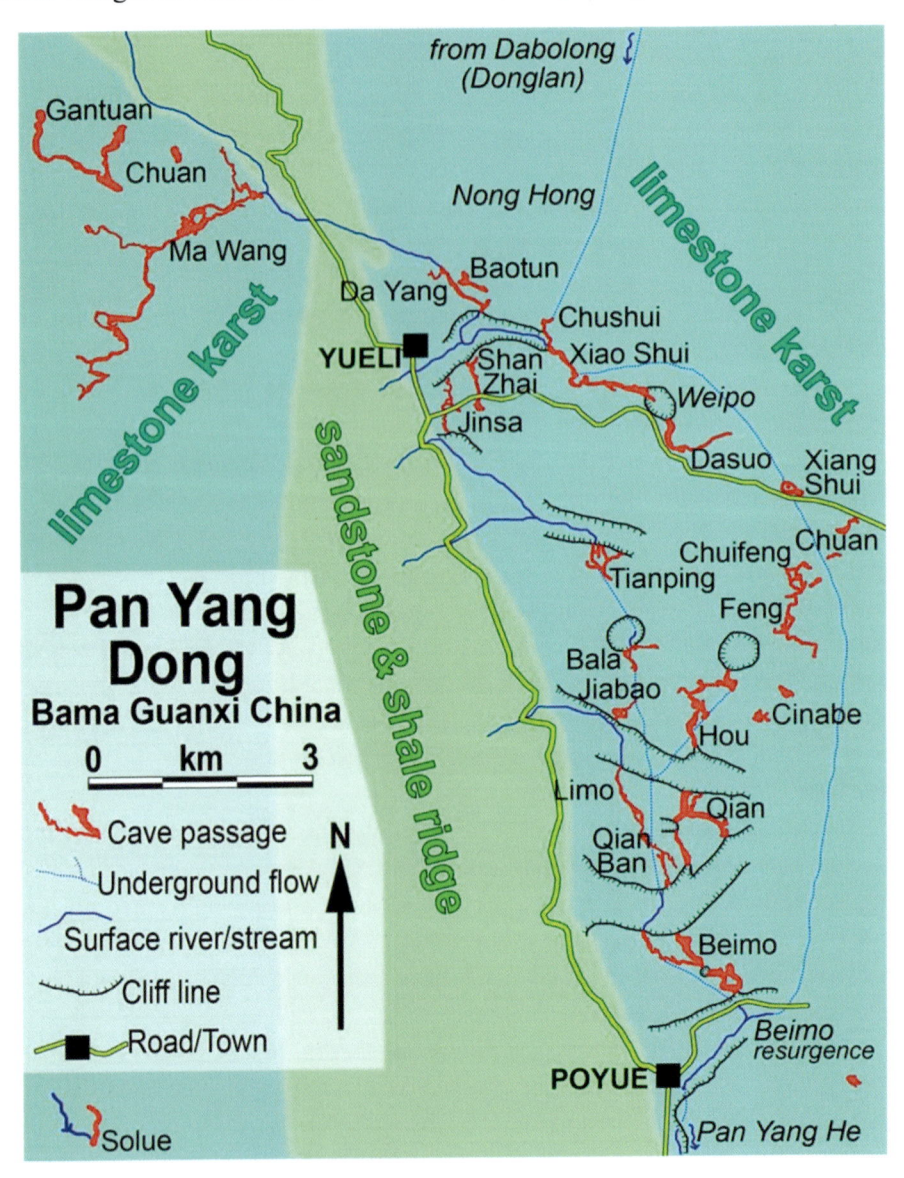

The Pan Yang Dong System, Bama county, Guanxi, China.

    We at last found the village of Nong Gang and descended a massive jungle clad doline which we could scramble down for about 300 metres. A great towering limestone cliff dominated one side; it reminded me of the massive holes in New Britain, Papua New Guinea. At the bottom of the doline was Nong Gan Dong, a nice large cave which led us to yet another lake, but a side passage terminated in a climb with a passage about 10 metres up. Without bolting equipment it looked impossible to climb as the walls were smooth. Just as I was about to leave, I heard a noise from the passage above and Steve Jones magically appeared at the top. They had returned to Hou Dong and found the way through from the big chamber they had entered yesterday. The short drop into Nong Gang was rigged with a rope and they descended to join us amid much jubilation. The villagers had indeed been telling the truth, there was a way right through the mountain. We shook hands and took a few photographs.

Andy Eavis had arrived in Bama and walked over to the village of Long Wang but had been unable to find us so had returned back to Bama. I had promised to join a few team members to conduct a reconnaissance to another region for a future expedition and was due to return to Duan the next day which meant I would miss completing the through trip from Nong Gang to Hou, Qian, and Beimo Caves, a traverse of six kilometres through some of the largest caves on earth. Ben, Mike and Charlotte kindly offered to carry my equipment back to the road head and Steve offered his SRT equipment so I could ascend and descend the roped pitches and he offered to come with me. We were back at the jeep by 6.30 pm after a fantastic three hour trip.

In just 14 days we had explored and mapped some of the greatest caves many of us had ever seen, a very successful expedition. Mike had commented that he was in danger of caving himself out of a job if he continued to explore the giant caves of Bama County as Gunung Mulu National Park Sarawak where he worked had some of the largest caves on earth. I was soon to find out exactly what he was talking about.

We decided to call the caves collectively as the Pan Yang Dong System considering they were all directly associated with the Pan Yang River and we vowed to return at the earliest opportune moment.

On Saturday 16th January, I handed over to Ben to finish off the work over the next few days which is all they had left before returning to the UK. Steve and I returned to Duan and discussed the plans for the reconnaissance. The plan was that Steve, Gavin, Tim and I would travel to Hunan Province and meet up with personnel from the Black Metal Mining Institute in Changsha with a plan to split into two groups. Steve and Gavin would conduct a reconnaissance to Chenzhou while Tim and I would go north to Luota.

On Sunday 17th January, we travelled to Nanning by bus but missed the first train to Changsha so spent a boring day wandering around the town and visited the Friendship Shop but there was little to buy of any interest.

During the 1980s it was possible to buy products in Friendship Shops using tourist money called Foreign Exchange Certificated or F.E.Cs. Changing US dollars at a bank with your passport, was the currency issued at the time to foreigners. It was not possible to obtain Chinese currency, the Yuan, but of course being cavers we did find a way around this. As the expedition provided all accommodation, provisions and transport via payment directly to our Chinese hosts, it was not necessary for us to carry much money around. Buying anything in China during this time was ludicrously cheap as one Yuan was equal to about 16 pence and the Yuan was divided into 100 Fen. You could buy things for a few Fen; a fraction of one pence.

We caught the sleeper train and by 11 am the following morning arrived in a very cold and snowy Changsha to be met by our hosts from the Black Metal Mining Institute. We stayed at the Institute as our finances for the reconnaissance were strictly limited.

That afternoon we discussed the plans with the director but found it was impossible at that time of the year to get to Luota because of the snow on the high mountain passes. The alternative was another possible area at Jiuyishan. They asked for far too much money but after a great deal of haggling we set a price for our trip. I checked over the maps of the cave at Luota and it appeared from their very basic map to be extensive with a possible depth of 900 metres; 51 underground streams had been traced totalling 82 kilometres in length.

We had an uncomfortable sleep that night in freezing conditions as there was no heating in the rooms.

The following day, they arranged for our travel permits but were unable to find a vehicle to take us until the next day so we visited a museum with a 2,100 year old mummy of a queen found in a tomb with bits of her preserved in glass jars.

On Wednesday 20th January, we finally got underway for a 500 kilometre trip taking 12 hours to reach Jiuyishan. We were treated to a sumptuous dinner by the Deputy Mayor and the Political Chief but on enquiring they were unable to supply detailed maps of the region. Then, of course, there was no such thing as Global Positioning Systems (GPS) so hard copy topographical maps were essential. These of course tended to be state secret, which is still the case in many South East Asian countries. In Guangxi we had been allowed to see the maps and make tracings so that the position of caves could be plotted with some accuracy.

A hand drawn map was finally produced and the next two days were spent trudging around the mountains in the cold and looking at possible cave sites but we were disappointed as the area was nowhere near comparable for extensive cave networks to that of Bama County.

China is an amazing country; vast and highly populated would be an understatement. It seemed at times that every square inch of land was cultivated. Even in the mountains of Bama County small terraces had been constructed clinging to steep hill sides. The villagers would climb a steep hill to a small terrace where a few vegetables grew in a little parch of soil, carrying a bucket of water or a shovel full of dung. Some villages used septic tank derived methane gas for cooking, piped from the tank to a small stove. Smiling friendly faces greeted us everywhere and we were always made welcome.

Of course, there were many frustrations, jeeps breaking down, delays, lack of fuel but these can happen anywhere. All signs were in Chinese characters, and trying to translate Chinese into English, the Roman and Latin alphabet was a nightmare, so many of our spellings of caves, villages and towns were hopelessly incorrect. Whenever we asked for a translation of a cave or village we seemed to obtain a different spelling every time. Labelling on maps was also in Chinese characters, now in the 21st century this is no longer a problem as maps of China with Roman characters are widely available. Few people spoke English, so it became imperative to always have a Chinese translator by our side. We were of course told not to take photographs of poor people as it was felt important to the Chinese for us to portray China in a good light. The English sense of patience and tolerance was a prerequisite for any expedition into the heart land of China. Some team members did have a problem with this but for most of us having explored caves in various areas of the world we could handle the frustrations involved in exploring caves in China during this early period of exploration, after all we were the first there.

Food was interesting as a Chinese idea of a banquet, which we had to attend on many occasions, consisted of dog, river snails or some other exotic dish and large quantities of foul smelling distilled rice fire water. First the Political Secretary would propose a toast, all had to down a glass to the Chinese equivalent of *cheers,* which is *ganbei*. The same procedure would be repeated over and over again by each official until everyone was legless. The wine as they called it could be tasted for days after and the hangover seemed to last forever.

On one occasion we stopped at the Chinese equivalent of a transport café for something to eat with a huge sign above the door and lots of rather pretty ladies who appeared to be touting for business.

I asked the million dollar question, 'Are there prostitutes in China?'

'Of course not, it's against the law,' came the firm reply.

I then asked my other Chinese friend what the sign above the door said.

'Good food, clean beds, clean girls, very cheap.'

Well I suppose that said it all, I did not ask how cheap.

While in Bama I called at one shop selling liquor with some strange bottles in the window with a variety of colours and strange things inside the bottles, snakes, lizards, worms and other creatures and plant roots I did not recognise. They were all different varieties and colours of their fire water distilled rice wine. I asked what they were all for and was told they were medicines which was the reason why the people of Bama County had the reputation of longevity and lived over 100 years. I bought a bottle and took it home to give a small glass to visitors I wanted to get rid of. It worked every time and some of them died young.

On Sunday 23rd January, we set of back to Beijing by train, a 30 hour journey. Hu Mengyu and Zhu Xuewen were to accompany me back to the UK as our guests and I had fun on the plane teaching them how to use a knife and fork and drink soup with a spoon instead of the Chinese culture of slurping the soup straight from the bowl. They soon picked up the English cultural style of eating. I had the pleasure of their company for a few days and took them along with the BBC Look North West TV film crew to Poole's Cavern in Buxton, the short news slot was transmitted that night. On the way back I took them to see a typical Derbyshire hill farm at Giants Hole.

How many people live here?' Zhu asked.

'Just three,' I replied.

He could not believe it, 'In China there would be twenty families farming here,' he replied.

19

Three Counties Expedition to China, 1989

'We act as though comfort and luxury were the chief requirements of life, when all that we need to make us happy is something to be enthusiastic about.'

Albert Einstein

After the huge success of the 1988 expedition I immediately started work on a return trip but was slightly waylaid by the October-November expedition to the Gunung Mulu National Park recounted in the next chapter. I was now clocking up two expeditions per year which was a strain on Maggie's patience and also my meagre finances.

This time, I gathered a team of ten. Ben, Steve and Gavin were straining at the bit to get back but unfortunately Mike could not make it as he was busy at the Gunung Mulu National Park, Sarawak. I recruited a few friends from Derbyshire in the form of Alan Walker, Dave Arveschoug and Dr Steve Ray. Julian Walker, Kevin Senior and Kenny Taylor made up the ten. Gavin Newman was our man with the camera and he agreed to accompany me as part of an advance team as it was important, considering where the caves were heading, that we had a base somewhere along the road north from Bama to Fengshan County. I christened the trip The Three Counties Expedition as from our drawn cave maps it appeared that this system extended into neighbouring Fengshan and Donglan counties. The expedition was organised under the auspices of the China Caves Project.

We set off on Tuesday 21st February 1989 via Hong Kong where we spent a few nights before catching a Dragon Air flight to meet our Chinese colleagues at the Institute in Guilin. The next few days were spent sorting out our equipment as we now had a stash of ropes and other caving hardware stored at the Institute from the last expedition. Arrangements were made for the expedition, with much discussion as usual on how much it was going to cost us. This time they were asking for 50 US dollars per man per day, way over the top. They claimed that they were under orders from Beijing with regard to the minimum amount they could charge. After much haggling we finally got the total cost down to £7,800.

Hu Mengyu and a student called Chen, along with a driver for the jeep, would take us to Bama while the main team would travel by minibus accompanied by Mr Tan, Lian and Fang.

This time they had the 1:50,000 maps which would help with plotting cave entrances, but the main problem was still transport. The Institute asked if we could supply a minibus and a car from Hong Kong as their jeep was now in a bad way, this could be arranged for the future.

It was Sunday 26th February before we set off for Liuzhou as the jeep needed some repairs. The brake pipe burst on the way and after some temporary repairs we topped the brake fluid up with Chinese fire water spirit as we had nothing else. There was no petrol available in Liuzhou so we headed towards the next town of Xin Cheng where we found enough fuel to get us to Bama. Spending the night in Xin Cheng we were once more on the road in the early morning, this time the back wheel of the jeep seized up, probably due to using booze instead of brake fluid.

Spending the night in Bama we set off on 28th February after having the brake pipe welded and headed north along the road from Poyue to Fengshan County. Beyond one of the caves we explored in 1988, Tian Ping we observed numerous valleys and dolines where the underground river emerged into daylight and disappeared once more underground.

It was then that we saw it at the other side of the road. A river emerged from a cave near a small village but above was a large cave entrance followed by an even bigger one above the first. The upper entrance was larger than any we had ever seen previously anywhere in the world. From our position it was impossible to estimate its dimensions. To describe it as huge was an understatement. That night we stayed in the main town of Fengshan County, Feng Cheng and we were told we that we were the first Europeans ever to visit their county.

At a meeting the following day with the Deputy Director of the town he explained that during the wet season they had problems with flooding in the dolines that were farmed to the west of Feng Cheng, and asked if we could help by exploring and mapping the underground rivers. The cave and the massive entrance we had seen from the road they called Ma Wang Dong.

To the north of the village we mapped a large cave called Chuan Leng Yan with a river and a road going through it to a doline. The river emerged from another cave at the far side but was blocked by boulders after 150 metres. The cave had a good strong wind, so it was possible there was a route somewhere through the fallen blocks. Above was a mined tunnel and the river had been utilised as a hydroelectric plant that fed a small factory.

On Thursday 2nd March, we retraced our route south back down the road and crossed to the other side of the valley to a small village called She Geng. Above the village was Chuan Dong, a massive spectacular natural arched bridge with the short cave going right through the mountain. Ma Wang Dong was next on the list situated close by. The underground river was an amazing pale blue colour, a series of deep lakes through natural arches open to the sky; we both remarked what a wonderful tourist attraction this would make. There were a number of bamboo rafts, but we headed off for the big entrance, which was impossible to resist. Climbing up a rocky slope we reached the first cave about 100 metres high, this was another short cave that went right through the hill. On the other side we climbed further to gain the entrance of the main Ma Wang Dong. The view down into the entrance chamber was indeed spectacular with dimensions of 160 metres wide and about 80 metres high. We walked down a steep slope to a deep gorge crossing the passage. At the bottom was the river we had seen at the base of the cliff. A thin bamboo pole stretched across the void against the right-hand wall and a man-made wall guarded the pole bridge. There was no way we fancied balancing across a flimsy pole with a great drop below, but a villager joined us and proceeded to waltz across in his plimsolls. After all we were the expert cave explorers from the other side of the world so we just had to follow him; if it held his weight it would hold ours. We gingerly and nervously made our way across.

We began mapping into the chamber and found evidence of occupation. Looking back towards the entrance and the man-made wall it looked like the perfect fortified hideout. Only one person at a time could cross into the chamber from the entrance, easy to defend from an enemy.

We mapped the ongoing passage with our village friend holding the tape along a tunnel 100 metres high to another deep drop down to the underground river; our Chinese friend soon got the hang of it. The passage continued on the far side of the gorge but could only be gained by climbing and fixing rope protection along the left-hand wall. There were many leads to follow, a job for the main team when they arrived. The translation of Ma Wang Dong was interpreted as Horse King Cave or House of the King and without doubt this was one of the largest entrance chambers and cave passage in the world.

It was now important that we found a base close by so on Friday 3rd

March we met the Director of Da Yang village who was also the Police Chief for the area. He offered us the use of a basic building with six rooms where we could set up our base at a small village called Yueli. The building was two storeys high with rooms above with a few bunk beds and downstairs a room where we could store equipment and draw up our maps. This was ideal as it was situated next to the road and only four kilometres south of Ma Wang Dong. We arranged for a man to cook breakfast and a dinner in the evening for the team.

The river flowing from Ma Wang Dong flowed across the sandstone and shale capped valley and sank below ground in a cave near the village of Da Yang. This proved to be a beautiful river cave where we used a bamboo raft to cross a lake. It emerged to daylight at the other side of the hill in the valley just north east of Yueli village. The river crossed the valley to flow into yet another cave called Xiao Shui Dong. The following day, we mapped this cave to a large lake where we were amazed to find a man with a candle and a fishing pole. The lake was a sump, but a bypass was followed leading to a collapsed doline window up a steep climb to day light. The passage continued beyond and we could just make out daylight ahead, yet another job for the main team.

Another river flowed from a cave entrance joining the main flow from Da Nang Dong emerging into the valley from the north side. The number of caves to explore and map was mounting up dramatically.

On Sunday 5th March we looked at another valley system further to the north where we had noticed the river flowing on the surface. Sure enough the river flowed into another great river cave called Xiao Jingli which we mapped to a deep fast flowing lake about 40 metres wide. With the aid of a rope we crossed to the other side without reaching the end after a distance of over one kilometre. A massive ramp up boulders with lots of mist was followed again without reaching any end. At the north side of the valley the river emerged once more from a cave entrance, but we did not investigate for lack of time.

During the course of the expedition this area was not revisited as the team had so many other caves to explore and map and as far as I know, no one has ever been back there. That night the main team had arrived at Bama. Gavin and I had already surveyed over six kilometres of cave passage in just five days and the potential for connecting up these caves into the 1988 expedition discoveries looked promising, the Pan Yang Cave System seemed to be as suspected of immense length and very complex, a world class ranking system of caves. The next day we set up base at Yueli village.

Yueli village was an interesting place to live; it had electricity at night as the source was a hydroelectric supply but the dam drained dry after a couple of hours, so the lights went out. When the local engineering shop used an electric arc welder the lights dimmed to a tiny glow. They even had a cinema showing ancient Chinese movies which always seemed to feature a European with a black beard as the villain dressed in a long tailed black coat, but the villagers loved it. The village hall was another strange place where the men would gather in the evenings drinking tea and playing a finger game to much shouting out of numbers; I presumed it was a little like the children's game of Scissors. We joined in but could never quite figure it out.

One of the main objectives was Feng Dong, the deep shaft found the year before with the wind and mist blowing out resembling a smoking chimney. This time we had plenty of rope so Ben, Steve Jones, Julian, Alan, Kevin, Lian and Chen set of with six porters to bivouac near the windy hole in the hill.

Dave and Steve Ray mapped the Chushui cave where the river emerged from the mountain but it hit a sump after only 250 metres. They mapped another 250 metre cave close to the village of Yueli.

Kenny, Gavin and I continued with the exploration of Xiao Shui Dong to the daylight we had seen a few days previously. We emerged in a massive doline containing a small village called Weipo. On the far side of the doline the cave continued, called by the villagers Dasuo Dong, and again this led through the mountain to yet another doline with the isolated village of Xiao Suo Qiang nestling between the mountains. We returned back to base after mapping just short of two kilometres of fantastically large cave passage.

Dave and Steve continued clocking up caves near our base mapping Shan Zhai Dong for 750 metres, while Gavin, Kenny and I returned to Weipo finding three shafts. One was a huge jungle clad shaft near the road with a five second drop when a boulder was thrown down. It reminded me of the giant shafts in the jungles of East New Britain, Papua New Guinea and was named Xiang Shui. A river could just be seen at the base of the shaft but no cave entrances. I descended a steep slope with the aid of a rope tied to trees through the undergrowth and arrived at the edge but was still about 100 metres from the bottom. Kenny rigged the shaft later on during the expedition but did not reach the bottom as he could see that the river emerged from a flooded cave and disappeared down a similar one. Another collapsed hole was found just to the north of the road with a deep drop into a cave.

The following day it was discovered that the road had been constructed right over the top of Dauso Dong breaking through the roof of the cave. It was pointed out how important it was for caves to be mapped before construction takes place so events like this could be avoided. The workers blasting a route along the mountains could well have fallen through to their deaths. We rigged the pitch through the roof for a photographic session and explored a beautiful side passage with calcite dams full of crystal clear blue water.

The shaft in the Weipo doline was rigged down to a stream but unfortunately the stream entering emerged from an impenetrable small hole.

On Friday 10th March, Steve and Gavin mapped Xiao Bolong to the north of Yueli. A mini hydroelectrical plant had utilised the river so the cave had been flooded by construction of a dam. A cave on the south side of the valley was mapped for 500 metres while Dave and I investigated the same river where it disappeared underground finding a large cave entrance and a lake which we crossed on a bamboo raft to a totally flooded section. A few side passages were mapped with the draught disappearing up into the roof probably to a higher entrance.

That night Ben's team arrived back from their bivouac at Feng Dong. They had descended the shaft for -320 metres using 400 metres of ropes in the process. Arriving at the base of the roped shaft they explored a series of steeply descending passages going up and then down with the wind still howling through to a 20 metre pitch, but by this time they had run out of rope so were forced to retreat. The pitch was described as awkward and dangerous with some loose rocks as there was nowhere to escape in the event of a rock fall.

A few days later, Steve Ray, Kenny and Alan along with Zhu returned for a three-day bivouac. Kenny rigged the 20 metre pitch to two passages continuing into the unknown and called it a day as to progress further would involve an underground camp which we were not kitted up for. They de-rigged all the ropes and returned to base.

On Monday 13th March, Julian and Steve Jones began the climb in Ma Wang Dong across the chasm in the floor. Julian fixed numerous 6mm bolts and hangers in the left-hand wall so he could fix a traverse rope skirting the chasm.

Dave and Ben hiked across the mountains past Feng Dong and descending into a doline found a group of ladies drying their long hair at a small cave entrance which they called Chuifeng, Hair Dryer Cave. A very powerful inward wind provided a steady stream of hot air. They said excuse me and passed the ladies having great trouble trying to keep their carbide lamp flames lit as the flames kept blowing out in the wind. The small entrance opened up into a nice roomy passage which they mapped for 500 metres with no end in sight.

The next day Julian and Steve Jones finished the bolt traverse and entered the massive beautifully decorated continuing passage beyond mapping it for over one kilometre with no end in sight while Ben and Dave continued with the exploration of Hair Dryer Cave, Chuifeng.

Kevin and I were led across the mountains near Hair Dryer by a large group of children to two large high-level caves called Chuan. They were only short in length but contained huge stalagmites where it was possible to get lost by going around in circles. One had a massive entrance with clouds in the roof.

On Wednesday 15th March, Julian, Steve Jones and Kenny were back in Ma Wang Dong and reached a doline after a further 1.7 kilometres with an old bamboo ladder leading up into the daylight. The ladder was crumbling away and far too dangerous to ascend.

Professor Zhu, while walking near Ma Wang, had discovered a large entrance 200 metres above the road beyond the bridge cave of Chuan. Dave, Ben and I investigated and discovered a magnificent very large cave passage to a steep slope down requiring a rope after one kilometre. We called it after the professor, Gantuan.

The cave was fully explored over the remaining days of the expedition; the slope was rigged with a rope but was completely blocked at the base but Steve Jones followed a traverse above the floor of the passage and discovered a 23 metre pitch which again was rigged with a rope. An old bamboo pole was found at the base of the pitch and a huge chamber with massive stalagmites was entered.

A few days later, I returned with Julian, Steve Jones and Dave and continued mapping the large chamber at the base of the pitch but could find no way on. With Steve Ray and Kevin, I returned on the 25th March and we finally found a way on to 1.6 kilometres of beautiful large passage into a massive chamber. The chamber was dominated by huge black soot stained stalagmites with bright orange tops and soot also marked pathways everywhere with a number of burnt sticks lying around. We could find no way on from the chamber as calcite formations completely blocked any passages which may have been open a few million years ago. It was obvious that the cave had been explored many years previously by Chinese, we had no idea why and the few metres of orange stained calcite deposited on the stalagmites indicated just how long ago this was as calcite is deposited very slowly and this deposit occurred after the cave was explored with lighting from burning sticks. They must have descended to a 23 metre pitch using a bamboo pole. It was possible that this cave was used as a hide out for bandits.

The main entrance chamber of Ma Wang Dong was surveyed around the walls in order to give us some indication of its dimensions and Alan and I continued with the exploration of Dasuo mapping a 400 metre side passage to a wall which needed climbing aids to reach a high level passage seen at the top.

Fencong karst, classic scenery in Guanxi, China. Photo: Jerry Wooldridge.

On Friday 17th March, exploration began of the river below the Ma Wang Dong entrance. These magnificent pale blue lakes explored using bamboo rafts led through rock arches into more lakes open to the sky. A side passage was mapped for 800 metres to a small entrance close to the road. There was no way on beyond the lakes as the continuing passage was completely flooded beyond the last one. Gavin produced some incredible photographs of a couple of cavers balancing on a bamboo raft and poling the raft across the lakes. One was made later into a fine poster for sale in aid of the China Caves Project. I had it proudly taped to my wall at home for many years.

Two days later, Alan and I joined Gavin, Julian and Steve Jones taking photographs in Hair Dryer. We mapped a few side passages which crossed the main passage, upwards to blockages and down to the water table, any possible passages below this level would be completely flooded. The end point of the cave terminated in some huge Gower Pools. These are calcite dams full of deep blue water and Gavin produced some stunning photographs with a man in one of my RFD red dinghies which had been used in New Britain, Papua New Guinea boating across the lakes. Some of these dams were high and climbing was necessary to reach the pools. When one was crossed another appeared, the last one found that day was six metres high and could not be climbed without bolting equipment.

Alan, Dave and Steve Ray passed this obstacle a few days later and rigged the wall of the dam with a rope. The passage continued beyond which they followed for 180 metres until they found recent footprints that must have been left by the explorers of Feng Dong. It began to look like a connection had been made and the source of the wind in Feng Dong originated from Hair Dryer because of the difference in barometric pressure due to the great difference in height. The natural flue and the chimney had been connected.

Julian and Steve Jones returned sometime later and explored a further 500 metres of passage with no end in sight with many passages left to explore and confirmed the connection.

We were not yet finished with our most important discovery, Ma Wang Dong, and during a mass photographic session with Gavin we discovered a passage leading off from the main chamber which reached an entrance overlooking the valley after 800 metres. The river at the base of the entrance gorge where the flimsy bamboo pole was situated was reached and the dinghy lowered down to Gavin and Kevin. The lake was explored for 500 metres but was flooded in both the upstream and downstream direction. Julian and Steve Jones descended the gorge which Julian had bolted across to reach the passage on the other side. Again, at the base they found a deep lake which was followed for one kilometre to an upstream sump. It was obvious that these two rivers connected back to the main river rising at the blue lakes.

The final wall with the old bamboo pole at the furthest point reached in Ma Wang Dong was finally passed by Gavin, Julian and Steve Jones into the doline open to the sky. This resembled a lost world and so was named as such. The cave continued on the far side and they mapped a further 2 kilometres without reaching a conclusion. Again, Gavin's photographs of giant 70 metre high stalagmites were spectacular.

This system has not been revisited as far as I know but other China Caves Project expeditions have found caves to the west which are most probably a part of this huge westerly continuation of the Pang Yan Cave System.

A few more caves were mapped just to tidy up in the remaining days, with another fine very large upper cave above Da Yang Dong called Boatun explored for 800 metres; this passed through the hill and was extremely well decorated again with huge stalagmites and was photographed once more by Gavin.

Jinsa Dong was mapped for 1.5 kilometres by Steve Ray, Dave, Alan and I and as we found in so many caves it passed right through the hill beneath the road popping out in the same valley as Tian Ping Dong.

On our last day exploration centred to the west of Gan Tuan with a number of caves explored but none to a conclusion.

The Political Chief of the area asked us if we could find coal, as the area was considered as being economically poor. We explained that they were sitting on a fortune as regards to the area's tourist potential. Ma Wang Dong is a unique cave and tourist trips could be developed with careful planning. It was pointed out that the main problem was access as the roads leading into the three counties needed upgrading, all problems which could be overcome.

The expedition had explored and mapped an outstanding 39 kilometres of some of the world's largest caves in just 28 days. Including the caves discovered on the first expedition, the Pan Yang Dong system totalled 52 kilometres at that time. Today the area has been recognised by the Chinese government as an area of outstanding natural beauty and protection measures imposed. Our advice was followed, and Ma Wang Dong is now an important tourist attraction with boat trip on the lakes and a restaurant on one of the boats. Once more we had contributed towards the long-term sustainable prosperity of this region and become a part of the history of exploration. It was satisfying when many years later one of the expedition members told me it was the best expedition he had ever been on.

Entrance to the Solue Resurgence, Guanxi, China. Photo: Jerry Wooldridge.

We would have liked to return to continue the work on another expedition, but the costs imposed by our Chinese colleagues precluded an immediate return. Another expedition was in the offering which would be partly sponsored by them as it was of interest for the Chinese to have a complete underground survey of an area in Yunnan Province where water supplies was a huge problem.

20

Gunung Mulu Expedition, 1988

'Nothing will ever be attempted if all possible objections must first be overcome.

Samuel Johnson

At last I had been invited by Jerry Wooldridge to join his expedition to this legendary park of giant caves. The team had great expectations of things to come and we were not disappointed.

It was shortly after one of my cave exploration expeditions in 1986, the Untamed River Expedition to New Britain in Papua New Guinea, when a colleague of mine, Ben Lyon asked me to be one of the judges for the International Caving Film Festival in the Vercors France. I had known Ben for many years, and he was now a successful businessman being the main UK distributor for Petzl caving equipment and a highly respected cave explorer in his own right. I agreed and spent a pleasant few days with Ben driving to the festival. On the way he happened to mention that Jerry Wooldridge, an old friend and renowned British cave photographer was organising a cave exploration expedition to the Gunung Mulu National Park in Sarawak.

Being a member of the federation of Malaysia, Sarawak is situated on the island of Borneo and is something of a tropical paradise. Large areas are still preserved as national parks, nature reserves or wildlife sanctuaries. I was well versed in living and working in tropical rain forests after my recent five-month expedition to New Britain and of course had always wanted to go to Gunung Mulu. The work of the three previous Mulu expeditions was well known and documented, every cave explorer worth his salt had read about the giant caves of Gunung Mulu and the spectacular tropical karst.

'Give him a ring,' said Ben.

On my return to the wilds of Derbyshire I did just that and Jerry invited me on the team. Matt Kirby, Richard Chambers, Tim and Pam Fogg, Jerry and I made up an ideal small team of six. The expedition was scheduled for

November of 1988.

At that time Mike Meredith worked at the park as the development officer, developing the park, including four caves, for tourism. Mike being one of the original expedition members from the 80's expeditions had been asked by the Sarawak Forest Department to take on the job, as no one in Malaysia knew anything about caves. Although Gunung Mulu was scheduled as a park in 1974, it was not until 1985 that it was opened to adventure tourists.

We contacted Mike and the relevant Sarawak authorities seeking permission. This proved to be a difficult task as letters and faxes went unanswered. In the end, on the way back from one of their travels, both Tim and Pam called at Kuching, the capital city of Sarawak. Just a few days before the expedition was due to take place, they secured an interview with the late Minister of Tourism, Datuk Amar James Wong Kim Min, one of Sarawak's most famous political figures.

The problem, as we all knew only too well, derived from the last expedition in 1984. A certain Swiss gentleman named Bruno Manser had turned up in Sarawak out of the blue. Claiming he was a cave explorer from Switzerland, he asked the team leader if he could join in the fun and games and indeed he proved to be a dedicated worker and a good cave explorer. Unfortunately, he disappeared into the rain forest after the expedition, recording in the log, *'I am going to find the Penan.'* The Penan he referred to were the last remaining true nomadic indigenous groups left in Borneo, their way of life fast disappearing.

Bruno became something of a celebrity, spending five years in the forest with the Penan. Evading capture by the Sarawak Field Force Regiments he organized resistance and blockades against the logging companies eventually to escape and return to Switzerland after being bitten by a snake. Up to a few years ago he ran a campaign against the use of tropical timber and promoted indigenous rights for rain forest dweller. Some years later he returned to Sarawak and went missing somewhere around a famous mountain called Batu Lawi and is now presumed dead. Bruno's actions had obviously tainted the reputation of British cave explorers and we were viewed with great suspicion. Would we do likewise and run off into the forest? Hardly likely but their concerns were completely understandable.

Tim and Pam eventually convinced Datuk James that our only interest lay in the exploration of caves, training local guides and generally promoting the Gunung Mulu National Park as an international tourist destination. Sarawak's logging policy was not our concern. Permission was granted and

Journeys beneath the Earth

we agreed to attempt a connection between two large cave systems, Clearwater Cave and Cave of the Winds. The reason for the interest in a connection lay in the fact that Clearwater was, until a few years previously, the longest cave in South East Asia at 48 kilometres in length. It had just been beaten by the Australian explorations in Mamo Kananda in Papua New Guinea. Under the leadership of an ex-patriot, Dr Julia James from Sidney University, Mamo Kananda had been explored for over 50 kilometres in length, pushing Clearwater into second place. This would not do, and Datuk James wanted a Gunung Mulu cave back in first place and rightly so.

Ater a meeting with the Director of Forest, Datuk Leo Chai who explained Sarawak's sustainable logging policy and the foolishness of Bruno Manser, permission was given.

Sarawak is a member of the Federation of Malaysia and is a fantastic tropical county with rainforests, huge rivers and high mountains situated on the Island of Borneo with a diverse population of 2.8 million with different groups, cultures and native tribes. It's almost as large as all the thirteen Malaysian States put together as it covers an area 124,000 square kilometres, just 6,400 square kilometres smaller than the whole of England.

There are large groups of Chinese, Muslim and Christians all living together in peaceful harmony, a beacon of tolerance which many areas of the world could well learn from. It is possible to see a mosque near a Christian church with a Chinese temple close by. This remarkable achievement has been brought about via a political coalition of the various groups in an attempt to give all groups an equal chance and a say in government. It is quite common to sit around a table with a Muslim, a Chinese and three or four other Christian native groups and all eat together with respect for each other's cultural and religious differences. Chinese, Muslim, Christian festivals and native festivals are all celebrated by all the population together. There are few countries in the world where this would be acceptable. Peaceful coexistence, respect and tolerance are the keys to the harmony found in Sarawak. The world would be a far better place if this could be implemented in other countries.

Sarawak is also famous for its high biodiversity and especially the orang-utan's that still roam wild in the protected forest areas and its many other Totally Protected Areas are all of unique value.

The history of the country is also fascinating and reads like a swashbuckling novel as it was largely formed under an English adventurer called James Brooke. He inherited a ship and decided to sail to South East Asia and make his fortune.

In 1841 James Brooke became the first British White Rajah of Sarawak, an area encompassing the Sarawak River basin where the capital of Kuching is situated. Before this period the whole of Sarawak as it is known today came under the jurisdiction of the Sultan of Brunei, but a deal was made for Brooke to control the warring native tribes and in return he would be made the first White Rajah. At this time there was much tribal warfare and head hunting was a popular pastime, this was banned by the Brooke administration and some measure of control imposed.

From 1868 to 1917, Charles Brooke became the second white Rajah of Sarawak and the country was greatly expanded to include in 1882 the Baram River Basin. This area of 30,000 square kilometres was ceded from the Sultan of Brunei for a perpetual annual sum and the majority of the Gunung Mulu National Park lies within the catchment of the Baram River. The northern sectors of the park lie within the catchment of the Limbang River. The Limbang River catchment was again ceded by Sarawak from the Sultan of Brunei thus dividing Brunei into two separate sections.

In 1888, Brunei became a British Protectorate and from 1917 to 1946 Vyner Brooke became the third white Rajah of Sarawak. From 1941 to 1945 the Japanese occupied Sarawak and Brunei and in 1946 after the succession of hostilities, Sarawak became a British Crown Colony as the infrastructure required rebuilding. Independence came in 1963 and Sarawak joined the Federation of Malaysia.

In 1858, Spencer St. John, the Consul General to Borneo, visited Gunung Mulu and attempted to climb to the summit but was thwarted by limestone cliffs, dense jungle and sharp pinnacles of rocks. In 1932 Edward Shackleton, the son of the famous Antarctic explorer, with Tom Harrisson's Oxford University Expedition was led by a Berawan called Tama Nilong to the summit of Gunung Mulu following an old white rhino trail. In 1951, a Sarawak Museum expedition lead by the then Curator, Tom Harrisson, obtained bird and mammals specimens. The story of Tom Harrisson is a remarkable adventure story in itself, as he and other very brave men were parachuted into the heart of Borneo to organise a resistance movement of native groups during the last war to fight the Japanese with considerable success.

The first geologist to visit Gunung Mulu was Dr Gerry E. Wilford in 1961 who at that time was working for the Borneo Geological Survey. He mapped and explored, Deer Cave, parts of Wind Cave and a few other caves of Gunung Api and Benarat and in 1964 published what was to become the catalyst for future expeditions to Gunung Mulu, The Geology of Sarawak and Sabah Caves.

In the period from 1960 to 1973, Dr J. A. R. Anderson and Dr Paul Chai of the Sarawak Forest Department carried out a series of expeditions, which revealed the areas remarkable biodiversity, with over 100 new botanical species. Their findings resulted in the recommendations for the Gunung Mulu National Park to be constituted as a totally protected area. National Parks and Wildlife is administered under the Sarawak Forest Department and the Gunung Mulu National Park is considered as one of their crown jewels of biodiversity, geological landforms and outstanding natural beauty. The park is dominated by the mountain of Gunung Mulu, a sandstone formation, but overlying is the Melinau Limestone's containing massive caves. The park ranges in altitude from 28 metres to 2,377 metres above sea level with huge areas of primary rainforest with different vegetation zones so is a prime area for research.

In 1977 to 1978 the first major foreign expedition organised by the Royal Geographical Society UK and the Sarawak Forest Department spent over 15 months in the field. Over 100 scientists took part and all the inventories of species and the Management Plan was compiled under the leadership of Robin Hanbury-Tenison. A few cave explorers took part and over 45 kilometres of caves were explored and mapped during this expedition revealing Deer Cave as the largest cave passage in the world at that time.

Exploration of the caves continued with a follow up expedition in 1980 from the UK with a further 50 kilometres explored and mapped by cave explorers helped by local Berawan guides. The world's largest underground chamber was discovered which was named Sarawak Chamber in a cave called Nasib Bagus, and geomorphologic and cave biological studies was also undertaken. Gunung Buda to the north was visited and a few caves explored and mapped; this expedition ascertained the potential of the Gunung Buda limestone for further cave exploration as this area was not within the park boundary.

Another major British caving expedition took place in 1984 bringing the total of cave passages explored to 160 kilometres with the Clearwater Cave System reaching a total length of 48 kilometres.

Deer Cave is one of the two largest cave passages in the world with dimensions of 120 to 150 metres with one of the largest colonies of bats at several million individuals and numerous different species. The other contender for the world's largest diameter cave passage is called Hang Son Doong which has recently been explored in Vietnam by Howard Limbert and his UK team of cave explorers.

Sarawak Chamber found by the British expedition is the largest natural underground space in the world, measuring 600 metres long by 415 metres wide and 80 metres high, with a floor area of 162,700 square metres and a volume of 12 million cubic metres. The chamber is larger than any man-made structure with an unsupported roof so is of great interest for geological study on why it does not collapse.

Deer Cave, Sarawak, Malaysia. Photo: Jerry Wooldridge.

I travelled out with Richard Chambers on Monday 31st October 1988 and we slept on the floor of Kuching airport on the night of the 1st November as we arrived late at 11.30 pm so there were no flights until the following day to Miri. Kuching is the capital of Sarawak while Miri is a boom oil city to the north, close to the border of the neighbouring independent country of Brunei Darussalam. We flew to Miri and met up with two of the team, Pam and Tim Fogg, they had been sorting out our permit with the Forest Department in Kuching and Jerry Wooldridge and Matt Kirby were to join us the next day. On Wednesday 2nd November, we caught the ferry up the mighty Baram River to Marudi town, a trading town situated on the banks of the river where we spent the night.

We were met by Mike who had offered to arrange logistics at the park during our stay and the following day we purchased our food supplies and cooking equipment and again by ferry boat travelled upstream to the tributary of the Baram River, the Tutoh River. We arrived at a Long House called Long Terawan, which is occupied by a native group called Berawan.

There are numerous native groups living in Sarawak and the Berawan are classified as Orang Ulu along with many others, which can be translated as Up River People. Many of them were employed at the Gunung Mulu National Park as their ancestors had occupied the area for a few hundred years so they knew the park well. From Long Terawan we travelled up the Tutoh River by longboat, passing rapids, and arrived at a tourist lodge called Tropical Adventure where we could eat and consume large quantities of alcohol situated on the banks of a tributary to the Tutoh called the Melinau River. At the opposite side of the river was the temporary park headquarters where we were provided with a bunk house.

On 4th November, we decided to conduct a preliminary familiarisation survey of Clearwater Cave. Our main objective was to attempt to increase the total length of this cave so it once more became the longest cave in Asia; one way of achieving this aim was by finding a connecting passage from Wind Cave situated close by. Both Wind Cave and Clearwater are accessible by longboat upstream along the Melinau River. The entrance sections of Clearwater are open to the public as a show cave where tourists can descend to the spectacular underground river.

Mike had a few boats in the underground river of Clearwater, so we paddled our way upstream for about one kilometre to a large passage on the right called Battleship, so named because of a massive boulder with stalagmites sticking out at an angle pointing towards the enemy. It was here we found a note left by the original explorers signed by none other than Bruno Manser. We found the way up a steep boulder slope and a climb to the huge main upper series called Inflation. Fun was had on the way back when the river flooded and the boat capsized. I just had to remark if this was in the Nare cave we would all be dead.

One of the nice things about caving in the tropics is that the cave temperature is high as caves normally have an average temperature for the area where they are situated. Alpine caves are very cold, some containing ice and in British caves insulated clothing is worn as hypothermia can be a problem. In the caves of Gunung Mulu we can cave in a tee shirt and shorts and still sweat.

Mike assigned a park guide called Wan Kulay to accompany us and we spent the next few days in Wind Cave searching for a possible lead which would take us into Clearwater Cave. Wan was a good caver as most Berawan seem to have a natural aptitude for moving safely through a cave. All we found was another small entrance leading into a jungle covered doline not far from the final chamber which had been named Illusion by the original explorer.

On Sunday 6th November, Matt, Jerry, Pam and I were back in Wind Cave. I followed the bedding passage steeply up the dip of the beds of limestone and mapped 200 metres from Illusion Chamber but with no way on at the top. Pam and Matt found a passage going down steeply through loose boulders with an encouraging draught while Tim, Wan and Richard searched Hyperspace passage in Clearwater for a likely passage which may connect. Anything with a wind was considered to be the most promising lead to follow.

The following day, Tim, Pam, Richard and Wan returned to Hyperspace and at the very end found a narrow hole going steeply upwards through loose boulders with a good draught of air. Matt and I along with another Edmund, one of the park guides, carried on searching in Wind Cave and after mapping to the new tiny entrance we headed off to the final Illusion Chamber where we heard voices from the distance. Tim and Wan appeared having succeeded in climbing upwards at the narrow hole through the loose boulders following the wind. The connection had been made so Tim, Matt, Edmund and I completed the first through trip from Wind Cave to Clearwater Cave amidst much jubilation. We called the connecting passage Wan Way Street after our park guide. The Clearwater Cave System was once more the longest cave in Asia and we informed the Minister of Tourism, Datuk James Wong and all got rather drunk that night along with two tourists. Charlie Marvin was from the USA and liked the park so much he had returned to Marudi to renew his permit. I was to meet him again a couple of years later in a totally different country.

It soon became obvious to us that the Mulu caves and the jungle are hard on clothes and boots. Nothing dries out so leather goes mouldy; cloths rot and boots fall to bits. The rock in the caves is sharp and the floors covered in boulders so caving equipment does wear out fast along with skin. Cuts need to be treated as a bacterial disease is present in the caves called leptospirosis. This disease in Britain is known as Weil's Syndrome and is transmitted through the rats' urine. In Mulu it is probable that bats are the carriers, it is therefore not advisable to drink the water in the caves unless it is first boiled. If a caver starts with a temperature the disease can be treated with antibiotic so we made sure our medical supplies were up to date with drugs and antiseptics which proved to be a good move as we were to find out later.

Next stage of the expedition was to search for entrances in the thick jungle slopes of the mountain of Gunung Api as the Clearwater cave system only extended less than halfway inside the mountain. Vast areas in the central and northern parts had no recorded caves. It seemed obvious that the cave system extended to the north, the problem was finding it. Previous explorations of Clearwater to the north had petered out but with a vast complex cave system, it was easy to miss a possible continuation. A careful examination of possible leads might lead into the projected continuation. To this end a jungle camp was established over the next few days with the help of Penan porters along the western flanks of the mountain near a known cave called Leopard Cave, which contained a river issuing from within.

We asked Wan to find us a cook and he said he would ask his cousin, who surprisingly turned out to be a very pretty young lady called Helen who did not seem to mind living in the jungle for a few weeks with a load of uncouth cavers.

On Wednesday 9th November, we trekked through the forest from Clearwater Cave for two hours continually pulling off leeches; they seemed to have a preference for European blood as our Penan porters did not receive any bites. Leeches cannot be felt as when they bite through the skin, they secrete an anaesthetic and if wearing shorts can suck blood from very embarrassing places without one knowing until a very fat, blood-filled leech is found guzzling away from one's private parts. The best way of getting rid of them is salt or a singeing with a lit cigarette, but this can be a tricky operation if they are situated on the delicate parts of the body. They also liked to sneak into socks so when we pulled off our boots we often found a boot full of blood and very messy socks but the bites did stop bleeding after a while.

One of our porters was a young Penan man called Miry, and Wan told me that when he was about 12 years old his parents passed away so he disappeared for years and lived alone in the forest with little more than his blow pipe and parang. One night at our camp he borrowed a torch and a short while later returned with a few fat toads which he cooked, as he was not all that keen on our western food. I declined his offer of a toad and stuck to our own food.

The following day, we located the entrance into the far reaches of Clearwater which had been named Snake Track. These caves are inhabited by Racer Snakes which navigates in the dark following trails left over thousands of years by their ancestors so the rocks where they slither along become polished and easy to recognise. They coil up on a rock and detect bats or cave swiftlets as they fly past grabbing one for a tasty dinner, presumably by detecting a change in air pressure as unlike cave explorers they do not have a helmet and light. The snakes can be aggressive if disturbed and can grow to a few metres in length so are best left alone as after all this is their domain, not ours. The caves are also occupied by bats, swiftlets and troglobitic insects, some of the insects can be extremely poisonous, again best avoided, so it is important to watch where you place your hands on the rocks.

Over the next few days, armed with the original cave maps many areas were investigated and a few short unexplored passages explored but nothing leading on into the unknown northern blank spaces under the mountain of Gunung Api. Right at the very northern end a very small entrance was discovered during the last expedition but seemed impossible to locate from the surface as it was tiny and situated in a jumble of rocks and none of the team members had ever been in this area before. If we could locate this it would provide an easy route into the furthest reaches of the cave system, but we failed to find the correct route through into the northern sections of Clearwater. We did eventually locate a very small hole in approximately the correct place on the surface with a powerful wind, but it was so small we presumed it had collapsed.

Jerry and Mike planned to produce a book of the Gunung Mulu caves illustrated with colour photographs so Jerry bivouacked in Clearwater for a few days with Pam, Tim, and park guides Michael Dapa, Wan and Edmund. Matt, Richard and I along with park guides Simon Lagang and Joshua began the difficult task of searching the flanks of the mountain to the north, looking for cave entrances. Most open entrances are situated 30 to 50 metres above the alluvial plane and are impossible to see through the dense vegetation so the only way of detecting an entrance is to detect a breeze or a smell of guano. If leaves are seen moving or bat droppings can be smelt, there is probably a cave entrance close by and we found one.

I mapped it the following day teaching park guides Joshua and Simon how to survey caves. Unfortunately the cave terminated back at base level and was only 200 metres in length. Considering 12th November was my birthday, I called it Birthday Cave. Matt and Richard had better luck as they continued searching along the mountain flanks for a further one kilometre and found a couple of promising looking entrances. That night Tim and his team returned from Clearwater after exploring beyond a 100 metre deep pitch called Ronnie's Delight to yet another 100 metre deep pitch which he called Deep Thought but by then he had run out of rope. This area is leading into a blank area on the map but is extremely remote so it was not visited again.

Next day along with two park guides, Simon and Joshua, I mapped a short cave found by one of the park guides called Noah, so it became known as Noah's Cave. It was beautifully decorated with various cave formations which unfortunately completely blocked the continuation of the passage. The popular book being read at the time was Douglas Adams The Hitch Hikers Guide to the Galaxy, so I spent some time back at camp designing a fictitious cave which I promised we were going to find, Matt started to call me Slartibartfast after the designer of planets.

The two entrances with a strong wind found by Matt and Richard looked very promising. Tim and Pam explored the higher of the two which we called Dapa Entrance and found that it dropped into the lower cave which was being explored by Matt and Richard at the time. The lower entrance received the name Centipede. There were many good leads to follow so the following day we were all back mapping the main continuation of a typically large Gunung Mulu cave passage to a short 10 metre pitch down into a large chamber with a few ways on. The chamber had a nice flat sandy floor with water close by so was an ideal underground camp site.

All survey stations were numbered and most marked on water proof paper with the date, name of explorers and the station number. At junctions a small cairn was constructed so that at a later date explorers could find the survey station and number to continue with the mapping from a known point. The chamber was at station number st47 so Wan and I mapped on from there across a narrow sediment gap between two massive holes in the floor into a huge tunnel approximately 15 metres in diameter heading into the unknown. It terminated in a blank wall after 500 metres but with a steep low passage descending on the left side which needed a rope but did not appear to have a draught of air. As I roll my own cigarettes, I called it Old Holborn.

Tim and Pam went from st47 in a downward direction rigging a pitch to arrive at a stream which they explored for 800 metres both up and down stream naming it Slip Steam. Matt and Richard followed another massive tunnel to an area with walls covered in gypsum flowers which received the name The Flower Shop and from there into a chaotic area, Damocles Hall. A three metre high passage led off which they named Fire Fly as the walls were covered in sparkling selenite needles. Beyond they entered an area of sandy pits in the floor to Brighton Beach so named because of all the sand and turned back at a steep slope descending down with loose boulders where they built a cairn. During this period Jerry concentrated on photography helped by a few park guides.

Back at camp that night it was obvious we had hit a huge cave system without a name. Various names were suggested but our Penan porters called this area Black Rock so Black Rock Cave came into existence.

It was decided to camp underground but our pretty cook Helen did not fancy staying on her own in the middle of the jungle so insisted of coming with us, as she was a good cook and we had a spare helmet and light she followed us down the cave along with a few Penan porters carrying equipment, food and cooking gear and Helen settled in well to life below ground.

On Wednesday 16th November we set up our bivouac in the chamber which we called Milliways better known as The Restaurant at the End of the Universe and once more began mapping. Matt and Richard asked me to map the passage they had found but it had to be pointed out that the unwritten law is that passages explored had to be mapped by the original explorers, I would continue with the exploration from where they had left off and built their cairn.

Accompanied by Wan, I descended the boulder slope from the cairn which was loose and dangerous resembling a quarry face into a very muddy area which was awkward to traverse along. We mapped as we went and arrived at a great black space where I could just make out the walls and roof. It turned out to be a junction with a huge passage far larger than anything yet discovered disappearing into darkness both to the left and right, below us was a lake with a sandy shore, which received the name Blackpool. We had hit the jackpot as it followed the strike of the beds of limestone, 90 degrees to the dip which was the direction of the majority of the major trunk routes of massive passages within the mountain.

I marked a cairn as Station Junction DWG34 and we both strolled along side by side ecstatic with wonder. The passage went basically in a straight line to the north and into unknown territory and after a kilometre or so we hit another junction with a small stream. We followed it downstream for 180 metres to a sump but a side passage close to the junction led up a steep climb for 30 metres which contained a good wind with a passage branching off which looked to be bypassing the sump. I built a cairn at the junction and had a look upstream where the passage could be seen to continue, then mapped the gallery for 800 metres on the way back to Milliways. I had become quite friendly with Wan Kulay and he told me the tragic tale of his wife who was bitten by a spider and died not long after their wedding. I named the passage after her, Rudang Gallery.

Tim and the park guide Edmund completed the exploration and mapping of Slip Stream where it terminated in a sump pool after 450 metres while Matt and Richard surveyed from Milliways to their cairn near the quarry. The horrible muddy section beyond the quarry we called Slarti's Revenge.

The following day, 17th November, Tim and Edmund came with us to Rudang Gallery and while Wan and I finished off our mapping, Tim climbed the steep sloping passage near the sump and sure enough it dropped back down rejoining the stream. Downstream went back to the sump but upstream was followed along a stream way with jet black dolomitic limestone which they called Black Silk which they mapped for 600 metres to another sump. Matt and Richard along with the park guide Philip Lawing turned right from Junction 34 and Wan and I joined them. Again, the passage this time heading towards Clearwater was huge passing a massive dam of sand which they named the Hoover Dam. It terminated in a large boulder pile leading upwards for 136 metres to a solid wall with no apparent way on. Another large passage led off to the left so Wan and I began mapping down into a very muddy area which we called Purgatory but we could hear a river running somewhere ahead. We arrived at a huge river running from left to right; there was little doubt that we had found the upstream section of the Clearwater River which I named Black Magic. Wan and I set off swimming and wading in deep water downstream where we turned back with no end in sight after 200 metres.

The following day, we all made our way back to our surface base camp after a stay underground of three days. Tim and I began a surface survey from the two entrances of Black Rock which we called Dapa Entrance after Michael who found it and Centipede Entrance. It was important that we fixed the entrances with respect to Leopard Cave as this point was known with respect to Clearwater Cave. It was also important to begin calculating all our measurements into co-ordinate data so we could begin drawing up the maps.

We would only then have some idea of where the cave was heading and the separation from Black Rock to Clearwater.

My feet were now a mess as I was suffering from Mulu Foot, as it became known, and Wan had the same condition. This manifested itself as a fungal infection; a raw red rash which if left without treatment started to bleed. It was akin to walking on red hot needles. The only treatment that worked was to dry the feet and smother them with anti-fungal powder for a few days. In these conditions, feet were permanently wet and never had much of a chance of drying out, similar to the condition experienced by soldiers in the First World War, known as Trench Foot.

On Saturday, the surface survey was completed while we started calculating and drawing maps and as suspected the cave was heading north into large blank areas on the map. The Black Magic River was without doubt an upstream continuation of the Clearwater River, which at its furthest point north was flooded to the roof; the jigsaw puzzle began to take shape. A few more park guides joined us, and they had travelled upstream by long boat along the Melinau River and then walked for a few kilometres to the camp. This was far shorter than the long walk skirting Gunung Api that we had used to establish the camp.

Sunday 20th November saw the team back down Black Rock accompanied by Yusuf and Noah two of the park guides. Wan and I were still suffering with Mulu Foot so decided to give it one more day for the sores to heal following them the next day with Philip, Noah, Helen and Jimmy Kebing another park guide. We spent the day taking photographs with Jerry and mapping a side passage off Old Holborn while Matt and Richard explored another side passage along the main tunnel. Tim, Pam and Yusuf continued from the stream junction exploring upstream which went on and on seemingly without end. They returned tired out after mapping over two kilometres of massive passage without reaching a conclusion naming it Firecracker.

The following day we all set off to explore and map beyond dividing into three separate teams to explore different sections. Tim, Pam and Yusuf stayed at camp as they were suffering after their mammoth exploration trip of the day before.

Great care was taken descending the loose boulder slope at the quarry, Wan and Jimmy followed on behind when I heard a rumble of boulders falling and a cry of pain. Dashing back, I found Jimmy cradled in Wan's arms and groaning in pain, loose boulders had given way under his weight and Jimmy had come crashing down to the bottom of the slope. The rest of the team joined me and it looked bad, Jimmy had a broken knee cap and had no chance of walking back out to the surface, he was a stretcher case but the nearest one was back at park headquarters, many kilometres away through the jungle.

The situation looked desperate as no one knew where we were, only those in the cave knew its whereabouts and we were many kilometres underground in a newly discovered cave far from daylight, which no one else in the world knew. There are no roads connecting Gunung Mulu to the closest town with a hospital which was by river over 100 kilometres away. All the UK team had experience of cave rescues as we were all members of various cave rescue organisations, so realised the difficulties facing us in order to get Jimmy out alive. Even if we managed to get him to the surface, we still had a day's journey to get him to the river through the jungle and down to a hospital. Jimmy was the son of the head man of Long Terawan and was a heavy well-built man, impossible to carry without the aid of a stretcher. We only had one choice; make a stretcher from what we could find.

Wan set off at a great pace for the surface to pick up the medical kit meeting Tim and Pam at the bivouac camp. They raced up to the quarry with food, a stove and one of our blow-up camp beds. Noah and Matt headed for the surface to cut poles for a stretcher and a leg sprint and bring back one of our nylon sheet reinforced camp beds. By threading poles through the sheet, it could be made into something resembling a cloth stretcher. I headed back to the bivouac with Jerry's photographic equipment and returned with ropes, slings and a sit harness.

When Matt and Noah arrived back, we constructed a makeshift stretcher and placed the blow-up bed on top so Jimmy had at least a little protection from being dragged over sharp rocks. After a few hours, Wan and Yusuf arrived with what little medical equipment we had so we dressed the wound as best we could and made something resembling a splint out of a few pieces of wood which was placed around the damaged leg. Dosing Jimmy with pain killers we set off up the dangerous boulder slope arriving at the top without major incident. We rested for a short while and brewed up, already exhausted.

Noah and the guides, Philip, Yusuf and Wan gathered around their friend and prayed as they did not think Jimmy would survive the long journey out. They did not feel confident knowing the remoteness, difficulties of the cave, the distance to the entrance and the total isolation of the team. I tried my best to reassure them that we would get Jimmy out alive; they seemed a little more assured and got stuck in with the long and difficult carry out.

We asked Wan to get back to the surface and try to reach the park headquarters to bring a team to the cave with a stretcher. He was an incredibly fit man and made it back out for the second time that day and navigating through the jungle in the dark found the boat on the banks of the Melinau River. He managed to travel downstream in the pitch black of night to the headquarters, an amazing feat of skill and determination.

While Pam carried all the bags of equipment, the remaining eight of us began carrying the homemade stretcher with a very heavy Jimmy tied to the pole frames along the difficult terrain. It was a case of carefully passing the stretcher forward over rocks and other obstacles as those at the back ran to the front, again to pass the stretcher onwards. We only stopped for Jimmy to have a pee while we were instructed to turn our backs, then dosed him with sleeping pills and pain killers. We covered the 1.2 kilometres back to our bivouac camp in around seven hours arriving at 10 pm that night; Helen already had the stove lit to feed the very hungry and tired explorers.

Tim Fogg is a professional cave instructor and an expert on Single Rope Techniques so offered to rig the pitch with the help of Richard. They rigged a clever Tyrolean and pulley in order to get the stretcher to the top. The pitch did not have a completely free hang and the rope went over a few rock projections so pulling a stretcher up with a very heavy man strapped inside would prove to be impossible. The stretcher had to be kept clear of the rocks. The next problem was our home-made stretcher which would without doubt fall to pieces on the way up the pitch.

We waited for five hours for the other team with the good stretcher to arrive from park headquarters and at 3 am on Wednesday they arrived so we could finally get Jimmy safely to the top of the pitch. I then directed the passing of the stretcher along the entrance series which consisted of a short-roped traverse across a vertical hole in the floor and a flat out crawl where we attached a rope to the stretcher and directed it through to the far side. We reached the surface at 8.30 am it had taken us 23 hours to carry Jimmy out and, as promised, he was still alive.

A large group had assembled on the surface and they carried Jimmy back to the boat and shipped him to hospital in Marudi. We collapsed at our surface camp with bleeding feet and the following day hobbled slowly back through the jungle to the boat and park headquarters. Tim made himself a crutch which he used to reach the boat.

The following day we got very drunk and had a party celebrating the rescue of Jimmy seeing just how many empty tins of beer we could build into a mountain on a table. From Tropical Adventure tourist lodge, we had to cross the river on a boat at night to reach our bunk house but we lost Tim when he fell overboard but luckily we saw his light still shining below the waves.

Clearwater Cave, Sarawak, Malaysia. Photo: Robbie Shone

On Saturday 26th November, we were back down Black Rock at the bivouac camp this time with Mike Meredith who wanted to see the Black Magic River. On the Sunday Mike and I pushed down stream in the river passage but the river was in flood and we did not progress far. We reached an area of very deep fast-moving water where is proved difficult to swim out against the strong current. The walls were covered in mud which seemed to indicate that the river backed up during periods of heavy rain, the probable cause being a constriction ahead, possibly a sump. We mapped the river on the way back and explored upstream, but the river emerged from boulders with no way on. Above the boulders we did find a steeply descending passage which required a rope and another which reached a traverse again requiring ropes. My feet were not yet completely healed so I tried wearing polythene bags next to the skin, which helped to reduce the pain.

Richard and Matt explored a side passage off Firecracker heading west towards the cliff face for one kilometre to a steep climb upwards which they called Racer Series after a rather large snake guarding the passage; this seemed to indicate another entrance not far ahead. Jerry, Noah and Philip obtained some stunning photographs of the Firecracker passage for the planned book.

Next day, Mike, Jerry and I started carrying the camp equipment out of the cave and back to our surface camp while Tim and Philip continued the exploration and mapping of Firecracker, they turned back at a large bank of loose silt which could not be climbed after mapping a further 800 metres of huge tunnel.

Over the next few days, we dismantled our surface camp and travelled back to park headquarters where we partied the night away in thanks to our Berawan park guides. On the way back to Miri we visited Jimmy in hospital and decided to name the quarry where he fell after him, Jimmy's Quarry.

Calculating the co-ordinates, Black Rock Cave came out at just over 14 kilometres in length and along with the other discoveries this small team of six men had discovered and mapped over 15 kilometres of previously undiscovered cave passages.

Before travelling back to the UK we had a meeting with the Minister of Tourism, Datuk Amar James Wong, who took us out to dinner at the Hilton Hotel but his driver felt very embarrassed when he had to pick us up from a very cheap run down guest house in Kuching, which was all we could afford. The press and TV were in attendance and a good story appeared in the New Straits Times written by James Richie. It appeared we had made a good impression and Datuk James asked us to return another year to continue the work. Unfortunately, I was not able to make it as I was in China at the time of the next Gunung Mulu expedition.

21

China Caves Project, Yunnan Province, 1990

'Our greatest glory is not in never falling, but in getting up every time we do.'

Confucius

By this time, my partner Maggie was getting a little pissed off with my constant wanderings and moved out, buying her own house. The Halifax Building Society was good to me and I was once more able borrow money and re-mortgage my house. I now owed six times more than I had originally borrowed 21 years ago. My eldest son Mark still lived with me and looked after the house while I went on my journeys. At the time, work was going well with some industrial contracts. Twelve hour days seven days a week were common but it enabled me to manage two expeditions a year.

Andy Eavis asked if I was interested in leading an expedition to Yunnan Province, mentioned by our Chinese hosts from the Karst Institute during the last expedition in 1989. He suggested a reconnaissance first in order to ascertain the potential and logistics. I of course agreed and left the UK on Saturday 13th January 1990 for a three week trip to China.

The reconnaissance was postponed for one week due to the official invitation from China not arriving so I could not apply for my visa permit to enter China but when it finally arrived, I booked my ticket.

Again, I travelled on the cheapest airline possible, Pakistan International Airlines to Beijing via Islamabad, Pakistan. This was a grave mistake as from the start nothing went right. The plane landed at Amsterdam to pick up more passengers and eventually after some delay took off on its way to Pakistan. After about one hour I noticed that the sun which should have been on the starboard side of the aircraft had changed to the port side. This could only mean one thing; the aircraft was going north not south. I made a discreet enquiry to the stewardess pointing out that we were going backwards and I needed to catch a flight from Islamabad to Beijing. It appeared that a Pakistan lady had been taken ill and the aircraft was heading back to

Amsterdam but I was assured the Beijing flight would wait as there were many passengers flying on to Beijing and Tokyo. We landed at 8 pm and two hours later we took off again, there was nothing wrong with the sick lady from Pakistan.

The flight arrived in Islamabad at 8 pm Pakistan time on Sunday, three hours behind schedule. A large group of passengers milled around for a few hours with nothing happening and after a great deal of asking I found a man who seemed as if he knew something. He eventually informed me that the aircraft to Beijing had left at 730 pm. We had missed it by 30 minutes. When I enquired when the next flight was, he replied next week. After another few hours with nothing happening, I finally tracked him down again and persuaded him to fly us to Karachi where we could pick up a flight to Beijing. I returned to the group and informed them, as for some unknown reason they thought I was in charge of Islamabad airport, I had to inform them that I was just a passenger.

By 1 pm we were on our way to Karachi where we were booked into a free hotel and I met a nice Japanese lady who was in the same boat and was on her way to Tokyo. We jumped in a taxi and visited the markets and the impressive Karachi Mosque and we then finished off my bottle of whisky as there was no booze in town.

My flight to Beijing the following morning, after having all my batteries confiscated by Pakistan officials, was impressive, flying over the Karakoram Mountain Range and K2. I flew over Mongolia with fine views from the scratched window of this very ancient Russian-made Rumanian Airlines flight, most of the seats were falling off their hinges and I was amazed it still flew. The communist dictator of Rumania Nicolae Ceausescu and his wife Elena had just a few days before been put up against a wall and shot for genocide.

I was now one day behind schedule and at Beijing airport tried to buy a ticket to Kunming but the ticket office wanted cash only and would not except plastic cards. Managing to obtain cash from the money change office, I dashed back to the ticket office but when I was a few feet away they saw me coming and slammed down the shutters. This meant another wasted day as I had to spend the night in Beijing.

I managed to get a bus into the city to the China Airlines office but as expected it was closed. A taxi took me to the old hotel I had stayed in previously but it had burnt to the ground; luckily I was not in it at the time, so I persuaded the taxi driver to take me to a cheap hotel for the night. The following morning, I found the China Airlines office and this time it was open but all flights that day were fully booked. Another wasted day, so I booked the flight for the next day Wednesday 17th January and went for a walk to the Forbidden City via the back gate where the guard kindly let me through considering this was the exit. Tiananmen Square had a few days previously been vacated by the Chinese Army as it had been closed during and after the demonstrations, so I was able to take a wander around without being arrested and deported.

The following day a telex message was sent to Kunming saying I was on my way and after a great deal of trouble found the Pakistan International Airline office but what a surprise, it was closed. I could see this trip was going to turn into an epic and I was not wrong.

I caught my flight to Kunming and thankfully was met at the airport by the Director of the Hydro and Geological Department; they'd expected me to arrive one week ago. We discussed the arrangements for the reconnaissance and the following day travelled the 320 kilometres south to Gejui where I was met by the Director of Water Recourses and Hydraulic Power. He supplied their geological and hydro geological maps of the area they wanted us to investigate.

It appeared there were several stream sinks and a large river rising, between which was a productive agricultural area but in the dry season there was a distinct lack of irrigation water as it all disappeared underground. A few bore holes had been drilled to find the depth of the water beneath the surface but without a great deal of success. A huge dry limestone plateau dominated the area and the stream from a major sink was suspected as flowing beneath this plateau. The project suggested was for a team of UK cave explorers to attempt to gain access and map the projected underground river.

On Saturday 20th January I began investigating the area armed with the Chinese maps. We drove for one hour to the town of Mengzi which was known as Mongtseu during the period when the area was a French colony. From Mengzi we drove to a small village called Mingjui where a seven kilometre walk passing a very old Chinese Temple, led to the main stream sink called Shi Dong. The associated cave had two entrances and descended steeply down to join the underground stream where I followed a 60 metre high passage for a couple of kilometres to a sump, a job for a diving team with compressed air bottles.

The following day we spent wandering around on the 2,000 metre high plateau. This huge area called Xi Bei Le Township was inhabited by thousands of Yi minority people living in 32 remote villages. I was informed that I was the first European to be seen in the area; this became apparent when the people dressed in their beautiful coloured traditional clothes ran away as soon as they saw me. One large shaft was found with a ten second drop, probably about 200 metres deep, and the next day I looked at the other sinks many kilometres away to the south. These were small with no apparent cave entrances and the majority of the water had been captured by a dam in an attempt to form a reservoir. The problem was the dam was leaking through fissures in the limestone and was fed by a river cave which they asked me to look at during the planned expedition.

Nearby was a walled French built village established about 100 years ago with an abandoned railway line which in years gone by connected into the French colony of Indo-China. The border with Vietnam was just a short distance to the south as the Tropic of Cancer ran through the village. The railway line was littered with very old, rusting, abandoned French railway engines and in my opinion they were of great industrial historical interest.

We looked at a few other possibilities but with no penetrable entrances so on the 23rd January we investigated the resurgence, where the river reached the surface, this they called Nan Dong. A small park and a short show cave had been developed with boat trips through a series of underground lakes but the main cave, according to the maps, appeared to be hidden behind a military concrete installation. I was told the local authorities would obtain permission for us to enter explore and map the cave as an underground river could be reached some way inside.

It became apparent at a series of meetings the following day that they were very keen for us to conduct a thorough investigation of the area along with a team of divers to penetrate the flooded sections. I agreed, if I could raise a team from the UK, providing logistics would be provided and we could conduct a reconnaissance to a different area after the expedition. They agreed and the expedition was suggested to take place during the dry season around May.

All I had to do now was get back home which was not going to be an easy matter as the Chinese informed me that their Spring Festival, better known as Chinese New Year, was on 27th January and everything would be closed.

On Thursday 25th January, we arrived back in Kunming to find all flights to Beijing had been cancelled due to the holidays. The only way back was by train which would take around three days. I managed to obtain a ticket on a sleeper and set off at 10 pm along with two elderly ladies in the same carriage. They could speak some English and both turned out to work at the

Research Institute in Beijing. One was a Doctor of Micro-Biology and the other a Doctor of Medicine and we had long interesting conversations over the next two days about China at the time of the Cultural Revolution. I asked them what they were doing during this turbulent period of Chinese history, one was forced to be a stoker in a factory boiler and the other had dug ditches. It caused stagnation and put back the development of China for over ten years, so they said. I also brought up the reported massacre in Tiananmen Square during the student demonstrations in June, just a few months previously but they both insisted that no one lost their lives and the reports in the western press was pure speculation and anti-Chinese propaganda. They did not believe that films of injured and dead had been shown on western TV and claimed that the pictures were falsified but there again the purges were still in progress so I suppose they had to say that as the walls have ears, even in railway carriages.

The following day, we passed through the Province of Guizhou and the capital Guiyang passing through some amazing karst scenery and on into Hunan Province but the next day, Chinese New Year, the onboard restaurant was closed. We starved and shared a couple of apples as we crossed the Yangtze River in the snow in a freezing cold carriage.

After a 57 hour trip, I arrived in Beijing on 28th January in time for my Pakistan International Airline flight back to the UK but again, what a surprise, the airline office was closed so I went for a walk through the snow to a park where I played snow balls with the Chinese crowd.

The next day I went to the airport to catch my flight, booked my seat and weighed in my baggage but four hours later I was still sitting there in what appeared to be an empty airport. I managed to find someone who spoke English and was told the flight had not arrived from Tokyo because of the snow. Finding the PIA office, the one person there told me to call at their office in the city. Jumping once more in a taxi I arrived at the office to find the same man who informed me the next flight was next week. When my blaspheming ceased, he said his computer was down but there may be Swiss Air flight tomorrow to Karachi then London. Refusing to pay for a hotel I stormed out in disgust before I clobbered him.

On Tuesday 30th January, I found the Swiss Air office and obtained a one way ticket to Zurich for that evening. As suspected from the beginning the trip had been something of an epic, I made sure I never flew with PIA again as I had only completed one quarter of the journey with the airline from London to Islamabad.

22

Yunnan, China, 1991

'The man who moves a mountain begins by carrying away small stones.

Confucius

This story is out of sequence as it follows on from the last chapter as I was a participant of two expeditions in 1990.

Once again, I had a great team of highly experienced cave explorers, interested in the project. Paul Seddon, Kath and Steve Jones, Gavin Newman, Steve Dickenson, Stuart Whitmey, Dick Willis, Kenny Taylor and Pete Francis. This time we imported diving bottles so the sumps could be investigated.

We set off on 16th March and flew into Kunming via Hong Kong. From Kunming we set off driving to Coaba, after fourteen hours and six breakdowns we finally arrived exhausted. On the way we looked at the famous Stone Forest, a mass of limestone pinnacles surrounded with concrete paths. This was a highly commercialised area with camel rides, masses of tourists, markets and female guides in traditional dresses. It was eventually inscribed on the World Heritage List but I suspect after much alteration.

After the usual meeting with County Government officials when they stressed the importance of finding the further reaches of the underground river in order to increase food production, we settled into our basic accommodation. The town market was interesting with the Pau minority group of women dressed in their colourful traditional outfits and the steamy silk factory.

The first objective was Da Dong which contained a lake. Dicky and Paul swam around for a while without finding any way onwards. We found out later that the Chinese pump out the water in the dry season passing four perched sumps terminating in a small bedding passage. Obviously, this was not worth diving. Dick and I looked at a cave called Ping Shi Ban but it was flooded to the roof after 100 metres, this was probably worth diving when the rest of the team arrived with the equipment.

That day the team arrived with the diving bottles and began charging them with compressed air. A few more promising caves were investigated the following day. Wuli Chin was a resurgence cave and open to the public with some electric lighting. The cave was mapped but disappointingly no major extensions were found. Over the next few days, a number of shafts were descended but all were choked and none going into the postulated underground water course. The next objective was to dive the sump in a cave called Jan Ping Ban. Steve and Gavin dived in very bad visibility to a low passage too small to get through. We had the usual trouble returning to our base with a broken-down truck blocking the road. This seemed to happen often in China.

The following day Dick, Paul and I explored and mapped Da Ta cave for 400 metres to a day light shaft. The cave contained many bats which proved to be eventful later on.

The main cave system in the area was called Nan Dong, again this was a resurgence cave with a large active river. There were two major branches; the right-hand branch contained the river. On arriving we were refused entry but after prolonged negotiation we were allowed in but banned from entering the river passage as this was classified as a military installation. Not to be outdone, Steve and Gavin explored the river to a lake. The remainder of the team began the exploration of the left-hand tunnel but after a short while the cave was raided by the army carrying stun guns. Everyone was ejected at gun point. Considering we had come all the way from the UK with our equipment at the request of the Chinese authorities, this seemed to be ridiculous. The next day, we again attempted entry but once more it was refused. Our hosts from the Karst Institute eventually sorted out the problem convincing the military that we were not capitalist spies working for the British Secret Service.

By the 25th March, we had permission to continue with the work and began the mapping of Nan Dong. Steve and Gavin set off upstream with diving bottles followed by Stuart, Dicky and me surveying as we progressed. All the other members of the team began mapping all the other left-hand passages. We progressed well up stream through deep water canals, short climbable waterfalls and rapids but began to suffer from headaches. Our carbide lamp flames reduced in size and kept going out. Only one thing could account for this, high concentrations of carbon dioxide. Steve and Gavin met up with us and confirmed this. They had managed to explore a further one kilometre upstream without reaching the sump, passing eight stream inlets all seemingly containing diesel. It was far too dangerous to continue so a hasty retreat was made. It appeared that the old military dumps above the cave were leaking diesel into the ground water. The survey was completed for the other cave passages but an old electrical wire running through the cave and steel fittings gave false compass readings.

On Wednesday 27th March, I returned to the major sink of Shi Dong with Stuart and our two Chinese compatriots, Zhang and Chen. It is a long drive over rough roads of two and a half hours, followed by a further walk of one and a half hours. We surveyed the cave to the static sump I had seen on my reconnaissance visit one year ago. We met five Chinese with a couple of sticks of gelignite; they said they were going fishing in the static sump. Attempts to climb above the static sump failed as the climb required bolts fixed into the rock as anchors. We placed non-toxic dye in the stream in an attempt to trace the underground flow and find out where the stream emerges. That day a further trip into Nan Dong with more surveying and a dive through a flooded passage was conducted by Steve and Gavin. They passed two sumps into a large passage but could not make much progress as once more bad air prevented exploration.

The following day Peter, Stuart and Paul accompanied by two of our Chinese compatriots bivouacked at the entrance of Shi Dong in order to attempt the climb above the sump. Paul fixed a few rock anchors and explored beyond into a well decorated section terminating in a very tiny passage with no way onwards. Kath, Kenny and Dicky bivouacked up in the high mountains and descended the large shaft with a ten second timed drop, they descended 150 metres with another huge deep shaft beyond. Later in the expedition, Stuart, Dicky and Paul returned using horses to carry the equipment but the shaft terminated in a soil blockage at 205 metres in depth. Three more deep shafts in the mountain were descended but again all were blocked without intersecting the postulated underground river.

Gavin became ill with large red blotches over his body. At the hospital they wanted to inject him with antihistamine, which he flatly refused sensibly fearing old previously used needles.

Steve, Dick and I investigated the stream sinks to the south called Yong Li Dong, sadly blocked with mud. These were situated on the Tropic of Cancer close to an old French abandoned railway station. Old French trains were lined up along the tracks, a testament to the colonial days when the French occupied Vietnam situated close by. This was a possible tourist attraction that could be considered for the future.

The next day, Steve dived in Wulcun Dong but the underwater passage in bad visibility closed down being far too small for progress.

The entrance to Shi Dong, Yunnan, China. Photo: David Gill.

It was decided to have an excursion to another area for three or four days to see if we could find any important cave systems as we were not having much luck in Coaba. We drove to Luxi where we settled into a hotel. This is a big busy city which kept us entertained with a huge parade and many speeches by Chinese dignitaries. At one point, we were completely surrounded by staring people and police with stun guns moved us back to the hotel. We visited Alu Dong, which was a highly decorated show cave with formations everywhere and open to the public. The boat ride along the underground river looked promising for diving into the flooded sections. The Chinese maps indicated numerous stream sinks and risings but on investigation they were blocked with debris. One was an 80 metre deep shaft with a huge stream cascading down, the spray and condensation rising into the air like a smoking chimney. It was close to the road and the Chinese claimed that six people had accidentally fallen down, never to be seen again. Gavin produced some impressive photographs of Kath descending, engulfed in spray.

We returned to Alu Dong, but it was a festival day and we estimated 40,000 people were milling around the cave. Gavin dived in the upstream sump in zero visibility only reaching a small chamber, the way on was blocked with mud.

That night, the team gave an impromptu performance in an outdoor stadium to a crowd of many thousands. I am not sure if the audience understood Peter's rendering of 'swing low, sweet chariot' but there was much laughing and clapping. Dick and Paul had retired to the hotel with a high temperature and I felt the same.

Dr Zhang, our main Chinese liaison scientist from the Institute of Karst Research, asked us to continue the work at Coaba as they did not want to lose face with the Director of the Prefecture of Hong He, which covered thirteen separate counties. We agreed and returned to continue with the work with Stuart, Dicky and Peter descending shafts up on the plateau. Gavin, Steve, Kath, Peter and Kenny bivouacked at the stream sink of Shi Dong and Peter and Steve dived through a ten metre low passage to 1.7 kilometres of huge tunnel with many climbs and calcite encrusted pools to a small very muddy sump. They mapped the cave, surveyed a few side passages and photographed the find.

Dick and I spent a few days collecting and replacing the dye detectors with Zhu Wang and poking our noses into a few totally blocked caves.

We now had permission from the military to dive in a bore hole called Ming Tunnel, which intersected a fast-moving stream. Gavin dived but the passage both up and down stream was too small after some 20 metres.

We drew up our surveys of the caves and handed in a report of our activities, also giving a presentation of our finding to the local officials. We had a visit that evening from 40 youngsters learning English where they sang to us a Chinese ballad. Sadly, one of the girls fell into a septic drain on the way out as it was pitch black with no lights. We pulled her out and the girls cleaned her up. She smelt a bit.

The expedition had been a little disappointing considering all the mammoth caves we had discovered in Bama County but this expedition was considered as a diplomatic exercise with the hope that the work and opportunities for cave exploration in China could continue for many years to come which is exactly what happened.

Paul was very sick and on returning to the UK was diagnosed as having histoplasmosis as explained in Chapter 13. Dick and I were sick with a high temperature but soon recovered, indicating our immunity. I had contracted the disease in Mexico and Dick must have contracted the disease somewhere else during his long and very active caving career.

The reconnaissance to Xingwen County, Sichuan was a great success and another expedition carried on with the work of the China Caves Project.

23

High Trikora Expedition, Irian Jaya, Indonesia, 1990

'You can never cross the ocean until you have the courage to lose sight of the shore

Christopher Columbus

The other half of New Guinea had been a part of the Dutch East Indies until it was annexed by Indonesia in 1969 and had always been a mystery as it is a vast area of jungle and high mountains inhabited by various indigenous tribes. It was known that it contained high mountains of limestone which extended across the border into Papua New Guinea and a couple of British expeditions had investigated remote areas in the search for caves, with some success. Permission to explore caves was not easy to obtain but in 1990 the late Dave Checkley organised another expedition into the high mountains of Trikora which reach an altitude of 4,730 metres in the Jayawijaya Range where he had searched for caves on the last expedition. Streams were sinking in the limestone south of the Baliem Valley and the area looked promising for a major deep cave system. Further to the west of the range the mountain of Puncak Jaya, Carstensz Pyramid reaches an altitude of 4,884 metres and before the advent of global warming had a permanent ice cap, but by 1960 the Trikora ice cap had also disappeared.

The Baliem Valley is about 80 kilometres in length by 20 kilometres in width and lies at an altitude of 1,600-1,700 metres, with a population of around 100,000 Dani tribespeople. The valley was first recorded by Richard Archbold during his third zoological expedition to New Guinea in 1938. On 21st June, an aerial reconnaissance flight southwards from Hollandia, now called Jayapura, found what the expedition called the Grand Valley with a surprising number of previously unknown people living there, basically they were still living in the Stone Age.

Dave asked if I was interested and he did not need to ask twice. At this time British cave explorers were organising expeditions to the remotest places on earth where limestone occurred, and Dave was one of the most experienced having numerous expeditions under his belt. The team consisted of Dave Checkley, Sheila, Steve Jones, Roo Walters, Kevin Senior, John Wyatt, Paul Seddon, Colin Jackson and me.

I offered to travel out in advance of the main party to meet with Dr Roby Ko, the President of the Federation of Indonesian Speleological Activities, and attempt to gain an interview with the Director General of Tourism. Colin Boothroyd and John Wyatt were both working in Jakarta and offered to meet me at the airport. John was going to come with us to Irian Jaya but Colin was too busy and unfortunately could not make it.

I travelled out via Frankfurt and Singapore arriving in Jakarta on 23rd June and met with Roby the following day but was unable to reach the Director of Tourism as he was not at home or in his office. My time in Jakarta was limited as I had arranged to meet up with the rest of the team on Tuesday 26th June so left on a 3 am flight to Ujong Paneng in Selewasia and from there to Jayapura, the capital of Irian Jaya, where I met up with the team. They had been on the go for 48 hours as their flight went via Los Angles, Honolulu, Biak, Bali and then to Jayapura.

We spent the rest of the day purchasing food supplies and trying to obtain carbide for our lights but to no avail as the shop was closed, so Dave and Steve Jones offered to remain an extra day to obtain the carbide as it was a case of no carbide, no light. Carbide is usually obtainable from welding shops as when mixed with water it produces acetylene gas used with oxygen for welding. We booked our tickets to Wamena in the high lands with the rural airline Marpati for the following day after obtaining the police stamp on our Surat Jalan, which is the required Indonesian permit to travel into remote areas of Iran Jaya.

Trouble was still brewing with the indigenous Dani tribe and other tribes in the mountains as the country was being inundated with Indonesian immigrants taking over native lands. Java has a very high population and as Irian Jaya is sparsely populated the government have a transmigration policy to relocate citizens to Iran Jaya and Kalimantan in Borneo. At that time a few million had already been relocated. The tribes wanted independence as they claimed the country had been taken over illegally after a trumped-up vote for Irian Jaya to join Indonesia but all dissension had been successfully and ruthlessly put down by the Indonesian Army.

We sent our freight separately and flew to Wamena at 1,650 metres in an old short landing and takeoff Hawker Siddeley 748, which I had helped to build way back in 1969 when I worked as an aircraft electrical engineer at Woodford Aerodrome; it still flew and flew well. We booked into a guest house called Syahrial Jaya Losman and who should I bump into but Charlie Marvin, the guy I met in Gunung Mulu, Sarawak during the expedition in 1988 A small world indeed.

The next few days were the hard bit, trying to get our permit stamped by the police and arranging for air transport into a small village air strip called Kiawagi in the Tiom District. Kiawagi is situated in the Baliem Valley dominated on both sides by high limestone mountains which was our ultimate destination. The Missionary Aviation Fellowship (MAF) flew light planes into these remote village airstrips, the Cessna 206 had a payload of only 400 kg but they also flew a Caravan with a much greater payload of 1,200 kg, which worked out at £266 per hour to hire. The grass runway at Kiawagi was long enough for a landing with a full load but not for a takeoff where the load needed to be reduced to 400 kg. It was therefore important that we weighed all our equipment and food supplies, there were also a number of helicopters around but at £1,212 per hour were a little expensive although they had a payload of 1,400 kg but this figure had to be reduced to 500 kg at 3,000 metres altitude. Dennis, the pilot of one of them, was stranded somewhere by a river having broken down and attempts were being made to fly in a spare part to the stranded pilot. The Caravan sounded the best option once we could weigh our equipment. Dave arranged for a short helicopter reconnaissance at a later date.

The police were a little more of a problem as they did not want to stamp our permit which had been issued from Jakarta. The police officer in charge telexed the authorities for permission and told us to call again tomorrow. Steve and Dave arrived a few hours later after obtaining the carbide but had to fly out of Jayapura in a small Twin Otter as the 748 flight was full.

On Friday 29th June, the police finally stamped our permit but certain areas in the mountains were out of bounds to all, probably due to the troubles. Oksibil, Okbibab, Kiwirok, Pase Valley and Arch Bold were all closed but Kiawagi was still open for us.

At last our freight arrived but we were a little overweight for the Caravan. It was therefore decided that four team members would walk in, which would take around four days. This reduced our total weight to 1,260 kg, just right for the Caravan. Roo Walters, Paul Seddon, Kevin Senior and Colin Jackson set off at 7 am the following day with a local English speaking guide called Johna while Steve and I went cave hunting.

We had been informed that a large rising issued from the Cone Karst to the east of Wamena so we hired a guide and crossing two rivers on canoes, reaching the resurgence called Minimo. The river was in the order of 12 cubic metres of water a second but issued from boulders. A large cave above full of fruit bats proved to be a flood overflow but hit a flooded passage after only 100 metres. This cave must drain a large area of karst and is almost certain to contain an extensive cave system. The cave was situated about eight kilometres north of a village called Mapinduma. A large river sink had been reported at Oksibil but the police had informed us that this area was closed to all visitors.

While waiting for the Caravan to be available, the next day Dave, Sheila, Steve and I went shaft hunting in the Cone Karst region. We crossed a large river via a very dodgy-looking suspension bridge that was falling to pieces. Local Dani tribesman told us of a large shaft with many bats but by mid-afternoon we had not been able to locate it. While Shelia and I returned to move our equipment to the MAF airfield, Dave and Steve continued searching and discovered a 70 metre deep shaft but had no rope to descend. They also found a 5 cubic metre a second river rising from the limestone mountain and followed it for 100 metres with no end in sight, a good project for a future expedition.

The Caravan was at last available so on Monday 2nd July we loaded up and took off at 11.40 a.m. flying over the Pyramid area then west over a huge river sink and rising. Between the sink and the rising were a few immense collapsed dolines but no rivers could be seen in the jungle-covered base of the shafts however, a trail was seen passing close by the giant holes. This was most probably the Baliem River sink and rising that had been visited by one of the previous UK expeditions and was described as the largest river sink on earth at an estimated flow of 100 cubic metres per second of water which disappeared underground at the end of a valley. The whole river sank in boulders with no apparent open cave passage.

My expedition to New Britain had explored the Nare cave with a flow rate of 20 cubic metres a second which was probably the most dangerous and technically difficult cave in the world to explore. An underground river five times larger would probably be impossible for normal men but an exciting prospect. I was determined that whatever happened in the high mountainous area we intended to explore, we needed to get into these huge collapsed dolines to see if any cave passages led down to what could be the largest underground river in the world.

After a flight of little over 35 minutes, we landed on the grass runway to be greeted by the whole Kiawagi village of 200 people all milling around. A mad scramble followed as everyone tried to grab a bag of equipment to carry down to the Mission House where we could store our equipment and find some space on the floor to sleep. It was complete pandemonium. We negotiated a price with the village pastor to rent the house which worked out about £3 per night and we paid the porters who had carried our equipment and food supplies from the airfield down to the house.

Our next problem was to hire 16 porters for the following day to carry our supplies up the mountain, which was easier said than done. The Dani in these remote areas are subsistence farmers and can be awkward to deal with. They try their best to get the best deal possible which is completely understandable as expeditions or rare tourist visits are their only chance of earning ready cash. Patience and diplomacy is the key, but with a certain degree of firmness.

I had some experience of negotiating with similar native groups in East New Britain, Papua New Guinea as the indigenous population of Irian Jaya are the same basic native group and follow approximately the same cultural traditions with some slight differences. They are closely related to the indigenous aboriginal people of Australia. In these circumstances it is important to pay the going rate for labour as it is far too easy to inflate the prices, which would set a precedent when others followed.

The houses in the villages are typical rounded Papuan dwellings of timber with a grass roof. A cooking fire is usually in the centre with a hole in the roof to let the smoke out and they sleep around the fire as at 3,000 metres it can be very cold at night even in the tropics. They have very few clothes, the men wear the traditional penis sheath and the ladies a grass skirt. The sheath is a hollowed out elongated seed pod called a gourd, tied with a piece of string around the scrotum and the waist covering the private parts and very uncomfortable to wear as we were to find out later. When the men wished to pass water, they hid at the back of a tree so they could not be seen when removing the sheath. This attire is open at the top and is used as a pocket where the man can keep his tobacco and money if he has any. The adult men have large ones and the boys small ones as can be expected.

Missionaries throughout these areas of West Papua and West Papua New Guinea supply old clothes and encourage the people to wear them. This has caused problems with hygiene as the clothes are not washed and when they sleep too close to the fire these tend to suffer from burns.

The following day I fixed a price at 5,000 rupees a day, which was approximately at that time just less than £2 and employed the required number to carry the bags. Kiawagi is situated at an altitude of around 2,000 metres and we were heading for a lake called Gulangun at 3,500 metres above sea level which Dave had seen on his last expedition into the area.

Having flown in we had no time to acclimatise to the altitude and being a smoker with the after-effects of histoplasmosis, I was suffering from altitude sickness before long so managed to get a passer-by to carry my bag. After a ten hour slog it was getting dark so we pitched tents in the rain and tried to sleep. The area was named Alaya with a few streams sinking underground close by so we established this as our Alaya sub camp where supplies and caving ropes could be stored and explorations conducted from the sub camp at a later date.

The next day we headed off towards the lake after a prolonged argument with the porters who all wanted to stay with us. This was out of the question as we would have to feed and pay all 16 of them and our food supplies and finances were limited. Their spokesman was a hard negotiator called Nokie and an agreement was eventually reached. Four would stay with us during the entire expedition and a further four would be employed for the day to carry sacks of equipment to our planned base camp at the lake.

Two hours later we arrived at our planned base camp near the lake and pitched our tents then began searching for cave entrances. We hacked through the thick scrub up a ridge to the west of the lake for a kilometre then, descending to the lake, we encountered a large doline just beyond where the overflow from the lake sank underground against a cliff face but the stream sank in boulders with no cave entrance. A short distance away a small cave entrance beckoned but proved to be only 50 metres in length to a tiny narrow passage. A rumble could be heard beyond which was probably the underground stream but there was no way we could reach it.

Steve Jones along with a few porters continued cutting tracks up to the west of the lake but the moss forest which is normal in the tropics at this altitude proved very difficult to cut through. They reached an area of razor sharp clints, water worn grooves in the limestone that can enlarge to man size shafts, but there were none to be found large enough for a person to descend. This was a potentially dangerous place as the holes were covered in moss and rotting vegetation and on crossing tended to give way beneath the feet. The limestone had been eroded into sharp knives of pointed rock. On returning to camp we found that John had arrived after getting a lift into Kiawagi with a group of research workers from Australia and the men that had walked in were on their way.

The following day the helicopter arrived for Dave to conduct an aerial reconnaissance of the range. but the weather was far too poor for any useful observations. Dennis, the pilot, kindly agreed to do a food run back to Kiawagi for us at a very reasonable price and decided to stay the night to see if the weather was better tomorrow while the rest of us continued searching and track cutting. Steve and I returned to the east ridge where the progress was a little easier with small stunted tree growth.

On Saturday 7th July, the weather was good so Dennis took off in the Helicopter with Dave. They flew across the peak of Gulangun where the mountain dropped off on the south side in a massive steep cliff with pinnacles of karst and many rising from underground streams but no open caves were observed. To the west looked much more promising with many sinking streams and dolines.

Steve and I along with two of our porters, Jaus and Pineus, continued exploring the eastern ridge. Dave, John and Roo Walters joined us later and we found a large doline covered with knee deep moss but no open caves. Further on we at last found an open shaft with a small stream requiring a rope followed by a few more near a small hut constructed of stones and sticks with a moss roof. This was probably a stopping off place for people walking across the mountain from villages on the far side then down into the Baliem valley.

The following day, Steve and I decided to bivouac at the Dani hut at an altitude of 3,900 metres and descend some of the shafts. There were a number of obvious trails through the moss which had been made by the giant high mountain rat locally called a Cus Cus. These are hunted by the men of the villages as it is their only source of meat besides the few pigs they keep around the villages.

The first shaft descended for 15 metres down a series of cascades with the stream to a 22 metre pitch. We rigged a rope and descended but the passage at the base narrowed being far too small to follow. Steve descended the next one which was inhabited by a small colony of swiftlets but a rope descent of 14 metres petered out in rocks with no way on. We retired to a cosy night in the hut which was just big enough for two huddled around a fire then dosed ourselves with a few sleeping pills.

The following day we were back shaft bashing and found a very wet narrow rift to a pitch. Steve placed a bolt in the rock to attach a hanger for the rope and descended 80 metres but again the cave was very immature and petered out at a tight muddy rift. Another shaft was descended by Steve using a cut tree to get to the bottom but again it was blocked. We returned to camp in the rain disappointed, finding the other team members equally disappointed after descending numerous shafts all blocked.

The following day separate teams scoured the area in all directions and a few more very wet shafts descended but again all were blocked after a short distance. One had looked very promising with a large stream but hit a sump in a large stream passage after only 60 metres. That night there was much discussion on what to do next.

Typical karst scenery, Irian Jaya, Indonesia. Photo: David Gill.

A promising looking canyon had been found further down the valley from the Alaya sub camp with a flat area and water which looked good for a bivouac camp from where the area could be thoroughly explored. Steve and John set up base at the sub camp the next day while Kevin and I continued cutting through the very dense moss forest along the ridge but again we reached an area of sharp and dangerous pinnacle karst. Dave and Sheila set up the bivouac and began searching for cave entrances in the canyon. That night it never stopped raining and the following morning little could be seen in the dense mist. A good sink had been found but proved impossible to descend because of very high water levels. Paul had descended another four blocked shafts and there seemed plenty more to look at providing the weather conditions improved and water levels dropped sufficiently to descend them.

I joined up with the team at the Alaya sub camp the following day and walked over to the main sink in the canyon where an impressive amount of water was disappearing underground. I found Paul and Steve, who had descended yet more very promising looking shafts but again all petered out to nothing. However, Dave and Shelia had found a deep one again in the canyon, which looked like the best bet for a big, going cave. The ground was good for walking with no moss forest or limestone pinnacles. Then we received some bad news, Kevin Senior had seriously cut his leg while slashing through the moss forest, and the cut required stitching. Dave set off back to our main camp at the lake with the medical kit but the message we received the following day was that the wound could not be sewn up with the stitching kit we had. Kevin would just have to take it easy and hobble his way back down the mountain.

John had to return to Wamena as his time was up and he needed to get back to work so I accompanied him back down to the Baliem River as it appeared according to the maps that the river disappeared then reappeared again three kilometres away. This was well worth investigating if true and needed to be checked out before the expedition finished. John had a few days before setting off walking back to Wamena so it was arranged that when John left, I would return back up the mountain to continue with the search for a going cave.

We set off with three porters on Saturday 14th July. It was much easier going downhill and we arrived at a small shelter down in the valley where we left our supplies and started to explore. We found a large rising with a two cubic metres of water a second issuing from the mountain but the associated cave hit a sump after a short distance.

That night we slept at the shelter and the following morning John set off on his long walk back accompanied by Samuel, one of our porters while I began searching for the Baliem River as my Dani porters reported that the river did disappear into a cave. Arriving at the steep banks I tried to cut a way down through razor sharp rattan vines and reached close to the riverbanks. The river was huge with white water rapids and traversing along the banks I could just see that it appeared to flow into a very narrow canyon. Although it was impossible to reach without a major effort requiring a few days, no cave entrance was seen. I retreated along with my three porters, Paus, Pilaman and a 16 year old boy called Weoi for a four hour walk back to a small village which they called Luraren, where I intended to spend the night. Crossing a river on the way I followed it up stream, but the river just issued from boulders and no cave could be seen. The next river had a strong flow but again issued from rocks. I had not crossed these two rivers on the way in so must have skirted around them and they must drain the limestone mountains to the south.

Before we reached the village Pilaman passed his bag to his friend and dashed off cuscus hunting leaving the very powerful Paus to carry two very heavy bags. The cuscus is a giant marsupial of the genus *Phalanger*, with thick fur, long thought to be extinct in the region and one of the very few animals to be found in these inhospitable mountains; although in 1997 the Australian extinct marsupial *Thylacine,* which resembles a striped dog, was recorded.

I pitched my tent just outside the village stockade and Pilaman returned just with the tail of the giant cuscus rat; the trap had worked but an eagle must have stolen the rest of it. I paid off the two porters and kept Paus with me so he cooked the tail over our fire and as we were ravenously hungry enjoyed a little fresh meat of rat's tail accompanied by some cooked pig and sweat potato which I purchased from a lady in the village.

A large cave called Yugupuru had been reported at the other side of the Baliem River so the next day we set off crossing the river on an amazing long wood and vine suspension bridge. A steep ascent following a stream up to 3,100 metres led to a large cave entrance with the stream appearing inside from a blocked passage after only 60 metres, yet another disappointment.

Returning back to Alaya sub camp the story was not good, Steve had dropped a few more pitches in the big sink but it had bottomed out in a small hole with the entire stream disappearing down. Other team members had again been attempting to cut further up the mountain on the west ridge while the big shaft again came to nothing at a depth of 55 metres.

Colin and I descended a good-looking hole the next day placing a rock bolt and hanger for the rope. The pitch led to a large passage with a stream flowing down steeply to another drop. Again, a bolt was drilled into the wall and the pitch descended but it only led to a large chamber at a depth of 40 metres with the stream sinking in gravel with no way on.

The expedition was now drawing to a close and it was decided that three of the team would walk out back to Wamena while Dave, Kevin and Sheila would return to Kiawagi to sort out flights back to Wamena for the transportation of our equipment. Steve and I would walk over to a village called Wanunga at an elevation of 2,850 metres where the Baliem river sink was situated and attempt to find the big shafts which we had seen from the Caravan flight on the way in.

On Friday 20th July, Steve and I set off at 8 am with four porters, caving equipment and food for four days. Ten hours later just before dark after crossing the Baliem River on yet another home-made suspension bridge we pitched camp just outside the village where we managed to purchase a few eggs from the headman.

The following day we explained why we were at their village and they offered to show us the way to the big shafts. Accompanied by about twenty people from the village we set off along the main track to Tiome village going over the mountain above the sink. The sink was something special, the whole river of well over 100 cubic metres of water a second sank between massive boulders in a foaming mass of white water. We had never seen anything like it before; if the underground river could be entered it would certainly dwarf anything yet found on earth and present a unique caving and technical challenge to explore.

We branched off from the main track and 15 minutes later arrived at a huge collapsed doline, estimated to be at least 150 metres deep. A steep climb down led us to a cave entrance on a shelf well above the bottom of the shaft. They called this Gua Wanugwa, which proved to be a nice dry cave about 300 metres in length with a couple of blocked shafts. There was no draught of air in the cave, so it was not going to lead us into the underground river. Back on the shelf we tied our rope to a tree and abseiled down to the bottom of the doline to find all the villagers waiting for us. They had free climbed it. Feeling rather foolish, we searched the base of the jungle-covered doline but it was just a jumble of fallen blocks and no draughts could be detected. Back up the steep slope another cave entrance led us to a steeply dipping slope to a chamber about 40 metres below the entrance. We found a small hole which contained a draught and Steve managed to get down to a section completely blocked. The villagers insisted that at times the underground river could be heard rumbling away below but today it was silent. The villagers on the surface appeared to be enjoying themselves lighting fires and throwing rocks but the smoke was being sucked into the cave so we could not see a thing. We retired back to camp coughing and insisted we did not need the entire village to come with us the next day.

Next day dawned bright and clear and once more we were led up above the sink following the trail to Tiome. This time we only had two men from the village with us. We climbed steeply up to the right of the track to a small clearing where we found a shaft. Steve drew the short straw and descended on our rope but the shaft was blocked after ten metres. We explained to Eti, our man from the village, that we were looking for another huge hole like the one we found yesterday. Sure enough he knew where there was one and led us through the forest to the second collapsed doline. These two dolines were definitely the holes we had seen from the aircraft. This one did not need a rope to reach the bottom as the 100 metre drop could be climbed using trees for aid.

At the base was a huge cave entrance which dropped steeply down through loose boulders but appeared to be totally blocked at the bottom. It was lit by daylight, so we did not need our lamps to search around the sides. Eti pointed out a small hole with a draught but it was blocked with boulders so he started to dig them out revealing a small tube floored with rocks. As I searched for other holes, Steve crawled down feet first with a head torch as it looked impossible to turn around once you were inside. Eti shouted for me to follow Steve as he was shouting that he could hear the river. I followed and found Steve returning saying it looked good with a very strong draught of air. We retired back to the surface for some lunch and telling Eti to wait for us descended the flat-out crawl. Steve only had his head torch but I fired up my carbide lamp so we could see fairly well where we were going except it kept blowing out in the strong wind. Sure enough, we could hear the river which grew louder as we descended. We stopped at a steep muddy chute that required a rope. The river emanating from somewhere below sounded like thunder and the walls seemed to vibrate with the noise. The passage continued past the chute into a complex maze area with many passages leading off. We followed the largest passage to a pitch in polished black limestone that again required a rope then returned to the maze. Here we found an even larger passage where we lost sight of the walls to an obvious river passage with water-polished boulders. The passage was estimated at 80 metres in diameter and it terminated in a large lake with a nice beach, but where was the river? This was just an overflow passage probably only flowing during periods of very heavy rain. We managed to reach the surface before dark and back at camp congratulated ourselves on hitting the jackpot.

The expedition was over and the following day we walked back to Kiawagi hoping that Dave had fixed up some flights. We arrived four hours later but missed Dave as they took off just as we arrived so we could not pass on the good news. The following day, Steve and I flew back to Wamena with the news.

There was only one decision to make, when were we coming back to explore the Baliem River Cave and who was going to organise it? Steve lost and got the job.

I have no intention of publishing the photograph of all the naked team members traditionally dressed wearing their very large penis gourds with Sheila just wearing her grass skirt, a decidedly painful and mildly pornographic photographic session.

24

To Russia with Love, 1990

I believe in one thing only, the power of human will.

Joseph Stalin

This expedition to the Soviet Union (USSR) was the idea of the late Paul Deakin who fancied taking some photographs of caves in areas never visited by pampered capitalist westerners. The well-known Russian cave explorer Vladimir Kisseljov had close contact with the Eldon Pothole Club and he would be the leader and organiser, for a price. He was something of a professional caver, a large imposing figure reminiscent of our own late Ken Pearce. He had put together a small team of cave explorers with the intention of diving through the sump of Khabju Cave, a resurgence situated in the Caucasus Mountains not far from Sochi, a city on the Black Sea. The cave was just over the border of Russia in Georgia, now an independent nation.

It sounded like a good idea, so I joined up with Paul and Alan Walker and set off for Moscow on the 16th November. Moscow airport was a dark and dismal place as was the old car and trailer that attempted to take us through the snow to Vladimir mother and father's flat. Vladimir's wife Tatiana and family were very friendly, hospitable people and we could sleep on the floor.

We did the usual rounds of tourist trips in the snows of Moscow not least being shown the great department store with most of the shops closed, also the graves along the Kremlin wall and Lenin's army guarded tomb. There had been some suggestions to bury him but considering he was such a historical figure and a tourist attraction, it was best to leave him where he was. As we were from the west we had to stay at a hotel. Vladimir was a fixer and registered us. The Metro was impressive and good for getting around the capital, with Vladimir being so tall that when we lost him in the crowds we could spot him from a distance. The tomb of the Unknown Soldier seemed to be used mostly by couples getting married and having their photograph taken. I asked Vladimir what the one kilometre long queue of people in the freezing conditions was for. They are queuing for ice cream was the reply. Generally, the people did not seem to be a happy throng. These were the days of President Mikhail Sergeyevich Gorbachev, the last leader of the Soviet Union. It was obvious that compared to the decadent west under a free market economy, the USSR was in serious decline.

Some members of the team set off via a 36 hour train journey whereas we were going to fly to Sochi. Two hours later, we arrived via a very boring flight and stayed the night with an Armenian family just across the border in Georgia. The major hunt for transport on the following day proved to be unfruitful so we had a stroll along the Black Sea in a rundown holiday resort, much of it built during Stalin's era in the 1950's. It was 4 pm before we managed to hire a truck, and sitting in the open was decidedly a cold experience while travelling along the coast road.

Moving inland, we hit a dirt road with the massive karst mountains of the Arabika massif rising to 2,591 metres above sea level. This massif is now the site of the second deepest cave in the world, Krubera Cave at 2,197 metres deep, and the deepest cave in the world, Veryovkina at 2,212 metres deep. A huge rising seen from the track had been explored to -65 metres by a French cave diver, and was possibly the resurgence for the caves on this mountain. A strange site met us along the track as a funeral procession passed by with the body being carried separately from the coffin, a local tradition, it seems. By dark we hit a river where our driver just refused to progress any further. We unloaded the equipment into a nearby barn where a farmer appeared and offered us a room to sleep in. This Georgian family had lived in the area for generations farming and owned about one hectare of land, the rest was owned by the state. He reared turkey and cows, and grew maize, nuts, fruit and tobacco but had to give the state half of everything he produced from the land. Bears were a problem and he had been forced to shoot a few when they invaded his crops. For four hours we drank gallons of his home-made wine and consumed his freshly baked bread as we were starving.

With extreme hangovers we resumed our journey the following morning and after eight kilometres we halted at a densely wooded area overlooking a large river where we intended to camp. We were surrounded by huge mountains on all sides, many of them snow-capped and an imposing sight. The cave was on the opposite side of the river, which was in full flow but all attempts to cross failed as we were constantly being washed away. We had better luck the following morning when I managed to install a traverse rope across the river and we ferried the diving bottles to the Khabju Cave, a resurgence river cave with a high flow of three cubic metres a second. The sump looked deep and clear but was icy cold. Vladimir and two of his companions dived through sump 1 and passing through low sections and lakes laid a line through sump 2, returning to camp in the evening. We sensibly played at photographing the river passage then getting warm around the campfire. The following day, Vladimir and friends returned to the Khabju river cave while we set out on a search for Back Water Cave reported as a large stream rising from a flooded cave downstream of our camp site.

After much scrambling up steep wooded hills, we found the rising after a few waterfalls on the true left bank of the river. We spent the rest of the day searching the hills for cave entrances with no luck. The next few days were spent following bear tracks while searching for caves up steep mountains but nothing of significance was found. Vladimir's team mapped a further 400 metres in Khabju before we carried the diving equipment along a bear track to Black Water Cave entrance. Vladimir kitted up in his diving equipment and plunged into the sump for 75 metres with no end in sight in a flow of over one cubic metre a second.

There was little more we could do in this area so we arranged for the truck to pick us up and drove back down to the coast to Sokumi town passing our friendly farmer and collecting two jars of his excellent wine and some bread, which we seemed to be living on. Seventy kilometres along the coast road, we headed inland along a mountain road and some very rough tracks to the village of Amtqeli where we camped by the Shakuran river, a very pleasant spot. We left the majority of our equipment in a house in the village and hiked for two kilometres crossing the river.

Lower Shakuran cave proved to be photogenic with some nice calcite gour pools and deep water leading to a sump. The pools contained some black eels but to the left a steep muddy climb led to large muddy chambers. Vladimir and his friend Victor inspected the sump with a view to diving. The following day Victor made attempts to recharge the diving cylinders while we searched for Upper Shakuran cave only finding a small 100 metre long cave to a sump but the walk back was spectacular through a magnificent gorge with a 30 metre waterfall. Paul enjoyed photographing the tufa dams in heavy rain.

The next day we intended to look at a sink cave upstream situated in a gorge, so we retrieved our equipment and collected some food left in the very basic house in the village. This was occupied by an old man with three young sons. As a thank you we parted with a gift for the sons of toothbrushes and toothpaste, while the cigarettes went to the old man.

We managed to get a lift in a lorry and parted with a gift to the driver of a packet of Marlborough cigarettes. We had been advised to bring a carton with us as a small gift goes a long way. The driver seemed very pleased. The diving bottles had now been recharged with compressed air, so Vladimir and Victor prepared to dive the sump in Lower Shakuran while we set up our new camp in the gorge. Alone, I looked at the sink on the true right bank that seemed promising, a very wet passage to a cascade with a pitch and a way on over the top of the drop. Returning to collect my single rope technique equipment, Victor and another one of Vladimir's team members called Ilja joined me. Placing a couple of hangers for a traverse rope across the pitch and bolting the wall with another hanger, gave me a dry descent of the pitch out of the force of the water. Unfortunately, my rope was too short and reached nowhere near the base of the pitch. I returned and re-rigged the rope at a lower point so it reached the bottom. A large passage followed but, disappointingly, was blocked with granite boulders after a short distance. I left the rope in for a photographic trip planned for the following day and the three of us investigated another sink downstream. This was a large entrance to a tight rift blocked with boulders and much flood debris. That night we huddled around the fire in the rain drinking the local brew, which can only be described as fire water. My whisky had been totally consumed long ago.

The next day was horrific with very heavy rain, impossible to safely descend the sink which appeared to have a strange name, Female Bear Cave. We finished the fire water in order to keep warm while Ilja trudged a few kilometres to a house to try to obtain a stove and some fuel as keeping the fire lit for cooking was out of the question.

It rained most of the night but the following day the sun broke through the clouds. Alan rigged the wet descent in Female Bear Cave for a Paul Deakin photograph and we de-rigged the cave when Paul was happy with his photographs. After dark we investigated the next sink on the opposite side of the gorge called Cold Cave or Kholoduaja. This was an entrance crawl to a vadose passage leading to a 15 metre deep pitch. We used a natural anchor and a couple of bolt belays for a very wet descent followed by another even wetter pitch as streams poured down from the roof. I fixed a bolt anchor in the rock and we descended for about 18 metres to a series of muddy tunnels. Paul had fun taking his brilliant photographs.

Vladimir and friends decided to descend and de-rig the cave later. On arriving back at camp, we were greeted by two men who seemed to be very drunk. As they had brought along their home-made wine and fire water we joined in the merriment around the fire. One man was from Georgia and the other was Greek but after a while the Georgian became rather angry, we had no idea what for as we did not speak his language. We thought it prudent to disappear into the tent to avoid a confrontation. Vladimir's wife Natalia told him where to go and eventually he disappeared.

The author in Bol'shaja Medreditsa, Georgia, USSR. Photo: Paul Deakin.

The next day we packed up our camp and walked back to the road. A half hour, very crowded bus journey dropped us off at a small village called Oktomberi from where we walked up the hill to an old lady's house where she said we could stay for the night. Leaving our equipment, we set off hiking towards the gorge where Paul had fun photographing the tufa falls. A dry valley led us to Lavrentijs Cave, a phreatic maze developed along the strike of the beds of limestone with mud and pools of water. The cave obviously flooded to the roof in wet weather. The main valley had many risings and tufa dams popular with visitors as steps had been cut into the tufa for ease of climbing. We decided not to stay at the old lady's house and set off walking in order to catch a bus to Sokumi. After waiting for a few hours in heavy rain it became obvious that the buses had stopped running for the night. We had tea in a watchman's hut across the road roasting to death grouped around a very hot stove. A kind local man offered us the village hall where we could sleep the night.

A long wet wait the following morning at last saw us on a very packed bus into Sokumi. A few buses later, we arrived at our destination, the show cave of Nuofom where we had special permission for free entry and to take photographs. A tunnel has been driven through the mountain in order to intersect the cave and it was opened for tourists in 1975. It appears to be formed by thermal water with lakes that seem to flood as markings could be seen 20 metres above the floor level.

That evening we sat down in an outside bar drinking vodka when four young men joined us, two from Siberia and two from the Ukraine. They said they were miners but had served in the armed forces in Afghanistan. Paul gave one of them a £5 note, which produced yet more bottles of vodka. After a few hours we were very drunk, including the four men, when the conversation, via a translation from Vladimir, seemed to become heated. They most probably did not like the fact that the decadent west had helped the Mujahideen, secretly but directly, during the Soviet Afghan war 1979 to 1989. They had my sympathy, but it was wise to beat a hasty retreat and attempt to jump on a bus to Sochi. We managed to get about halfway there then stood in the rain by the road trying to flag down any passing car but no one wanted to stop. I could quite understand this as we were plastered and finding it difficult to stand upright. At last a taxi turned up but Alan decided to fall over towards a ditch full of mud. He made a desperate grab for my arm but only succeeded in pulling me in. I landed along with Alan headfirst. We emerged laughing and covered from head to foot in wet smelly mud. The taxi took one look at us and disappeared fast.

Vladimir flagged down a empty bus and explained we had been splashed by a passing truck. We did get some dirty looks from him as all three of us could not hold back the laughter. He kept telling us to shut up. We were all now congregated in a house in Sochi where we spent all night cleaning our muddy clothes and packing all the equipment. The final day saw us dashing from place to place trying to get our flight back to Moscow.

The Soviet Union did not last for much longer breaking up on 26th December 1991. We did not have anything to do with it honestly. The great thing about this expedition was that we rarely stopped laughing.

The entrance to Bol'shaja Medreditsa, Georgia, USSR. Photo: Paul Deakin.

The saddest part of this story is that Paul Deakin is no longer with us. I spent so many years caving with him and helping to take many of his wonderful photographs. The amazing Vladimir Kisseljov also lost his life on 11th March 1995, while diving in the ZhV-52 cave in the Pinega Region of Northern Russia. He ran out air due to a faulty valve and drowned whilst trying to exit the cave. He was an Honorary Member of the Eldon Pothole Club and quite rightly so.

25

Gunung Mulu Expedition, 1991

'The greatest use of life is to spend it for something that will outlast it.'

William James

The last expedition to the Gunung Mulu National Park in 1989 was led by Matt Kirby who again agreed to organise this one, unfortunately I was not able to go on the 1989 trip due to my expedition to China but this one was rather different as by now I had been offered the job as Development Officer for the park. It was therefore important to decide on a start date as I was already committed to two expeditions in 1992, one to Vietnam with Tim Allen and the other back to Irian Jaya with Steve Jones and I did not intend to miss either of them.

This time we had a science element in the shape of Dr Peter Smart, Fiona Whitaker and Andy Farrant. Andy was studying under Peter and his work in the Gunung Mulu caves would be a major part of his doctorate. Matt's team besides me and the three scientists consisted of Tim Allen, Peter Boyes, Dick Willis and Richard Chambers.

We travelled out on 1st October 1991, but Matt and I stopped off in Kuching to see the Director of Forest Datuk Leo Chai, as our permit stipulated that we needed first to pay a courtesy call. The meeting went well the following day but there was a problem for me taking unpaid leave during my two planned expeditions as the Forest Department wanted me to start work on the 1st January. I arranged a meeting with the State Secretary for the 4th November when the expedition finished, which would mean another trip to Kuching. Matt and I then caught a flight to Miri meeting the rest of the team, once more Tropical Adventure, had agreed to arrange our logistics for the expedition.

By Sunday 6th October, the team assembled in the park having travelled from Miri via Marudi and Long Terawan by boat. We set up our main base at the Tropical Adventure Tourist lodges at Long Pala not far from the new park headquarters which had now been constructed.

That evening we had a meeting with Oswald Braken Tisen, the Chief Park Warden and Victor Luna Amin, the Officer in Charge of the park, to discuss the science and exploration objectives of the expedition.

The science would involve paleomagnetic dating of mud samples from within the caves in order to determine the age of the various levels of passages; this can be achieved by looking at the magnetic orientation of the ferrous metals within the sample. As sediment in a stream or river settles to the bottom, the ferrous particles align pointing to the north and it is known that the earth's magnetic field has flipped a number of times in the geological past, then flipped back again and the ages of these magnetic reversals is known. If samples of sediment made at various levels show a reversal pointing away from north, the age of deposition can be calculated, thus the age of the passage development can be determined.

Also discussed were the exploration objectives to attempt to connect the Clearwater Cave System to Black Rock Cave discovered by the 1988 team which had included Matt, Richard and I. A connection would bring the system to over 100 kilometres in total length and the two caves were close to each other and were obviously part of the same system. A major extension had been discovered in 1989 called Phoenix in Black Rock, which was heading towards the far northern parts of Clearwater Cave. Two other caves could potentially connect to the main system which we could investigate; these were Racer Cave and Lagang Cave, both within close proximity.

The work began the following day with two separate teams searching for a connection between Racer Cave and Lagang but without success. This elusive connection still remains to be found. Ipoi, one of the park guides, accompanied Matt, Peter Boyce and I to the Melinau Paku River and the south side of Gunung Api where we found a small cave on a shelf that appeared to have a draught of air. We mapped the cave which we named after Ipoi, our guide, through a crawl for 200 metres to a larger passage blocked with clay with the draught disappearing up a tight rift passage too narrow to follow.

Braken wanted to construct a walkway between park headquarters to the tourist caves of Cave of the Winds then to Clearwater Cave. These caves were only accessible by long boat. The problem was there was a cliff in the way called Batu Bungan with no way over the top. We were asked if we could find a route either over or through the cliff.

There was an interesting legend attached to the cliff as the Melinau River passed by this beautiful cliff with stalactite formations hanging down from ledges. The legend goes something like this. A beautiful woman called

Bungan lived on one of the ledges and a hunter came to woo her every day but could not persuade her to come down from her lofty perch. All attempts to reach her by the hunter failed and in a fit of desperation and depression he killed her with a poison dart. So her ghost still haunts the cliff; a good story to tell tourists.

Tourist boat in Clearwater Cave, Sarawak, Malaysia. Photo: Jerry Wooldridge.

While the scientists collected clay samples in Cave of the Winds, we searched the cliff for entrances and about 100 metres above the river we found three but all were blocked with no way on. On descending through the very thick jungle, I brushed my arm against a nasty plant with small hairs which left behind tiny crystals of acid. The pain lasted for days as every time the skin is touched, acid is secreted and there did not seem to be any way of neutralising it. Down at river level close to Racer Cave we did find a few base level small sized stream caves that required mapping at a later date.

Mike Meredith was still around training Tropical Adventure guides, so I was able to pick his brains with regard to my forthcoming job. We then travelled upstream along the Melinau River to our camp, which had been constructed by Tropical Adventure. This was situated by the confluence of the Lutut and Melinau Rivers and on the true right bank opposite the park boundary from where we could conduct trips into Black Rock and Clearwater Caves.

It appeared that two expeditions had taken place around 1990, one from Korea and one from Indonesia. Both expeditions had received permission from the Forest Department and the State Secretary's office, but no reports had been received by the park authorities. As we had discovered in the past with expeditions to complex caves, it is very difficult if not impossible to decide where the last expedition finished or where to begin exploring unless you are accompanied by the original explorers. It is essential that all cave exploration expeditions write up their findings along with cave maps, descriptions of what has been found and photographs. which is the rule for all expeditions. This has always been the case for British expeditions to the Gunung Mulu National Park with comprehensive reports supplied. This serves a number of useful purposes; the foreign authorities receive information on their caves and the follow up expeditions know what has been done and what needs to be looked at. It is also essential that there is continuity with the team members. Some of the original explorers should be included in the team and new cavers that have not visited the area previously can be introduced and become familiar with the complexity of the cave systems. In the case of the Gunung Mulu National Park it is obvious that the British cave explorers are the experts and know the possible leads that remain to be investigated as all the caves have been explored and mapped by them over a period of many years. We therefore had no idea what the Koreans or Indonesians had discovered, if anything.

The intention was to camp underground at Milliways in Black Rock Cave and continue with the exploration of Phoenix. This was an upper section of passage that had not been completely explored by the 1989 team and seemed to be heading towards Clearwater Cave. It was thought that a thorough search in the northern sections of Clearwater might also prove fruitful as we had not entered this area during the 1988 expedition.

Tim, Petrus, one of the park guides, and I entered the Snake Track entrance leading into the middle parts of Clearwater and found the route through to Beckoning Finger Passage, which contained a good draught of air. A rope climb down followed by a 20 metre pitch led us into the sand-filled Dune Series of passages. A traverse ledge followed above a 50 metre deep hole in the floor, which went down to a lower passage called Sheer Delight. Passing across a very exposed section by clinging to holds on the right-hand wall I slipped and lost my balance as I was carrying a heavy sack containing our ropes which shifted position. Falling backwards, I went careering head first, sliding on my back down the slope towards the black space and a certain end but by sheer luck the strap on my caving sack caught on a small protruding stalagmite no more than a few inches long, sticking out of the rock wall. I came to a surprisingly sudden stop and, amazingly, it held my weight as did the strap. Hanging upside down, I managed to grab hold of a small delicate looking stalagmite and right myself. Freeing the strap, I was able to climb gingerly back up to the traverse ledge by clinging hold of some very small stalagmites, fired on by a dose of adrenaline. The caving sack strap certainly saved my life as it seemed a long way down to the passage far below.

Dick and the scientists joined us and we spent a great deal of time searching the far reaches in some magnificent large and well decorated passages called Gnome Oxbow and Troll Caverns but all leads appeared to be blocked with masses of stalagmite and flowstone calcite deposits. East Passage was at last found and noted for further investigation as this seemed to be the closest point to Black Rock Cave. This time it was much easier to find the North Entrance from the inside as daylight could be seen filtering in from a very tight crawling passage. We exited from this entrance and headed back to base camp, a long walk through the jungle.

The following day, we headed off to camp underground in Black Rock and set up our bivouac in our 1988 camp Milliways, this time with park guides Edwin, Noah and Petrus. Richard, Matt and I looked at the sloping pit at the end of my discovery of 1988, Old Holborn, but it petered out after 140 metres, blocked with sediment with no draught of air which indicated it would not go anywhere.

The next day, the 12th October, the team set off for Phoenix, the upper passages that we hoped would lead us into Clearwater. Tim climbed a couple of ramps ascending steeply just near the Flower Shop found in 1988. Halfway up the first ramp he found footprints that must have been left by the Koreans. On the second ramp he found a hawser-laid nylon climbing rope. Again, this area must have been looked at by the Koreans ,which emphasised the importance of continuity of different expeditions to complex caves such as this.

The end of Phoenix Passage had only been visited once and at the time, a large amount of water was falling from the roof at the terminal point called Broken Hope Hall. This time there was little water and a further 200 metres of passage was followed with no end in sight and running parallel with Clearwater's northern passages. The separation was estimated to be 90 metres between the two caves so it looked promising as the passage had a strong draught.

The following day, we pushed on beyond the end point along a nice roomy passage passing several greasy traverses protected with ropes and a few roped descents. The draught was strong and some amazing horizontal metre long stalactites protruded from the walls as the droplets of water were blown in one direction. A white walled canyon followed to a three metre climb down rigged with a rope to a large pool of water which appeared to be a few inches deep but turned out to be thigh deep mud at the edges and impossible to cross. We did not test the depth of the mud but as the walls are vertical it could be many metres deep. A fall into this could be fatal so Tim rigged a roped traverse along a one inch ledge around the edge of the pool. At the far side of the obstacle another pitch of seven metres, again rigged with a rope, led into a large boulder strewn chamber.

I mapped a large passage to the right but it terminated in a mud blockage but way above was an inlet passage that later proved to be directly below the nearby Leopard Cave. A connection to this cave would add another 3.7 kilometres on to the total length. The area had a number of other leads, but all were pitches requiring ropes and by now we had completely run out. The best lead was a 30 metre high canyon passage with a deep pit in the floor with the passage continuing at the far side of the pit. The only way to reach this was a very dangerous traverse along the wall which did not appear to have any hand holds. We retreated after mapping all passages found that day and retired to our underground camp at Milliways, tired but satisfied that we were heading in the right direction. There was no doubt that to reach our end point was exceptionally hard going, technically difficult and certainly remote. Any slight accident in this region would probably prove fatal.

By this time my boots had fallen to pieces along with a lot of skin and as I could not cave in bare feet I just had to find another pair somewhere so headed out with Richard and travelled back to Marudi. The jungle and the Mulu caves are without doubt unforgiving places.

I managed to find some cloth army boots which is all they had, and on the way back I bumped into my friend Wan Kulay who had been with me in

1988. He had now left the park and was working as a medic for a seismic survey company. We reminisced about finding Rudang Gallery together.

Richard and I headed back to our jungle camp and then made our way up to the Melinau Gorge at the northern end of Gunung Api while the rest of the team continued with the work in Black Rock and Clearwater.

No caves of importance had been found at the northern end of Gunung Api and any cave heading south could potentially connect with Black Rock as it was obvious that the cave system extended all the way through the mountain. The trip would kill two birds with one stone as it was important that I familiarised myself with this area of the park considering I was soon to live and work there. Mike had constructed a camp at a beautiful spot by the side of the Melinau River called Camp 5. This was used by tourist climbing up to the Pinnacles. The climb ascends through the forest for 800 metres, affording magnificent views of these massive 50 metre high unique limestone pinnacles, pure white and sharp as razors sticking out majestically from the jungle.

We spent a few days searching the northern flanks of the mountain but only found few short, blocked caves. At the time of writing this area has been searched by many during many expeditions but a connection through the mountain from the northern flanks still remains elusive although a large sink blocked with boulders where a stream disappears has been dye traced through to the Black Rock and Clearwater Rivers.

The good news on our return was that the team had made the connection with Clearwater on Thursday 17th October, Tim and Dick had rigged the pitch in the canyon, but it was blind and totally choked with no way on. They returned and by traversing along the right-hand wall with zero hand holds, which they named the Sweat of Fear Traverse, they descended the next pitch of 18 metres into the continuation of the canyon. A side passage led off up a greasy climb back to the level of the traverse and the passage continued for a further 60 metres to emerge in West Passage of Clearwater Cave just above a dry cascade in a hidden alcove that the original explorers of West Passage had missed. They completed the first through trip and emerged from the tiny North Entrance of Clearwater. The complete system was now an outstanding 102 kilometres in length and the 7th longest cave in the world.

On Saturday 19th October, Matt, Richard and I accompanied by two park guides, Edwin and Sulaman, returned to finish off a few remaining leads. We now had a faster route into the canyon area by entering via the Northern Entrance of Clearwater but had trouble finding the route through into West Passage which was not obvious as this was a squeeze upwards through a boulder collapse. We found the connecting passage in the alcove at the top of the dry cascade and descended the greasy slope into the canyon which resembled a Derbyshire mine, being highly shattered. then ascending the 18 metre pitch to the sloping Sweat of Fear Traverse which we decided was very aptly named. Although only six metres long, the traverse is a sloping ledge devoid of any handholds which requires a delicate balancing act where just a slight slip would prove fatal. We finished the mapping and exploring the remaining leads and the connection received the name, No Justice. The original explorers had missed discovering over 20 kilometres of cave passages by not searching the walls of West Passage, but this is not hard to do as the passages in Mulu are so large that the exploration and mapping tends to take the easiest route along a given passage length so small obscure leads to either side are easily missed.

Drawing the maps back at our main base at Long Pala near the park headquarters, we found a discrepancy between the two caves probably due to surface mapping errors as this was before the advent of GPS and surveying through the jungle was always a problem as the trees get in the way, not to mention the bugs.

We still had plenty of time left before the scheduled end of the expedition and there were suspected leads left in Armistice so we bivouacked underground at Scumring just near the start of the Armistice series of passages. We met our scientists who had been camping underground for four days collecting sediment samples from all levels of the cave system. We then proceeded up to Armistice and headed north but all likely unexplored leads proved to be blocked. The next day, Pete Boyes, Baguly, one of the park guides, and I checked out a number of blank spots on the cave map all proving to be oxbows to the main passage some dropping down in Revival Passage way below. All this area was extremely complicated and at some time in the future a complete re-survey was required.

Matt's team returned to Armistice to investigate a four metre deep hole in the floor of the sediment filled passage that must have recently collapsed as it was not there during their original exploration in 1989. They descended for 108 metres down steeply dipping beds in a very complex region finally arriving at a 38 metre pitch which dropped into Clearwater 5, the fifth stretch of river passage that had been discovered the year before by another team from the UK under the leadership of Alan Weight. Matt called it Edwin's Long Cut after Edwin, our park guide.

The different sections of the Clearwater River are divided by flooded sections and a short distance to the north the river is once more sumped but this was passed in later years during a dry spell and Clearwater 6 was explored to yet another sump. Whether this is flooded all the way to the Black Magic River in Black Rock is unknown as the separation is over 1.1 kilometres between the two sumps and the river does seem to pop up into dry air-filled passages.

On arriving back at our bivouac, the scientists were a little concerned that 18 sediment samples had disappeared. This was not the first time we had noticed the disappearance of items, usually food. It was presumed that some strange species of cave-adapted animal frequented the Scumring area, possibly a rat or shrew or the very large cave crickets had grown to rat size. Whatever they were, they seemed to like noodles as some of our packets had been ripped open, but we had no idea why they liked sediment samples, unless of course they were engaged in some science.

On the way back to the surface I had a good look at the roof of the massive Revival Passage and noticed a black space that could be reached by a climb up the sloping right hand wall. An easy but exposed climb with stalagmite holds gave out at a smooth wall but the passage could be seen continuing above, with some large formations just below. These could be lassoed with a rope, a possibility for another time as there is a blank space on the cave map above this region.

We packed up our camp near the Lutut River and jumped on our longboats back down stream to our park headquarters base camp at Long Pala where I met up with none other than Ian James and John Lynch who were leading a group of 22 Ghurkha soldiers based in Brunei, the country next door largely protected by the British Army.

We still had one week left, so concentrated our efforts on the areas within reach of our main base. A new cave entrance that had been discovered by two park guides, Simon Lagang and Wilson Bala, in 1990 had been found in the Southern Hills that contains one of the world's largest diameter caves, called Deer Cave. Again, this was a blank area on the map so Richard and I were joined by the Officer in Charge of the park, Victor, and Tama Bulan who had worked at the park from its inception way back in 1974. Tama Bulan was an experienced cave explorer in his own right as he had been involved in all the expeditions to Gunung Mulu from the start. The cave entrance was found just off the Deer Cave tourist plank walk about 30 metres up the hill. There was a horse shaped rock at the entrance, so I gave it the name of Stone Horse Cave. A huge sediment-filled passage with many fruit bats was mapped for over one kilometres terminating in a sediment filled passage with no way on but with a few side passages.

The following day we were back and continued mapping to a higher entrance with nice cave formations while other team members mapped a new cave above Batu Bungan called Sago Palm Cave, which had five entrances and proved to be over 800 metres in length. More exploration also took place in the Clearwater River not far from the entrance and another few kilometres added to the length of the system.

Over the next few days, I completed the survey of Stone Horse with a respectable length of 2.6 kilometres. As I was soon to be on my way back, I stored most of my personal equipment with Victor and we of course had the final party with the guides on Friday 1st November which was the usual drunken affair. Jimmy Kebing arrived, the guide we had rescued from Black Rock in 1988. His broken bones had healed and he could now walk without a limp. His father was called Kebing and was the Tua Kampong, or Head Man of the Berawans from Mulu and Long Terawan, and he asked us to join him at his house close by for beer. He wanted to thank us for saving his son's life so Matt, Richard and I sat with him for many hours getting steadily drunk and listening to Kebing singing his traditional songs of thanks and praise. As fate would have it, I was soon to meet my future wife as we were joined by Kebing's daughter Martha and her cousin Betty Usang. Betty was the daughter of Usang Ipoi, the man who had built the Royal Geographical Expedition base camp in 1977 and I secretly hoped I would meet up with Betty on my return.

Once more, the expedition had been a huge success and pointed the way towards many more. I now needed to travel back to Kuching to meet the State Secretary and the Forest Department Director. Matt and I travelled back to Kuching and I struck a deal to work without signing a contract for the first nine months so I could join the planned expeditions to Vietnam and Irian Jaya, then I would sign a two year contract. The only drawback was I had to pay for my own flight tickets. I had two months to sort out everything with my son Mark back in Derbyshire as the start date was 1st January 1992. At the age of 50, a new chapter was about to begin.

26

Bac Son Massif, Vietnam, 1992

'Don't ask what the world needs. Ask what makes you come alive, and go do it. Because what the world needs are people who have come alive.'

Howard Thurman

I had now been working at the Gunung Mulu National Park for two months as the Speleologist and Development Officer and money was in short supply but I had a little cash left that I had brought out from the UK so joined Tim Allen's team consisting of Jim Abbot, John Palmer, Andy Quin, Bob North, and Steve Thomas, a good small team of seven.

There were to be two teams in Vietnam at the same time as Howard Limbert also had a team from Britain intending to explore the Phong Nha karst in the central region. The 1990 reconnaissance expedition had made contact with the Department of International Relations and the faculty of Geology and Geography of Hanoi University and had investigated four karst areas but had been told about a 1,300 square kilometre karst region 170 kilometres north east of Hanoi near the Chinese border. This area was generally out of bounds as the Chinese had invaded in 1979 so little was known about the region and it had never been visited by Europeans since the days of the French colonial period when Vietnam was a part of French Indo China. On the plus side, we had good US army maps that were available in the UK.

Tim obtained the permits to visit and we were to be accompanied by two geomorphologists from the University, Prof Nguyen Hoan and Mr Phai, who could speak some English, a cameraman and a reporter. At this time Vietnam was virtually closed to tourists and the sanctions imposed by the USA were still in force so it was important to cement good diplomatic relations with the Vietnamese as there were many areas of unexplored limestone which could reveal world ranking cave systems.

I travelled out from Miri in Sarawak to Bangkok, Thailand via Kuala Lumpur on 13th March and looked for a hotel as my flight to Hanoi was due the following morning. The airport hotel was far too expensive at £50 for the night so I flagged a taxi down to find a cheap hotel in the city. Unfortunately, the Thai taxi driver spoke no English and took me to a house of ill repute but after a great deal of arm waving we finally arrived at a hotel. The next day I arrived in Hanoi to be met by the rest of the team and received some bad news. The man I had been with on my first expedition, the infamous Dr Ken Pearce, had lost his life while diving in open water.

We booked into a hotel in the centre of Hanoi and changed our money into the Vietnamese currency, the Dong, the following day. This worked out at a ridiculous 18,000 Dong to the UK pound, so we finished up with several million in 2,000 Dong notes, the smallest currency obtainable, this meant emptying our caving sacks and filling them with notes. My £60 completely filled my bag with paper money, which was over one million Dong and at last I was a millionaire. Trying to pay for a meal for the seven of us plus a few dozen beers took over 30 minutes just to count the money and it only came to about £2.50 each. That night a Vietnamese guarded our room carrying an automatic rifle, but this did not stop one sack full of money from disappearing. Later the money was refunded by the hotel.

Hanoi was a fascinating city although a little drab and run down looking as it had been heavily bombed, but it certainly had character with the steam engines still chugging through the city and belching black smoke and rickshaws dashing around. The French influence was still in evidence. Normally I dislike cities but found Hanoi an exciting place to wander around.

I had promised to present a talk and slide show on caves and the tourist potential at the Hanoi University that was translated from my English to Vietnamese. We were all hoping to meet one of the greatest army generals of all time who had been invited to attend, General Vo Nguyen Giap but sadly he could not make it and I never got the chance to meet him before he died in 2013 aged 102.

This amazing man was a committed nationalist, along with his father who had died in prison in 1919 after having been arrested for subversive activities by the French colonials. His sister was also arrested and died soon after being released from prison; he had lost two members of his family before he was ten years old. Giap was arrested and imprisoned in 1930 for taking part in student protests then in 1940 when the French banned the communist party, he escaped to China where he met Ho Chi Minh the leader of the Viet Minh, the Vietnamese Independence League. After his escape his wife was arrested and sentenced to 15 years in prison.

He led the fight against the Japanese occupation during the last war starting in 1942 with just 40 men, the basis of the armed wing of the Viet Minh and was wounded during a battle. Their base was in remote caves in the north near Vu Nhai and they hid from French patrols by hiding in a cave beneath a waterfall. Ironically his fight against the Japanese was greatly supported by the USA with training, arms and ammunition and by the end of 1945 he had over 5,000 troops in the field and by this time had made many successful attacks on the Japanese occupiers and he controlled large area of the country.

After the war the country was sadly divided following the decisions made at the Potsdam Summit but the French returned once more to govern the country so the Chinese Nationalists left the north and the British left the south. Giap then fought the French and won the famous battle at Dien Bien Phu in May of 1954 against crack French troops from the Foreign Legion by carrying his artillery of 24-105mm howitzers up the mountains along with anti-aircraft guns, an amazing military feat.

Shortly after the defeat at Dien Bien Phu the French left and Vietnam gained its independence but the country was divided into the communist north and the capitalist south and the escalation of the struggle began in 1959 with the opening of the 2,000 kilometre long Ho Chi Minh trail as there were many thousands of communist guerrillas known as the Viet Cong in the south. The Vietnam War resulted in the defeat of the mighty USA and it was General Giap who was largely responsible for the victory of the Viet Cong.

Then, in 1978, he finished off the terrible regime of the Cambodian Khmer Rouge and Saloth Sar, better known as Pol Pot, who began in 1977 attacking the Vietnamese north. Pol Pot was responsible for the Killing Fields, the deaths of 25% of the population of Cambodia; he fled to the Thai border area and finally committed suicide in 1998.

General Giap was not finished yet as China attacked the north around Cao Bang in January of 1979 in retaliation for the defeat of the Khmer Rouge who were supported by the Chinese; this resulted in another victory for his armed forces by succeeding in pushing the Chinese back across the border within two months. By this time the Vietnamese were probably the most experienced army in the world and this man had won more battles than any other general in recent history by defeating five different armies, but he has never received international recognition, except of course in Vietnam, probably because it was always considered he was on the wrong side.

I asked Mr Phai one day what he did during the Vietnam War and all he would say was that he set off walking from Hanoi carrying rocket launchers and stopped walking two years later when he reached Saigon, now known as

Ho Chi Minh City. He could not understand why sanctions were still in force, imposed largely by the USA. I tried to explain that they had won and the USA had lost and the American armed forces are the most sophisticated in the world and had never in history lost a war. Considering the huge loss of life, he did not bear any grudges towards the Americans but the thought did cross my mind that the cost in life and US dollars of the Vietnam War was immense. If the Americans had paid every man woman and child in Vietnam one million US dollars each it would have been far cheaper in the long run and far preferable. Thankfully, our socialist Prime Minister at the time, Harold Wilson, refused to get Britain involved in this disaster, which was a wise decision.

The talk went well with a large audience and a meeting later with the relevant government officials about tourist development of caves gave us an opportunity to part with our advice.

That night, after a heavy drinking session, things became a little heavy when returning to our hotel in the early hours of the morning the gates of our hotel were locked. In the following order, two armed guards demanded money in order to open the gates and then we were accosted by a lady of the night and her pimp, then being woken up at 3 am by the sound of gun shots in the street just outside the hotel. A rickshaw was on its side and four men armed with pistols were being chased down the street by one of the guards with his automatic. It began to look like this expedition was going to be fun.

We set off in the general direction of Lang Son, the Provincial City, with our two scientists, the cameraman and the reporter on 18th March, our supplied transport was a yellow bus along with a driver. The journey was interesting, passing bombed bridges across every river we arrived at, so we crossed the rivers on ferry barges. There were hundreds of bomb craters full of water and utilised as duck ponds that lined either side of the road and hundreds of shell cases and unexploded bombs all being cut up for scrap metal, a good local business. At least they were making good use of American armaments. The other striking thing was the weather, cold, misty and dismal, a surprise as we were all expecting a suntan.

At Lang Son, the area was similar to some karst areas I had seen in China with isolated towers of Cone Karst with pagodas and short caves with Buddhist shrines. One cave had been used as a hospital during the Vietnam War and another as an ordinance store during the confrontation with China, yet another could not be entered as it was still used to store armaments. The longest cave, called Nhi Thanh, at 450 metres had an old war road going right through it. We mapped a few of them but the area did not look promising for long cave systems so we moved on.

The following day, we drove a further 60 kilometres to the town of Binh Gia, the District Capital situated on the edge of the karst massif. This time we were accompanied by another two men, My Hoan and Mr An, appointed by the Provincial Committee at Lang Son, who insisted we needed protection. They introduced themselves as historical recorders but it became evident they were Vietnamese Secret Police.

We passed through the town of Dong Dang only five kilometres from the Chinese border and arrived at our destination where we intended to spend six days searching for caves before moving on to investigate other areas of the massif. The usual meeting and tea drinking took place with the District Peoples' Committee and the party chairman when our travel papers were carefully scrutinised and we attempted to find out if there were caves in the area. This proved extremely difficult due the language problem, but Mr Phai did his best. In China if you ask a villager for a Dong they will usually point you in the direction of a cave but in Vietnam the word for a cave is Hang but if you get the pronunciation wrong it can mean a crotch or a gate post. Asking a villager if he knows where you can find a crotch could prove disastrous.

On the downside, we were assigned another two District Officers. We were now well outnumbered, which was proving expensive as we had to feed them all.

On Saturday 21st March, we started exploring with a vengeance by driving to a small village called Pac Nang. This was known by the local Vietnamese as One Hundred Girl Village as it had a reputation of containing beautiful girls where large numbers of men congregated looking for a wife. As we were looking for caves, we attempted to ignore the stunning beauties and were led to a nice very easy river cave with the same name as the village.

A cobble-floored canyon led straight through the hill with a few side passages that we mapped within a couple of hours for one kilometre. Looking for something a little more promising, we explored a few short caves all blocked then found one of interest which appeared to be more of a labyrinth of interconnecting passages which was called Tham Khinh. We mapped this the following day but met a few guards in the shape of a two metre long olive green and brown snake accompanied by two of his friends. I suspected they were probably pythons and not venomous but decided not to take any chances. The snakes did not seem to want us to leave so we had no alternative but to goad them into an alcove then make a mad dash for freedom.

Our next objective, after a long wait for the Vice President of the District Committee to join us, was to travel to the village of Coc Keo. The maps indicated a large river sink and resurgence four kilometres away. On the way we passed close to a very large cave entrance taking a river and of course stopped the bus only to be told that this was out of bounds and on no account could we explore it. No reason was given but it was presumed to be a military installation of some kind. The river had to emerge somewhere so we went in search for the resurgence, which we were told was four kilometres away but there were no caves, or so we were told. This seemed unlikely so we insisted on taking a look.

The bus came to a bridge across a river, which consisted of two small trees, but it didn't seem to bother the bus driver who drove straight across without seeming to care that a slight miscalculation could result in a watery grave. Skirting a large doline, we found a shaft called Na Pung that we rigged with ropes. The cave descended steeply down to a choke of boulders and a clean washed passage eventually leading to a sump with no way on. The cave had a draught and three different entrances, so the following day Steve Thomas, Andy Quin and John Palmer returned to finish the mapping while the rest of us continued looking for the resurgence of the river sink. We drove towards a valley and the presumed area where the river would re-emerge into daylight but another bridge looked like it had been hit by a bomb and there was no way we could get the bus across so we walked for a few kilometres into the valley through very muddy rice fields in the rain to the village of Pac Lung. The head official told us that the river resurged a few kilometres along the valley but there were no caves. This information was only a translation so at the time could not be verified. Our guides led us on another long trek through the mud to the end of the valley with only one 120 metre long cave choked with clay, and insisted this was the only cave in the vicinity. We were a little suspicious and insisted on looking at the actual resurgence of the river as we said we wanted to measure the flow rates. After some discussion, our Vietnamese protectors reluctantly agreed and accompanied by what seemed like a few hundred children we found the resurgence of the underground river, but sure enough there was no cave. The children seemed to know what we were looking for and kept pointing up the hill above the resurgence. Hidden by undergrowth we could just make out a huge cave entrance so scrambled up the hill and began to explore, at last it looked like a good find as there was a strong draught and it soon became apparent why our protectors did not want us to find it.

The passage was an impressive 30 metres in diameter with huge stalagmites and columns, and a river could be heard in the distance. A steep descent down boulders followed to the river, which looked deep and cold, but a by-pass was found over the top again with beautiful cave formations and pools containing cave pearls, small rounded calcite balls. A traverse along calcite ledges led to a bridge across the river and a ramp leading back to the river, the only way forward was to swim. Unfortunately by this time it was getting late and we had to navigate back to our base before dark as I doubted that the bus had lights. We also needed to pick up our team from the Na Pung Cave and when we arrived they had been waiting for a couple of hours and were slightly inebriated after drinking large quantities of the local fire water.

We all returned the following day to the cave that did not officially exist but had a name, Ru Mooc, and split into two teams, one surveying and photographing and the other pushing on through the river. Tim, Bob and I surveyed to another entrance while the remainder of the team tackled the cold water by swimming through three lakes which they called the Pimp, the Whore and the Gunfight after our escapades in Hanoi and could not resist calling a side passage the Bribe. The passage terminated in a huge boulder choke after one kilometre and was obviously the other end of the large cave entrance which unfortunately was out of bounds for us. There appeared to be a few possible ways on through the choke but considering that the other side was probably a military installation this area was diplomatically left as to be found on the other side could have had serious repercussions and no one fancied a few years in the notorious Hoa Lo Prison better known as the Hanoi Hilton. This fine cave was mapped for 1,560 metres and there is most probably at least another four kilometres of cave beyond the choke. As far as we know, no one has ever been back.

Our time was now up in the Binh Gai District as we had limited our explorations to a certain period of days in each area in order to cover as much of the limestone massif as possible. We moved on to Bac Son on 26th March after the usual meetings with the district officials and paying for our accommodation, which cost us the princely sum of 25 pence per night per person, a good deal.

Bac Son was only ten kilometres away and from the maps looked promising as the town was surrounded by a mass of Cone Karst, Professor Hoan preferred to call it Madonna Karst as he must have been watching some western music films.

After the normal meeting with the town officials we explored and mapped a couple of caves. One was used as a short cut through the mountain by the local villagers, rather like some of the caves we had found in Bama County, China. This one though was in total darkness for most of its length of 427 metres so the villagers lit grass and ran through before the light went out. At the other side, the stream emerged from another cave called Tham Kim but it terminated in an 80 metre long canal where we found a bamboo boat probably used for fishing in the cave stream.

At the end of a blind valley another stream sink called Nam Ru looked promising with some nice calcite floors and lakes that we could traverse around but it descended down a pitch and a sump after only 227 metres.

That night there was some argument with our Secret Police minders who wanted us to pay them a daily rate. We finally agreed, in order to keep the peace, to pay them providing they paid for their own food and accommodation.

The next day, we found a cave entrance called Tham Oay at the end of an overgrown road near a village called Ghien Thang. We were surprised to find a large chamber measuring 110 metres by 75 metres with a flat concrete floor and steps up to a balcony and roadway. The Vietnamese during the wars had scoured the area looking for caves that could be utilised as hide outs, ammunition depots, hospitals and safe havens away from the bombs and this cave was one of them. Unfortunately, all exits were blocked with rubble but the cave was certainly of historical interest and most probably had been used by General Giap and his Viet Minh forces.

Over the next few days many caves were explored but none were more than 100 metres in length. However, three stream sinks had been noticed marked on the maps with the likely resurgence being 15 kilometres away, these looked to be the best chance for the expedition to find a major cave system. We managed to get the bus within six kilometres of the first sink and set off at a fast pace. Depression set in when it was found to be completely blocked in a choke of mud and the many tree trunks that had been washed in. A fruitless search in the jungle only revealed a few shafts and a cave down to a mud sump after 100 metres. The other major sinks were a long distance away and would require a bivouac in the jungle as there were no roads but our permit stated categorically that we had to remain in government approved accommodation so we were unable to visit this region and as far as is known, no one else has.

Only two more caves were explored of any significance in the Bac Son District, a resurgence called Canh Tao which was a sporting through trip along a beautiful passage with clear water cascades and a few side passages and mapped for 991 metres. The second Tham Gang was mapped for 830 metres near the village of Duc Luong with some nice cave formations but terminated in a mud choke. Although the caves were generally disappointing, between us we must have covered a few hundred kilometres of walking through this beautiful scenic area of Cone Karst with friendly people living in remote areas in bamboo-built houses on stilts, where a drink of tea was always on offer.

Our next port of call was the Huu Lung District near the Trung River south of Bac Son where we met the usual officials and settled into our new accommodation on Friday 3rd April. Huu Lung was a small town but seemed to be full of young female children who all wanted to learn English so most of the time we were surrounded but they were very polite and never got in the way.

A long drive along a very rough road led us to the south-east and a massive cave entrance called Hang Doi near the village of Dong Nham. This measured 110 metres wide by 120 metres high and like Tham Oay had been used as a munitions store during the war. A road had been excavated through the fill on the floor of the chamber that had been levelled out and with a circumference of over 700 metres could certainly store much military equipment away from the constant American bombings. Hang Doi can be translated as Bat Cave and it certainly was full of bats with much smelly guano collected by the villagers for fertiliser for the nearby tobacco fields. Dangerous looking bamboo ladders rose up into the roof to alcoves where the villagers mined the nitrate-rich guano deposits.

Walking on further across wet rice fields and following aqueducts near the village of Dong Xa, we followed a stream which disappeared into a cave. This was a short muddy cave called Hang Tho which led us through to a doline with the stream entering a massive cave entrance and river passage. This was another through cave called Hang Toi, in English Dark Cave, which was not much of an original name as they are all dark.

Tim, Steve and Bob began the mapping and Hang Toi led into another doline after 234 metres. Across the doline the stream disappeared once more into a large imposing cave entrance after flowing across the surface for about 500 metres which looked very promising. I have to admit I was a little excited and ran off alone to explore just to see if it went anywhere, leaving Tim, Steve and Bob to map the cave. Sure enough it did, again passing right through the hill for a distance of about one kilometre to emerge in the main Song Trung Valley. This cave had the name Hang Ca and looked to have a couple of skylight entrances high up in the roof. Feeling guilty, I returned to meet the surveying team and with Steve explored a side passage which led upwards in Hang Ca with many leads remaining. Due to very wet weather the roads into this area proved to be impassable for a few days so we were unable to carry on with the work until the weather improved.

Over the next few wet days, we searched the southern fringes of the karst massive and found numerous short and enlarged caves covered in Chinese characters along the road. We were told that these had been constructed during the Vietnam War by the Chinese army as they had built the road in order to transport arms and ammunition for the Viet Cong. Many of the caves had been used as living quarters and one cave called Lo Voi near the village of Chuc Quan had been used as a cinema during this turbulent period of Vietnamese history.

By Friday 10th April, the weather had improved enough to get back to Hang Ca. This time we drove along the Song Trung Valley and walked for four kilometres to enter the cave through the resurgence that they called Hang Be; this was a much shorter route than when we had originally found Hang Ca. The main passage through was mapped for over 900 metres with some waist deep water and a huge natural bridge which spanned the passage and two skylights above. These were reached by some devious climbing and a high-level passage found with golf ball size cave pearls.

Bob and I surveyed from the river to a steep climb up a decomposed calcite slope with much bat guano to a huge upper passage measuring 60 metres in diameter. A unique group of cave formations was found which resembled something from an alien comic book, so it received the name Alien Chamber. These formations were in the form of metre high pedestals with cave pearls on the top. The passage eventually went up to daylight overlooking a jungle covered doline. Another couple of surveying trips brought the total cave length to a respectable 3,342 metres.

Some tidying up was done in a few short caves over the next few days and cave maps were drawn up between much drinking of the fine Vietnamese beer but a great deal of trouble was had with our Secret Police minder Mr An, as he insisted we were out of the bar by 9.30 pm. It was a dangerous place, he claimed, but it became obvious that what he really wanted was his palms greased so he was easy meat to wind up which I did with great relish. We also spent many happy hours teaching these wonderful children English as they had never seen Europeans before and they came to see us every evening, eager to learn.

One area was left for us to look at which was a large rising issuing from the main north massif which was marked on the map as a water resource. Crossing a river by wading waist deep we arrived at a lake which had been formed by a dam. At the far side a large cave entrance could be seen but the problem was reaching it as the lake was surrounded by steep cliffs. At the water's edge was a coracle made of reeds and pitch with a small paddle. Bob and I jumped in, but it sank beneath the waves before we had reached a few metres from the shore. Jim Abbot and John Palmer almost fell in the lake laughing. Not to be outdone, I stripped off and paddled gently across the lake trying with difficulty to keep in a straight line and not to let any water in the boat. Arriving at the far side was a little embarrassing when a group of young boys and girls pointed out the cave as I walked bare footed across the gravel just in a pair of wet knickers and wearing a head torch. They obviously thought I was just a crazy European or an escaped USA pilot. After all that the cave was only 50 metres in length and blocked with flowstone.

We left Huu Lung on Wednesday 15th April and drove over to the south east edge of the karst massif to Chi Lang. The children seemed sorry to see us leave and wrote going away cards. Chi Lang was more of a tower karst region with steep limestone hills rising from paddy fields and again striking scenery but a series of sinks with nice shafts and streams were all blocked after short distances.

The following day, Tim and I went back to Lang Son to report our findings to the Vice President and while waiting for the meeting spent some time in a sleazy coffee house showing a strange video set to music called Girls of Majorca with naked ladies just wandering around on a beach and swimming.

The meeting went well except that we had to sit through a very boring video that our cameraman had produced and after one hour to our relief the Vice President had to leave so we followed in haste.

On Saturday we set off for Hai Phong and Do Son and the one year old 70 square kilometre National Park of Cat Ba. This is situated on the Hong He, Red River delta and has 400 islands. We spent three days at the holiday resort and fishing town of Do Son and had meetings with the Director of the National Park and the Director of Marine Research advising on a tourism plan before leaving for Hanoi to present our findings at a seminar.

While in Do Son, I noticed a room just off the promenade with a lady speaking very broken, poor English. She beckoned me in and I found 40 young people all trying to learn how to speak and write English. They were repatriated boat people funded by the EEC who had escaped to Hong Kong after the communist take-over of South Vietnam and were being re-educated. The lady asked me to take a lesson, so I spent a very enjoyable few hours teaching English.

There was little doubt that Vietnam had a great future for tourism and for further cave exploration with stunning scenery and friendly people. It was only a matter of time before sanctions would be lifted and Vietnam could join the international community. I could also understand why the French did not want to leave as the ladies are indeed stunningly beautiful.

The expedition had been a huge success with the mapping of 93 caves totalling 13.5 kilometres in a completely unknown and restricted area and there is still plenty of karst left to explore.

27

Caves of Thunder, Irian jaya, Indonesia, 1992

'You don't get to choose how you are going to die or when. You can only decide how you're going to live'

Joan Baez

After the High Trikora Expedition in 1990 when Steve Jones and I had found the postulated way into the Baliem River Cave, I just had to get back. This could be the largest underground river in the world, if of course we could enter it, but the possibilities looked hopeful. I attended a few meetings with team members in the UK and the team was a good one with Colin Boothroyd, the late Dave Checkley, Adrian Gregory, Steve Jones, Gavin Newman, Kevin Senior, Simon Willis, John Wyeth and I. Due to the noise of the thundering river that seemed to shake the walls of the cave, we decided to call it 'Caves of Thunder Expedition'. We practised river crossings and Tyroleans and obtained radio transmitters and receivers inside a helmet so communication would be possible. The team also practised wall and roof climbing.

I left the UK just after Christmas to take up the position I'd been offered at the Gunung Mulu National Park Sarawak so getting to West Papua was going to be a problem with little spare cash. There seemed to be only one way, travel to Miri, then by road to Brunei, then fly to Jakarta, from there try to obtain a ticket to Ujang Padang and from there to Jayapura. Four separate flights, it took me five days to get there.

As usual we had a mountain of problems trying to obtain permission called a Surat Jalan from the authorities and spending eight days in Jayapura. The police seemed to need permission from the army. To make matters worse we had a five-man filming team from France. On 5th August we at last flew to Wamana where we hired a guide called Johnas who proved to be invaluable as a translator. Steve, Colin and Johnas set off the following day for a two day walk into Wanuga which would be our base for the expedition. The film team wanted to recreate the episode of Steve and me finding the cave two years ago. Steve decided that Colin should play the part of me for the filming as he was a much more accomplished actor than me. He played my part well although not all that accurately. The film story did not match up to the true tale, but there again it was just a film for television.

The next day we managed to get two flights in the Mission Aviation Fellowship Caravan aircraft which landed us at Kiawagi, the closest dirt runway to Wanuga. As usual we were surrounded by Dani tribe people all trying to grab a bag to carry down to the hut where we intended to camp for one night. Chaos ensued, as expected, as 85 of them wanted paying. I seemed to be in charge of the porters, a far more difficult task than the caving considering the amount of cave and filming equipment we had. I estimated 100 loads to carry to Wanuga, a two day trip, one day to get there and one day to return. We offered the standard daily rate but they demanded five times as much. Negotiations were getting us nowhere as they were holding us to ransom, but no porters no expedition. After a couple of days we managed to agree a deal at double the normal rate, identifying each porter with a coloured string wrist band. I also wrote down everyone's name. The walk started at 6 am the following morning and was uneventful except for the one kilometre long line of porters stretching along the valley which looked spectacular. At Wanuga we had the use of the school room, for a price, where we could store our equipment, cook and eat. It was though embarrassing being watched by numerous people through the windows while we were eating.

Colin and Steve had arrived at Wanuga after their long walk and had looked at the cave and the hole where the loud noise of the underground river seemed to be coming from. For some unknown reason they did not wish to tell us anything until the film crew could be set up to film the meeting as the story line for the film was that they had just found the cave, which of course was not true. The filming began and Steve explained that the thunder was not there any more; it seemed hard to believe that the cave was silent. The river was still in full flow and sinking in the boulders. Where was our anticipated massive river cave with an expected flow of water of 100 cubic metres a second? The next day Kevin, Adrian and I went looking for it. We investigated the Maze found by Steve and I in 1990 and free climbed down to a flooded section. Above, a draught could be felt issuing from a passage with another free climbable drop leading to a nice phreatic passage with pools of water. We mapped this as far as another pitch going down, which required a rope. The limestone was black and very cleanly washed. The other team surveyed loops in the main tunnel. The next day was even more exciting with Adrian and I rigging the pitch we had found. I foolishly lost my driver for fixing bolts into the wall for a good rope hang so used natural anchors instead which meant there were some rub points from the sharp rock on the rope. I explored beyond the base of the pitch where a large stream inlet entered and, joined by Adrian, we explored down to a sump pool. Beyond was an area of mud-covered boulders and a large passage beckoned us onwards. Because of the spray we could not see the walls or roof, but we arrived at a very muddy climb upwards into a massive passage, the main tunnel later named Akam Nggok. We traversed downward to a waterfall, an inlet pouring in from the roof where we eventually sat and had tuna sandwiches. We explored beyond without seeing a wall and built a small cairn for a survey station. We mapped out, getting lost at one point, and also finished the mapping of parts of the entrance series. The other team busied themselves with mapping the large upstream passages and the massive doline.

The next day was a filming day and the sump at the end of the upstream tunnel had reduced in size so a few pitches were explored but still no raging river. On Sunday, along with Dave and Adrian, we continued with the exploration of the massive passage we had found, mapping around the walls. The huge passage was full of large muddy boulders. Up to the left was a steep mud slope but at the top was only an alcove with no way on. On returning down, I slipped in the mud and went sliding down completely out of control. I came to a sudden stop when I hit a large boulder. We called this area Slip Sliding Away. We surveyed out with me battered and bruised. That day Steve, with Colin playing my part, filmed our original discovery of two years previously.

The next day, Colin looked at the sump Adrian and I had found on our first day but it had disappeared. He explored downwards to a pitch where he could hear the river and returned with back up from other members of the team and a rope. After an eight metre pitch they found a white water river, certainly not the total flow but only a small part of it but very sadly the river sumped both up and downstream. The amazing thing was that this sump had dropped by 51 metres in four days.

Then it started to rain heavily. The sink began to rise forming a lake that steadily increased in size. We photographed and filmed underground but the cave started to flood dramatically. Brown muddy water began to flow along the upstream passages, rising in level all the time. The low passages were quickly filling with water and we took some interesting photographs and film of Adrian and I standing on boulders watching the rise in water level. The boulder Adrian was standing on was lost beneath the flow and mine gradually disappeared until the water was up to my knees. We measured the rise in water level at approximately one metre per hour. The whole cave with its massive passages was obviously going to flood right up to the roof, it was time to beat a hasty retreat as the entrance series was low and flood prone.

The following day, it was still raining and the sink had turned into a lake over two kilometres long and about 500 metres wide. Islands in the centre of the lake gradually disappeared beneath the brown water. We did a little more filming and removed all our equipment from the cave. The cave was christened, Jugumen O Tinggina and although only 2,643 metres long it is spectacular due to the size of the sink, the largest so found anywhere in the world.

The bridge across the Baliam River, Irian Jaya, Indonesia. Photo: David Gill

It was obvious that little more could be done in this amazing cave as it would take many weeks for the river to drop in size. The restriction of boulders at the outlet of the river on the other side of the mountain must restrict the flow resulting in a rapid rise in water levels inside the cave. The chances of ever entering this river cave with the normal flow of 100 cubic metres a second appeared to be nil. Any lower passages would be in the phreatic zone and therefore full of water. This was a great disappointment as the film team needed dramatic shots of the team desperately crossing a mighty underground river, so we had only one choice, move to another location where we knew of a river cave that had previously been explored called Illu Resurgence Cave near a village called Wolo.

The big problem now was transporting all our equipment back to Kiawagi, which meant once more hiring numerous porters. Colin set off walking to Kiawagi to use their radio to book flights. It was decided due to the lack of flights that the team would walk back to Wamena with 35 porters. I got the bad job of organising the porters and film crew to walk back to Kiawagi with the remainder of the equipment. Again much discussion took place on the price per day of the porters. We were accused of causing damage to the crops as they demanded vast amounts, but we managed to agree a reasonable fee and finally were forced to kneel and pray for a safe journey. Sadly, this was not filmed as it looked hilariously funny. The organisation of 77 porters on my own was a nightmare but I managed it in the end by using the same method of recording everyone's name and using our coloured string as an identification tab. Colin met me outside Kiawagi with a nice present, a flap jack.

The next day we flew to Wamena and managed to arrange trucks to take us to the cave of Illu where we could film some river crossings. One other river cave was explored and mapped near Wamena called Gua Anelak, which unfortunately terminated in a sump after 1,025 metres. I left before the filming was completed as I had to get back to work at the Gunung Mulu National Park. Again, this exploration must go down as an important part of speleological history.

Just as I was writing this chapter I heard the sad news that Dave Checkley had passed away.

28

Ten years in the Borneo rain forest

'I have learned to use the word impossible with the greatest caution'

Werner Braun

This chapter is a book in itself, so there is no room to tell the story. I was involved in ten separate expeditions in this area. Five in Gunung Buda and five in Gunung Mulu, plus numerous expeditions to other major karst areas of Sarawak. On returning to the UK after ten years, I was involved in another four expeditions, two of those to New Britain, Papua New Guinea. I am now back in Sarawak still involved on a voluntary basis in conservation, world heritage and local community development.

How I obtained the job was not simple. In 1990 Mike Meredith, the development officer for the Gunung Mulu National Park, arrived back in Britain. Ben Lyon gave me a call and happened to mention that Mike was moving on and the Sarawak Forest Department had asked him to find a replacement for himself. I immediately phoned Mike and asked for details. Mike had decided to put two names forward for selection. Although I did not think I had a chance of landing the job due to my age, I applied none the less. The other applicant was another good cave explorer friend, Steve Jones. We had caved together in China and even though there was a large age difference had hit it off.

Steve was teaching in London and hated it. I wished him the best of luck but a year later we had still not even had a reply to our applications. We forgot all about it. Steve changed jobs in the meantime and started a new career with Ben Lyon in Dent, he had also got engaged. That summer of 1991 Steve received a reply from Sarawak Forest Department with the offer of the job. He turned it down due to his new circumstances; he was settled at Ben Lyon's and was due to get married anyway. The second choice was me and a few months later I received an offer letter. Although the salary was very small I accepted the position and during the 1991 expedition in the November negotiated the contract with the Forest Department. I was committed to two expeditions in 1992, one to Vietnam the other to Irian Jaya but the Forest Department wanted me to start straight away. After a meeting with the officer in charge of contracts at the State Secretaries' office, we decided I could start in January 1992 without signing a contract. When my expedition assignments in Vietnam and Iran Jaya finished, I would then sign a two-year contract based at the Gunung Mulu National Park. At the age of 50, a new chapter of my life was about to commence. Bets were placed by caving friends in the UK that I would not take the job; they lost.

I returned home to Chinley in Derbyshire and on New Year's day 1992 after emptying my bank account of what little money I had, I threw the keys to the car, the keys to my house and the mortgage book at my eldest son Mark and said my fond farewells to my youngest son Leigh, packed a rucksack and jumped on a plane to Sarawak. It was to be three years before I returned from Sarawak with a wife, a son, a one-year-old daughter, a suntan, a few more scars to add to the collection and a mountain of memories but still no money. It was one of the best moves I ever made.

I was fortunate and privileged to be a part of the conservation and development of the park with a number of major achievements, the research and formation of the Gunung Buda National Park and, after a period of 18 years, the completion of the Management Plan. I also completed the major project writing all the documentation for Gunung Mulu National Park to be nominated as a UNESCO World Heritage Area on all four natural criteria.

It's a long story.

Sarawak Chamber, in Gua Nasib Bagus, Sarawak, Malaysia; the largest cave chamber in the world. Photo: Robbie Shone.

Journeys beneath the Earth

Also by David William Gill

With Paul Deakin. 1975. British Caves and Potholes.
Bradford Barton Ltd. Turo, UK.

With Dr Trevor Ford. 1984. The Caves of Derbyshire.
4th edition. Dalesman Books.

With Dr Trevor Ford. 1989. The Caves of Derbyshire,
5th edition. Dalesman Books.

1988. The Untamed River Expedition to East New Britain.
Chinley, Derbyshire, UK. ISBN.0.9514004 0 1.

With Dr John Beck. 1991. Caves of the Peak District.
Dalesman Books.

1999. The Gunung Mulu National Park Nomination for
World Heritage Listing. UNESCO. Sarawak Forest Department, Malaysia.

2011. Untamed Rivers of New Britain Expedition, 2006/2009.
Rainforest Cave and Karst Consultancy, Manchester UK.

2013. A Master Plan, Eco-tourism Development Project
Metarae Kejin, Middle Baram Karst, Sarawak.
Rainforest, Cave and Karst Consultancy.

With a team of Consultants. 2017 Regional Integrated Highland
Development Master Plan for Upper Baram, Miri Division, Sarawak (RIHD
MP 2017-2030) AJC Planning Consultants Sdn Bhd, Malaysia.

2018. Management Plan for Gunung Buda National Park,
Limbang Division, Sarawak, Malaysia. Forest Department Sarawak,
Malaysia. 348 pages.

With a team of Consultants. 2018. The Nakanai Ranges
of East New Britain, Papua New Guinea. Cairns,
James Cook University, Australia.

Printed in Poland
by Amazon Fulfillment
Poland Sp. z o.o., Wrocław